ORGANIZATIONAL AND OCCUPATIONAL PSYCHOLOGY

Series Editor: PETER WARR
MRC Social and Applied Psychology Unit, Department of Psychology,
The University, Sheffield, England

A complete list of titles in this series appears at the end of this volume.

Scientific Management,
Job Redesign and
Work Performance

Scientific Management, Job Redesign and Work Performance

JOHN E. KELLY

Department of Industrial Relations
London School of Economics, England

1982

ACADEMIC PRESS

A Subsidiary of Harcourt Brace Jovanovich, Publishers

LONDON   NEW YORK
PARIS   SAN DIEGO   SAN FRANCISCO   SÃO PAULO
SYDNEY   TOKYO   TORONTO

ACADEMIC PRESS INC. (LONDON) LTD
24/28 Oval Road,
London NW1

United States Edition published by
ACADEMIC PRESS INC.
111 Fifth Avenue,
New York, New York 10003

Copyright © 1982 by
ACADEMIC PRESS INC. (LONDON) LTD

British Library Cataloguing in Publication Data

Kelly, J. E.
    Scientific management, job redesign, and work
    performance. — (Organizational and occupational
    psychology)
    1. Job enrichment   2. Work design
    I. Title   II. Series
    658.3'142   HF5544.5.J616

    ISBN 0-12-404020-9
    LCCCN 81-71573

Phototypeset by Oxford Publishing Services, Oxford
Printed in Great Britain by Galliard Printers, Great Yarmouth

Preface

In the 1960s and early 1970s the redesign of jobs (or humanization of work as it was more grandiosely known) became increasingly popular in management circles. Seminars and conferences flourished, numerous publications appeared, and national centres for 'Quality of Working Life' were established in one country after another. And even if there was a lot more talk about work humanization and not quite so much action, the 'problem of motivation' at the core of these activities was undoubtedly taken seriously by managements throughout the Western world. The traditional carrots and sticks seemed no longer to be effective, as employees absented themselves, filed grievances, or quit their jobs and moved elsewhere. 'Blue collar blues' became a familiar phrase, most of all for managers in assembly-line plants seemingly faced with a mounting volume of discontent and alienation.

One answer which emerged to solve these manifold problems was to humanize work: to redesign the jobs employees performed so that they would be provided with a challenge and with responsibility, and no longer have to suffer the deadly monotony of tightly controlled and highly fragmented tasks. It was envisaged that in this way, employees would be more satisfied and motivated, their job performance would improve and a series of benefits would thus accrue to employers as well.

From the vantage point of 1982 these concerns and discussions may seem quite remote, and part of an age that has now passed into history. Much less do we read or hear about the problem of motivation, instead we have mass unemployment. Cooperation between employers, workers and unions in joint ventures to promote a harmony of interests now seems to take second place to anti-union laws and government-backed offensives against strikers; and schemes to involve employees more closely in their jobs and in the goals of their enterprise are overshadowed by the harsh discipline of the market place. Those in work are widely thought to be glad of a job, whatever its psychological deficiencies, and they behave accordingly; real wages are falling, and strike levels are reaching an all-time low throughout Europe and elsewhere. Employers may no longer take recalcitrant workers to one side and point to the line of unemployed people waiting at the factory gate for the occasional vacancy, but the pressure of the unemployed is no less effective for being less visible.

Why then, in the face of such a tremendous transformation in the Western economies, write about job redesign and work humanization? Apart from the fact that material has been gathered over a number of years, there are two good answers to this question, one of which is obvious but the other less so. In the first place, there is no reason to suppose a recession is endless: at some stage the Western economies *will* witness an upturn, unemployment will fall, labour markets will tighten and the 'problem of motivation' will once again recur. But there is a second justification for the book, and one which strikes at the heart of conventional theories of job redesign. These theories (to be discussed later) all analyzed job redesign as a necessary response to tight labour markets: with full employment, workers could afford to take days off, hop from one job to another, or put in minimal levels of effort. With mass unemployment, such behaviour is no longer possible and techniques to counter it (job redesign among others) are thought to be redundant.

One aim of this book is to show that this contention is wrong, and, more importantly, to show that the theory of job redesign from which it is derived is thoroughly inadequate. To begin with, many firms redesigned jobs in response to competition in *product* markets, not labour markets, and this competition has, if anything, intensified in the course of the recession. Other firms were prevented from redesigning jobs by trade union power. Attempts to enrich the jobs of production workers by allowing them to perform tasks normally executed by skilled craftsmen foundered on union-maintained job demarcations. The weakening of trade union power consequent on the recession has provided many employers with an *opportunity* as well as an *incentive* to implement long-wished for changes in division of labour and working practices. The "leaner but fitter" industries that are supposed to emerge from the harsh monetarist policies are taking shape not least because of dramatic changes in the design of jobs. It is indeed a cruel irony that a set of theories and techniques developed in order to promote *inter alia* a more humane and democratic workplace is being deployed under the discipline of the market by managements who seem keen to exploit the transitory weakness of their union adversaries and force through changes that would otherwise be resisted.

Having indicated the continuing relevance of job redesign, it may be as well to explain my own interest in the field. The present study emerged from my interest in the workers' producer cooperatives that began to re-emerge in Britain in the late 1960s and early 1970s. I was attracted by the possibility of industry being organized on more democratic lines, and tried to combine this socio-political interest with my academic background in industrial psychology. I was particularly interested therefore in the relationship between involvement in democratic decision-making and job performance and job satisfaction. In short I hoped to transpose some of the classic and long-standing concerns of industrial psychology to a radically new setting.

Unfortunately the difficulties of carrying out research in a burgeoning and popular field seemed insuperable, and it was at this time that I was shown a copy of *Work in America* (1972). Its analysis of industrial problems and accounts of solutions based on job redesign, or work reorganization, were replete with questionable assumptions and shaky evidence, and the evangelistic promulgation lent the book a displeasing abundance of optimism. Despite (or perhaps because of) those initial reactions, my interest was stimulated. Over the next few years, I immersed myself in the literature of job redesign, conducted field research, and pursued several (more or less) useful digressions into adjacent topics. Despite variations over time, and occasional shifts and redefinitions of interest, my focus remained on job performance, that is on one of the classic and conventional outcome variables of industrial psychology.

At the same time however I held deep reservations about several prominent features of the contemporary Anglo–American tradition of industrial psychology.

Conflict in industry has been neglected, or inadequately reconceptualized in terms of inter-personal frictions and misunderstandings. Conversely, the potential for cooperation and interest-reconciliation has been (and continues to be) seriously over-estimated. At best these features may be regarded as theoretical shortcomings; at worst, as Baritz (1960) has argued, they signify an identification of industrial psychology with the interests of employers, and a consequent over-lapping of the technical problems of the latter (productivity, labour turnover, for example) with the major concerns of industrial psychology. Theoretically, industrial psychology has also persistently failed to take seriously the economic basis of employment, worker-management conflict, job performance and job attitudes. This omission is all the less pardonable when it is borne in mind that much of the research in the discipline has been conducted within organizations whose *raison d'être* is the production of profit.

If the following study is critical of the work carried out by industrial psychologists on job redesign, this is not because of any quarrel with the *objectives* of redesign, which may broadly be described as humanistic and democratic. Rather, my critical attitude owes more to the naive assumptions that are scattered throughout the literature in this field, and to the unwillingness of many industrial psychologists to take seriously some of the less attractive features of industrial capitalism. Many working people experience insecurity, and unemployment, throughout their working lives, and earn wages and work in conditions, that most observers would find unbearable. Yet for many years the attention of writers has been focussed almost exclusively on a delimited range of job characteristics — monotony, repetition and lack of autonomy.

My own approach to the design of jobs and the organization of work — the division of labour — and to new forms of work organization owes an enormous amount, both to Marx and Marxist writings in general, but more particularly, and more recently to the work of Baldamus, Lupton, and Woodward as will doubtless become clear in the course of the book. Both Baldamus and Lupton showed a sensitivity to the 'wage–effort' bargain and to the instrumental character of employment, that is so often missing in other accounts. Lupton in particular stressed the importance of locating organizational behaviour in a series of wider contexts: product markets, labour markets, and, internally, technological structure. This last point was developed in the classic study by Woodward (1958) whose distinction between mass, batch, and continuous process production informs this study. Of the other influences on this work, more will be said in due course.

Many writers on job redesign have begun their work with an account of the deficiencies of Taylor's 'scientific management of rational-economic men', and I have adopted the same convention. This starting point has several advantages: Taylor is rightly considered to have exerted a profound influence on the design of jobs, which is felt even today. But despite the simplicity of his ideas many job redesign theorists have not done them justice, as Chapters 1 and 2 will demonstrate. As a body of work Taylorism is complex and evolutionary, and its theoretical significance is greatly underestimated. Taylor's careful attention to the design of jobs and division of labour was picked up once more by industrial psychologists in the late 1940s after the hiatus of the human relations approach. The book continues with a delineation in Chapter 3 of the major assumptions underlying classical job redesign theory, and on the basis of a critique of these sets out the main features of an alternative theory of the origins and mechanisms of job redesign.

According to the classical theory, closely prescribed and narrow jobs lacking in variety or interest are subject to diminishing returns because of employee dissatisfaction, absenteeism and turnover. But if jobs were redesigned to provide satisfaction and motivation, employee well-being and the employers' economic interests would be jointly satisfied. The alternative theory espoused here suggests that it is production and cost problems, arising from competitive product and labour markets, that are primarily responsible for the adoption of job redesign. Personnel problems, such as absenteeism, are very much secondary and confined to specific occupational groups, notably white collar clerical workers. The theory further states that job redesign improves productivity through changes in wage levels and earnings; more efficient work methods; elimination of labour; and increased control over labour. Finally the outcomes of job redesign are distinctly uneven: on the employees' side, jobs have been lost, wage increases have not always been granted, and the intensity of, and employer control over work have increased.

Job redesign is classified in this book into three types according to the nature of the production system. In mass production, we invariably find *flowline reorganization*, which entails the reduction or elimination of flowlines. In continuous process industries we invariably find that job redesign takes the form of *flexible work groups*. And in services we most commonly find *vertical role integration*, the combination of work roles from different points on a job hierarchy.

This presentation then leads quite logically into the next four chapters which constitute the core of the book: my analysis of job redesign. Chapter 4 examines the reorganization of flowlines (often referred to as job enlargement) in mass-production industries, and Chapter 5 provides a detailed case study of this technique. Chapter 6 looks at flexible (or autonomous) work groups, and Chapter 7 at vertical role integration (or job enrichment). The new terminology developed for the different forms of job redesign is intended to avoid the value-laden connotations of the conventional terms, with their assumption that "enrichment" for instance is self-evidently a good thing. On the positive side, the new terms are designed to reflect more precisely the changes in work roles that are actually engineered irrespective of their putative psychological consequences.

The picture that emerges from my analysis is that Taylor's emphasis on financial incentives, work methods and work control remains vital for an understanding of productivity improvements issuing from job redesign. But an emphasis on the determinants of productivity improvements will take us only so far, and attention must also be devoted to the ways in which job redesign can be implemented, that is, to the processes of organizational change. Accordingly Chapter 8 examines the assumptions about organizations that under-pin different forms of job redesign theory, using the distinction between unitarist, pluralist and radical frames of reference established by Fox (1966). One assumption, common to most forms of job redesign theory, is that the redesign of jobs can simultaneously satisfy the interests of both workers and employers through its provision of improved motivation, satisfaction and performance. The final section of Chapter 8 casts considerable doubt on this view by examining several hitherto neglected costs of job redesign, such as job losses. The final chapter then draws together and extends the previous findings and arguments. After a summary of the main findings of the study, the chapter continues with a discussion of its implications for theories of motivation, and theories of organization. Several suggestions are advanced on the most useful directions that job redesign theory might take, and the chapter (as well as the book) rounds off with speculation on the future of job redesign.

Although this book discusses all the most significant published cases of job redesign and critically reviews the associated theories, it is not in any sense a standard textbook, such as those by Aldag and Brief (1978), Birchall (1975), Buchanan (1979) and Hackman and Oldham (1980).[1] That is not to say it cannot be used for such a purpose; quite the reverse, and I hope the book will serve to introduce students to the literature in this field. But the book has a clear point of view, which is radically different from most work in its field.

London
February, 1982   J. K.

Notes

[1] The reader may also consult any of the following orthodox texts: Dickson (1977), Katzell *et al.* (1975, 1979), Sheppard and Herrick (1972), Srivastva *et al.* (1975); or the following articles: Morley (1979), Wall (1978).

Acknowledgements

I would like to acknowledge a profound debt of gratitude to David Guest, who supervised the PhD thesis from which this book is derived, and whose meticulous and penetrating comments helped to eliminate many of the shortcomings in successive drafts. I would also like to thank Chris Clegg, Sue Llewelyn, Sylvia Shimmin, Toby Wall, Peter Warr, David Winchester and Steve Wood for their comments; and to acknowledge the people in several different companies who gave me their time and much information. Last, but not least, thanks go to Sue Allen for typing and retyping most of the final manuscript, and to Judith Hallam and the secretaries at the MRC/SSRC Social and Applied Psychology Unit, Sheffield, for typing earlier drafts.

I would also like to thank the following for permission to quote material in which they hold copyright: Tavistock Publications Ltd for excerpts from Herbst, P., *Autonomous Group Functioning*, and Rice, A. K., *Productivity and Social Organisation*; Monthly Review Press for an excerpt from Braverman, H., *Labor and Monopoly Capital* (Copyright © 1974 by Harry Braverman); Methuen & Co Ltd for an excerpt from Davies, D. and Shackleton, V., *Psychology and Work*; HMSO for excerpts from Chemicals Economic Development Council, *Economic Assessment to 1972* and House of Commons Select Committee on Higher Education Science and Arts, *The Funding and Organisation of Higher Education Vol. 1. Report*; Lawrence & Wishart Ltd for an excerpt from Marx, K., *Capital Volume 1*; Locke, E. A. *et al.*, An experimental case study of the successes and failures of job enrichment in a Government agency, *Journal of Applied Psychology* **61** (6), 701–711, 1976 (Copyright 1976 by the American Psychological Association, reprinted by permission of the authors); Hackman, J. R. and Lawler, E. E., III, Employee reactions to job characteristics, *Journal of Applied Psychology* **55**, 1971 (Copyright 1971 by the American Psychological Association, reprinted by permission of the authors); Granada Publishing Ltd for excerpt from Herzberg, F., *Work and the Nature of Man*; William Heinemann Ltd for an excerpt from Drucker, P., *The Practice of Management*.

J. K.

Contents

List of Tables

1 Origins and Development of Division of Labour in Work Organizations and of Taylor's Scientific Management

Division of labour, it is sometimes argued, is a characteristic of all societies, both primitive and modern, and indeed is a precondition for human progress and development. But just as we must distinguish the general features of a phenomenon, such as work, from its specific properties within a particular economic formation, so too must we distinguish different *forms* of the division of labour. Marx (1970) distinguished the division of labour in society (social division) from its division in work organizations, and it is solely with this latter form of division of labour that we are concerned.

The key contributions to our understanding of the benefits of this process came from Adam Smith (1776) and Charles Babbage (1835). In *The Wealth of Nations*, Smith wrote that increased productivity arose from division of labour for three reasons: first, because of the increase in dexterity arising from repeated performance of the same task; second, because of the time saved by no longer having to change frequently from one task to another; and third, because of the increased probability of the invention of labour-saving machinery. Just over 50 years later Babbage added an essential complement to Smith's view, because whereas Smith had showed how it was possible to increase productivity through influencing the *performance* of labour, Babbage (1971 Edn) was the first to explain how the same process could increase *profitability* by reducing the *cost* of labour:

> . . . the master manufacturer by dividing the work to be executed into different processes, each requiring different degrees of skill or force, can purchase exactly that precise quantity of both which is necessary for each process; whereas if the whole work were executed by one workman,

that person must possess sufficient skill to perform the most difficult, and sufficient strength to execute the most laborious, of the operations into which the art is divided. (pp. 175–6)

While acknowledging the principles outlined by Smith, and pointing out in addition the significance of reduced learning times for more detailed jobs, Babbage considered his additional principle to be crucial in the production of cheap commodities.

Marx's own view has often been taken to be simply a combination of Smith and Babbage, and it is true that he largely accepted their accounts of the advantages, and of the diffusion of division of labour in manufacturing industry. But in line with his view of the capitalist system as dynamic and contradictory he was able to grasp, at a general level, the contradictions within the labour process itself (Marx, 1867).

. . . Modern Industry, . . . necessitates variation of labour, fluency of function, universal mobility of the labourer, . . . consequently the greatest possible development of his aptitudes . . . . Modern Industry, indeed, compels society, under penalty of death, to replace the detail-worker of today, crippled by life-long repetition of one and the same trivial operation and thus reduced to the mere fragment of a man, by the fully-developed individual, fit for a variety of labours, ready to face any change of production and to whom the different social functions he performs are but so many modes of giving free scope to his own natural and acquired powers. (pp. 457–8)

This extraordinarily prescient view appears to anticipate contemporary developments in job redesign, but before examining these we must consider the first systematic attempt to derive and apply principles of job design in modern industry.

1.1   Division of labour and the context of Taylorism

The division of labour spread throughout manufacturing industry in Europe and America during the nineteenth century, albeit unevenly between national economies and between different industries. It would appear that by the 1870s, consumer-goods industries—clothing and mechanical appliances, for instance—had witnessed far more extensive encroachments by capital than producer goods, such as machine tools, metal manufacture or extractive industries (Berg, 1979; Hobsbawm, 1968; Phelps-Brown, 1959).

The advanced capitalist economies experienced a major slump in the years 1873–74 followed by a long period of stagnation, commonly referred to as 'the Great Depression' (Hobsbawm, 1968). It seemed during this period as if Marx's worst predictions were being borne out: the rate of profit was falling in many industries; unemployment rose alarmingly, though the wages of those in employment arguably held up better than profits (Landes, 1969); and the late 1880s witnessed the upsurge, in Britain, of the 'new unionism' in the form of militant union organization of unskilled workers (Pelling, 1976). The two major poles of the capitalist response were ably summed up by Sohn-Rethel (1978):

> . . . the first, an expansion of the markets by opening up new territories and resuming colonial expansion on a new scale, . . .; the second, a substantial increase in the rate of exploitation of the labour employed in the industries at home, . . . (p. 146)

In short, imperialism and rationalization, with the latter being most clearly expressed in the USA as Taylorism, or 'Scientific Management'.

1.2 Taylorism

It is a curious paradox that a 'movement' variously claimed to have been superseded, defeated or even indeed rarely to have implemented any of its major principles continues nevertheless to generate a seemingly endless series of studies and commentaries (Aronowitz, 1978; Burawoy, 1978; Edwards, 1978; Whitaker, 1979). Without being too cynical, it is not implausible to suggest that its attraction rests to a considerable degree on the ready availability of a small and easily readable number of texts written by Taylor himself and often taken as synonymous in their content with the movement, or doctrine, of Taylorism. Although many management theorists emerged at this time, notably Gantt, Emerson, the Gilbreths, Fayol and Follett to name only a few (see Haber, 1964, Chapter 3; Tillett et al., 1970), it was Taylor's own work that became the centre of controversy, culminating, in 1912, in a special hearing of the US Senate, convened under trade union pressure, to investigate the Taylor system.

Taylorism has been analysed in general terms as a rather unsuccessful management practice, as an expression of the logic of capitalism, and as a crude management ideology. Palmer's (1975) assessment of the lack of success of Taylorism, supported more recently by Nelson (1975) and Edwards (1979), argues that it was defeated largely by worker resistance and struggle. This does not preclude *elements* both of Taylorism and of other systems being widely implemented in the early part of this century, and suggests, once more, that the significance of Taylorism *per se* is prone to be overstated. By contrast Braverman (1974) has argued that Taylorism constitutes:

> . . . the explicit verbalisation of the capitalist mode of production.
> (p. 86)

and marks the culmination of the development of capitalist management, both in theory and practice. The view is, of course, incompatible with Palmer's.

Neither of these orientations is adequate in itself. We cannot conceptualize Taylorism as a *total* entity and *then* assess its impact, overlooking the differential implementation of sections of Taylorist practice. Nor can we deduce a particular management practice directly from the main parameters of capitalist development, because there is, as we shall see, considerable variation in management practices.

The description of Taylorism as a crude management ideology is only one of many criticisms advanced by psychologists (Schein, 1978). Researchers in job redesign have produced a series of criticisms, chief of which is that Taylorism promoted the fragmentation of jobs without proper regard for its consequences. This 'blind spot' in Taylorism was noted by Drucker (1968):

> The first of these blind spots is the belief that because we must analyse work into its simplest constituent motions we must also organise it as a series of individual motions, each if possible carried out by an individual worker . . . This is false logic. It confuses a principle of analysis with a principle of action.   (p. 339)

This, however, is only one of several misconceptions of Taylorism that are to be found in the literature of job redesign and industrial psychology. There also exists the view that Taylor had no conception of the social dimension of the workplace. According to a recent introduction to industrial psychology (Davies and Shackleton, 1975):

> Taylorism assumed that workers should be studied as isolated units. It argued that the main factors affecting their efficiency were either fatigue, or substandard environmental conditions or methods of carrying out the job which could be remedied by time and motion study methods. Such a

view completely neglects other equally important influences on work behaviour emanating from the social environment.   (p. 17)

Once again we shall see that this view is untenable, and that Taylor in fact adhered to a sociohistorical theory of low production, in which 'restriction of output' was *socially organized* by workers themselves. And yet even Aitken (1960), the author of a full length study of Taylorism, lapses into the same error of treating Taylorism as an individualist theory of motivation and performance:

> The idea of a norm of output as a universal feature of all organised groups, set and maintained by the group itself and often defended by highly effective sanctions, would however, have been entirely alien to Taylor, as to most others of his time.   (pp. 47–8)

Yet there are numerous references in Taylor's works to the organized character of restriction in the USA, and he was also familiar with similar phenomena, known as 'hanging out', and 'ca'canny', in England and Scotland, respectively.

Taylorism has also been discussed as if it consisted solely, or essentially, of time and motion study, an opinion reinforced by the famous remark of Taylor's (1903), in which he describes the study of unit times as '. . . by far the most important element in scientific management' (p. 58). The comment has often been quoted, for instance by Friedmann (1955), a critic of Taylor and exponent of 'job enlargement', by Sohn-Rethel (1976; 1978), and by Bell (1972), writing on work at a general level. Yet at other points in his writings, Taylor (1911, 1912) also referred to 'the mental revolution on the part of employers and employees' as the essence of his system, or again to the slide rule, developed by Carl Barth, as being '. . . by far the greatest value' (Taylor, 1906), in his system of management. The point to notice here (and it will be developed more fully later on) is that Taylor's thought cannot be treated as a complete, and finished, set of ideas, and we should recognize the possibility that his ideas developed over a period of years or that they were in parts inconsistent.

Another misconception one can find is that Taylorism consisted principally of an effort to exert managerial *control* over labour. This theme is prominent in the recent work by Braverman (1974), but it has also been reiterated by Davis, a writer more in the conventional job design mould. As we shall see, there is an element of truth in this idea, but it does nevertheless detract from, and perhaps obscure, some of Taylor's contributions to raising labour and machine output.

A theme related to this idea of control is that Taylor held derogatory views of workers and that under scientific management workers were reduced to the status of automata, and were considered too stupid to grasp the subtleties of 'science' (Dickson, 1974). The quotation used most often to justify this view is Taylor's description of the character of Schmidt, his highly trained pig-iron handler, in which he referred to him 'as being as stupid and as phlegmatic as an ox'. This reference to the requirements for a specific type of labour has been taken by some writers as indicative of the requirements for *all* types of labour under Taylorism, an interpretation that can be shown to be erroneous.

The idea that Taylorism is associated with fragmentation of labour is probably the most pervasive theme one can find in the job redesign literature, but in second place would probably be the idea that for Taylor, worker motivation was a question that reduced itself, essentially, to the issue of pay. Indeed this theme has been enshrined in the shorthand term 'rational-economic man' which is generally considered as the beginning and end of Taylor's thought on motivation at work. Yet the provision of pay was *not* the only incentive that Taylor recognized, as we shall see, and the suggestion that it was is a misleading one.

The following account will not attempt a concrete analysis of the modes of implementation, the conditions that made them possible or the efficacy of Taylorism per se. The account is subordinate to the objective of explaining post-War developments in division of labour, and for that reason will focus on two themes:
  (i) The development of, and contradictions within, Taylorism as a theoretical and ideological formation; and
  (ii) the relation between Taylorism, on the one hand, and division of labour and related contemporary management practices (such as 'Fordism') on the other.
Taylor's works and his practice will be analysed historically. No attempt will be made therefore to impose a false unity on his work either by arbitrary selections from his writings, or by concentrating on a single text as the purest 'expression' of Taylorism. Thus, P. Taylor (1979) identifies *A Piece-Rate System*, Sohn-Rethel (1978) *Art of Cutting Metals* and Bendix (1956) and Drucker (1976) *Taylor's Testimony* as key texts, thereby underplaying the differences between various expressions of view. As stated above, the account to follow will explore developments and contradictions in Taylor's work.

1.3 The origins of Taylor's scientific management

Taylor began his career as a labourer at the Midvale Steel Works in 1878 and after a short spell as a clerk, returned to the shopfloor as a machinist.[1] He remained in this job only a few months before he was promoted to gang boss, and it was not long before he was again promoted – to machine shop foreman. It was during this brief period 'on the shop floor' that he made several observations that were to be crucial in the development of his system of management. First, he located the inability of managements to raise labour productivity in their ignorance of the times in which particular jobs could, and ought to, be done; secondly, he became aware of the existence of and the rationale for output restriction by workers; and thirdly, he came to believe that existing payment systems did not provide sufficient incentive for workers to raise output.

Unlike some of his contemporaries, and indeed descendants, Taylor did not continue to regard output restriction as 'irrational' but endeavoured to find its causes. In describing output restriction he used the term 'soldiering' and distinguished two types (1903): 'natural' soldiering was apparently innate, but 'systematic soldiering':

> ... results from a careful study on the part of the workmen of what they think will promote their best interests.   (p. 32)

The fundamental cause of this latter (which Taylor considered to be more serious) lay in the fact that employers did not know, and had no means of ascertaining, the extent to which it was possible to raise output; and this deficiency was based in its turn (1903) on a:

> ... profound ignorance of employers and their foremen as to the time in which various kinds of work should be done ...   (p. 30)

There existed then no 'rational' basis for allocating given quantities of work over a certain time period, and employers were thus compelled to depend on the goodwill of their work-force in responding to wage incentives, and on their own cunning in cutting piece rates whenever there was a transitory, upward, drift in productivity. The workers in their turn soon learned the costs of raising their output, and thus they organized restrictive practices. Once rate cutting had been experienced several times, and restriction of output regularly practised, there developed, on the basis of these experiences, a more generalized feeling of antagonism between worker and employer (Taylor, 1903, pp. 34–5; 1911, pp. 23–4).

Taylor thus created what we may call a sociohistorical theory of output restriction, which turned on the economic relations between employers and workers, the accumulated and generalized experience of workers, and the ineffectiveness of 'ordinary' systems of management, arising from managerial ignorance of the shortest possible work times.

The fundamental novelty of Taylorism was that it entirely rejected the attempt to raise productivity through a ratchet effect on *existing* levels. In order to raise, and secure, a high level of output it was, said Taylor, necessary to determine what levels of performance were physically *possible*, and to link pay to *these*, rather than to existing or previous levels. Managements had little or no conception of possible levels, and even if the workmen did (and Taylor remained ambivalent on this point), it was in their direct interests to conceal the fact, for on the basis of their past experience, the only consequence of disclosing their knowledge would be a reduction in piece rates, thereby compelling them to work harder for the same pay as before. But if output *could* be raised substantially (and Taylor believed, initially on the basis of his own experience, that it could) then several benefits would accrue, the chief of which was that the workmen could receive higher wages, at the same time as their employers achieved lower labour costs. Both sides could then (1912):

> . . . take their eyes off the division of the surplus as the all important matter, and together turn their attention towards increasing the size of the surplus . . . (pp. 29–30).

The basis for this transformation of industrial relations rested on the willingness of workers to raise output in exchange for guaranteed higher earnings, and on the displacement of surplus workers following this increase in output.

At the most abstract level Taylor's answer to the lack of knowledge about work times was striking in its simplicity: he proposed the application of the methods of science to the arena of industry. In particular, he proposed to measure what workmen actually did, according to times taken, and to develop on that basis the 'one best way' of working (1911):

> . . . this one best method and best implement can only be discovered or developed through a scientific study and analysis of all of the methods and implements in use. This involves the gradual substitution of science for rule of thumb . . . (p. 25)

The measurement of work, however, was not peculiar to scientific management, but as Taylor pointed out, earlier time studies were neither systematic nor detailed (Copley, 1923, Vol. 1, pp. 223–30; Urwick and Brech, 1945). The Midvale Steel Works, at which Taylor was employed from 1878 to 1895, certainly held records of the times in which various different jobs had been completed, but were these the fastest possible times? And were they based on the most efficient methods? Taylor was convinced that neither was the case, and he therefore began systematic time studies of Midvale workers.

In order to answer his questions, he employed two principles: firstly, in timing any job he began by analysing it into constituent, or elementary motions; and secondly, he sought the quickest time in which the job could be done, as he thought, 'consistently and without harm or injury to the workmen' (Taylor, 1903, p. 25; 1912, p. 123). This work was carried out by the Rate-Fixing Department, whose primary function, as the name implies, was to measure and prescribe worker performance, and to set levels of incentive pay to induce it. As Taylor discovered, however, there was more to rate-fixing than the assignment of workloads and pay incentives. In the production systems where he carried out much of his early work, products were manufactured, shaped, etc., on individual machines, and the condition of the machinery was often a crucial factor affecting the workers' possible output. If it broke down, for instance was the worker to be penalized for lost production? or the employer? or both of them? So, in 1895 Taylor wrote that:

> . . . the Rate-Fixing Department has shown the necessity of carefully systematising all of the small details in the running of each shop; such as the care of belting, the proper shape for cutting tools, and the dressing, grinding and issuing orders for work, obtaining accurate labour and material returns, and a host of other minor methods and processes. These details, which are usually regarded as of comparatively small importance, are shown by the Rate-Fixing Department to be of paramount importance in obtaining the maximum output . . . (p. 73)

This was the case, both because defects in machinery prevented workers attaining their 'maximum' output, and also of course, because they reduced the efficiency of the machinery itself. Taylor's studies of machinery, as in his 1893 paper on belting, which originally formed just one part of the application of science to production soon became an integral part of his work (Aitken, 1960, p. 100ff; Copley 1923, Vol. 1, pp. 258–61; Hoxie, 1915, p. 22; Taylor, 1906).

This *systematic* character of scientific management is frequently overlooked (though see Copley, 1923; Rose, 1975) and it is not uncommon for it to be regarded as little more than a combination of time study and wage incentives. Taylor's 'technical' developments are either treated as interesting by-products of his main work, (Braverman, 1974, p. 110; Friedmann, 1955, pp. 51–2; Kempner, 1970) or else ignored altogether (Argyle, 1972). Yet these twin aspects of Taylorism, which we may call the 'social' and the 'technical' are interconnected in several ways. Both stem from the desire to apply scientific method to industrial production, and both have as their common objective, 'the cutting down of time to the minimum consistent with good work' (Copley, 1923, Vol.1, p. 254). And finally, as Taylor argued (above), the application of time study and wage incentives in themselves would be insufficient to realize the greatest possible gains in productivity, unless one also standardized the conditions in the shop to facilitate uninterrupted production.

By 1895, the time of his first important paper, several major features of his approach were already clear. He had argued for the necessity of a separate Department to engage in time-and-motion study and fix wage rates in relation to output, because the volume of work already performed by management, and particularly foremen, was so prodigious that they could not possibly devote sufficient time to either of these tasks. In any case, these activities required a degree of skill and expertise that only a specially trained man possessed. Secondly, Taylor had by now developed what he called the Differential Piece Rate System. Under this system, a rate of pay was set for a standard level of output, which only 'first-class' men would be likely to attain. The worker who fell short of this standard, if only by a small amount, received a proportionately greater cut in pay, whereas the worker who exceeded the standard received a proportionately greater rise in earnings (Taylor, 1895, pp. 64–5). Thirdly, Taylor had developed his revised political economy, in the form of the argument that with rising productivity both employers and workmen could grow richer simultaneously and would no longer have to fight over the distribution of the surplus. And, finally, he had argued that the problem of raising productivity required an investigation of machinery, as well as of men. This was the state of Taylor's science in 1895; over the next 16 years several points were to be added, and there would be several changes of emphasis, which we shall now consider.

In 1895, he moved to the Bethlehem Steel Company and a few years later in 1903 he produced a paper entitled *Shop Management,* in which he extended some of his earlier observations. The worker was now to be assigned a daily quota of work by management, and to ensure he performed it various 'functional foremen' would attend to aspects of his work. The emphasis on the payment system and on time-and-motion study as the fundamental tools of management in the pursuit of higher productivity, had now been thoroughly overhauled, and increased stress placed on the role of supervision and assignment of work quotas, and on *organization* more generally (Aitken, 1960, p. 120ff; Copley, 1923, Vol. 1, pp. 253–4, 358; Kakar, 1970, p. 121; Myers, 1932, pp. 12–13, 39). Indeed, Taylor (1903) explicitly compared the benefits of organization and technology thus:

> There is no question that when the work to be done is at all complicated, a good organisation with a poor plant will give better results than at the best plant with a poor organisation.   (p. 62)

This was no mere exaggeration on Taylor's part: the comment marked a significant development in his thought, as is revealed by the proportion of this work devoted to a discussion of supervision. Taylor recommended a division of labour within the role of foreman. Specifically, he argued there should be no less than 8 different kinds of foreman, each with his own particular function, such as repairs, product quality, speed of working, etc. The division of labour then, was extended, for the first time to management itself. Having described this new system of supervision, Taylor further underlined its importance by proceeding to discuss in some detail the psychological characteristics of good foremen, the details of which need not detain us here.

Further indication of the importance of organization is revealed by the changed name of the Rate-Fixing Department, which had now become the Planning Department, responsible for all the major details of the shop. It will be recalled that Taylor had commenced experiments on machinery at the same time as he began his time-and-motion studies at the Midvale Steel Works, but the most efficient running and standardization of the machinery was by 1903 an integral part of the management of the whole shop. For if the workers were to achieve a high level of performance in response to the incentive of higher pay and under the direction of the Planning Department and the foremen, it was necessary to ensure that they were provided with the means to work efficiently and without interruption.

Thus it was that Taylor undertook to overhaul and to standardize the tools and machinery of the shop, and to set up a special stores department, responsible for the issuing of tools. Equally, it was necessary to ensure the workman knew exactly what he had to do each day and how he was to go about doing it. This conception of a daily production target Taylor referred to as the 'task idea' and he considered the assignment of such a target motivating in itself (Taylor, 1903, p. 69). For this Taylor developed firstly, a branch of management whose duty was to train the workforce in the new methods, and secondly a branch of the Planning Department whose role it was to issue instruction cards each day to the workmen. At the same time the other departments of the workshop and other sections of the workmen would be issued with routing cards instructing them where to obtain and despatch materials.

These developments—leading to the establishment of an overall system for managing the production of an entire shop—marked the culmination of the development of 'scientific management'. What began as a search for ways of raising output through the study of labour and machinery finally resulted in a complete *system* of management. This system comprised time-and-motion studies and rate-fixing, the routing of materials, tools, etc., and the planning of production, the running and maintenance of machinery, a series of functional foremen, and, in overall control, a central Planning Department.

In 1911 Taylor codified his own conception of scientific management in the form of four principles:

    (i) development of a science of production;

    (ii) selection and training of workers;

    (iii) bringing together the science and the workers; and

    (iv) an equal division of responsibility and cooperation between management and workers.

These principles usefully summarize the central practices of Taylorism, and having described their origins and development, we can now proceed to a more detailed examination.

Notes

1. These and other biographical details are taken from the two-volume biography of Taylor written by Copley (1923). A good condensed account of Taylor's career is provided by Rose (1975), which is why I have devoted less space to this aspect of Taylorism than it actually merits.

2 Taylorism: theory, ideology and practice

Having described the development of Taylor's scientific management, it is necessary now to locate and examine this in a series of contexts. In line with the emphasis within Marxism on the employment relationship and the division of labour, these two themes will inform the present chapter. First, I shall trace the evolution of, and contradictions within, Taylor's conceptions of the employment relationship, and assess the implications of this analysis for the ideological character of Taylorism. Second, the relationship between Taylorism and division of labour will be assessed in theory and practice, and an attempt made then to characterize the unique features of Taylorism as a management strategy.

2.1 First period: the employment relationship as individual economic exchange (1895–1903)

In Taylor's early formulations we find all the basic elements of the classical economic conception of the employment relationship. The main concern of the workers is wages, that of the employer profits, and any other considerations are strictly secondary. So seriously was this view taken that Taylor firmly insisted men would *have* to be paid more money in return for higher productivity, otherwise the terms of the exchange relationship would be violated and men 'would not do an extraordinary day's work for an ordinary day's pay' (1895, p. 64). More significantly, he insisted that under his system it was 'men not positions which were paid in order to stimulate each man's *personal* ambition' (1895, p. 35). Collective reward schemes, such as profit sharing, would be of no avail because of their failure to embody this point. If individual ambition provided the key to economic success its operation was thwarted by the villain of early nineteenth century thought, combination among workers.

Had Taylor remained at this level of analysis, it is difficult to see how he might have developed beyond what were in effect rather commonplace ideas. What permitted him to transcend classical economics was his simultaneous observation of the underdevelopment of management, and in particular of management's *knowledge* of production processes. Once armed with this knowledge, productivity and wages could simultaneously be raised thereby promoting 'a most friendly feeling between the men and their employers' (1895, p. 37). The knowledge thus acquired would be acceptable to both parties because of its scientific character, and because it satisfied their mutual interests.

2.2 Second period: from individual exchange to control (1903–1911)

1903 saw the publication of *Shop Management*, undoubtedly Taylor's most detailed study of workshop organization and management. The emphasis on time-and-motion study was greater in *Shop Management* than in any of his other publications, and indeed he wrote : 'What the writer wishes particularly to emphasise is that this whole system rests upon an accurate and scientific study of unit times, which is by far the most important element in scientific management' (1903, p. 58). As with many of Taylor's statements, this has been quoted out of context and adopted at face value, by writers such as Bell (1972), Friedmann (1955, pp. 51–2) and Sohn-Rethel (1976, 1978) without recognizing that throughout his works as a whole, Taylor referred to at least two other components of scientific management as the most important and essential (see Chapter 1). If Taylor's insistence on gathering up knowledge of production signifies continuity with his earlier work, its meaning *in context* marks a profound break. *Shop Management* contains an extensive critique of 'the management of initiative and incentive', the best of 'ordinary management' in Taylor's view. It received this accolade because it constituted *one* solution to what was now seen as a key problem, *control* over production.

The transition from Taylor's early, and classical, view of the employment relationship was made possible because of the ambiguity of the concept of *knowledge*. In his first period it was construed as a neutral body of fact whose authority would lie beyond dispute, but Taylor's own experiences, at Midvale and Bethlehem Steel, led him to a more profound appreciation of the intimate link between knowledge and power. Under 'ordinary management' control was undisputed, and rested with the shopfloor workers because of their monopoly of knowledge of production. Henceforth, the development of scientific management techniques for raising production and efficiency simultaneously constituted an integral part of the struggle to wrest control from the shopfloor. In 1906 he wrote:

> The gain from these slide rules is far greater than that of all the other improvements combined, because it accomplishes the original object, for which in 1880 the experiments were started; i.e., that of taking the control of the machine-shop out of the hands of the many workmen, and placing it completely in the hands of the management thus superseding 'rule of thumb' by scientific control.   (p. 252)

Consistent with the new emphasis on the employment relationship as a site of struggle over control, that is, as a political struggle, was Taylor's lengthy discussion of foremen and their authority, and the conditions under which they were most likely to be effective. Equally he admitted to the use (which in fact went back to the 1880s) of dismissal as a means of enforcing new levels and methods of production. And the theme was reiterated in his most popular work, *The Principles of Scientific Management* published in 1911 at the height of the public controversy about his system of management:

> It is only through *enforced* standardisation of methods, *enforced* adoption of the best implements and working conditions, and *enforced* cooperation that this faster work can be assured. And the duty of enforcing the adoption of standards and of enforcing this cooperation rests with the *management* alone.   (p. 83, Italics in original).

There is a firm insistence on dealing with workers only as *individuals*, whether the issue is revisions in work methods, work allocations, or specific grievances. The refusal to deal directly with unions or with workers en masse was predicated on Taylor's conclusion, derived from his own experience, that workers were far more powerful and cohesive as a collectivity than as atomized individuals. Finally the 'task idea' expressed Taylor's view of a properly regulated and controlled relationship in which the worker was told exactly what to do, how to do it, and how quickly to do it, and was rewarded (or punished) accordingly.

2.3 Third period: from control to cooperation (1911–1915)

Less than one year later, Taylor was describing his system of management to the 1912 Special House of Representatives Committee in terms of a 'mental revolution' on the part of workmen and employers, and referred frequently to the cooperation essential for its success.

He had long ago evolved the material basis of this cooperation in the form of a continuously growing mass of wealth in which both workers and employers could receive ever larger amounts of wages and of profits. But this in itself was inadequate, for not only had there to exist some *basis* for cooperation, workers and employers had also to overthrow their acquired beliefs and *perceive* there was such a basis.

When describing the 'mental revolution' Taylor (1912) referred to it as the 'essence' of scientific management, and sought to distinguish it from the 'mechanisms' as follows:

> Scientific management is not any efficiency device, . . . not a new system of figuring costs; it is not a new scheme of paying men; it is not time study; it is not motion study; it is not divided foremanship . . . these devices . . . are useful adjuncts to scientific management . . .
> . . . in its essence, scientific management involves a complete mental revolution on the part of the working man . . .   (pp. 26-7)

Although it was in the *Principles of Scientific Management* (1911) that Taylor insisted on the *enforcement* of cooperation, it was in this same text that he spoke of the need for a revolution in the attitudes of workers *and* managers. Nor was this simply a public-relations exercise designed to ward off hostile reaction. Taylor and his associates were undoubtedly concerned about the mounting campaign against scientific management by the American Federation of Labor and its member unions, not least because of the support it received in Congress. Scientific management had achieved some acclaim as a result of its use against the railway companies' request to raise prices at the Eastern Rate case hearings in 1910. Proponents of scientific management had emphasized productivity improvements in the railways as an alternative to price rises. This favourable publicity was somewhat overshadowed in the following year by a strike of molders at the Government arsenal in Watertown, in protest at time studies of their jobs (Aitken, 1960). Following the strike, pressure was mounted on Congress by labour unions, and the 1912 hearings were the result.

Nevertheless, although some defensiveness is clearly evident in

Taylor's testimony, in the form of groundless denials of various charges and numerous inconsistencies, the basic ingredients of the 'mental revolution' were anticipated in one of his earliest works (1895):

> The greatest advantage, however, of the differential rate for piece-work, in connection with a proper rate-fixing department is that together they produce the proper mental attitude on the part of the men and the management toward each other. In place of the indolence and indifference which characterise the workmen of many day-work establishments, and to a considerable extent also their employers; and in place of the constant watchfulness, suspicion, and even antagonism with which too frequently the men and the management regard each other, under the ordinary piece-work plan, both sides soon appreciate the fact that with the differential rate it is their common interest to co-operate to the fullest possible extent . . . This common interest quickly replaces antagonism, and establishes a most friendly feeling.   (pp. 68–9).

One consequence of this new 'cooperative partnership' was to be the disappearance of trade unions. Taylor made many conflicting statements on trade unions, but the weight of evidence suggests he never abandoned a deep-seated hostility towards them, an attitude that was reinforced by their campaign against his system, and which resulted in strong differences of opinion with his more pro-union associates such as Robert Valentine and Morris Cooke. Both men supported the institution of trade unions and collective bargaining, and their new degree of cooperation in industry thus took the form of 'industrial democracy' (Copley, 1923, Vol. 2; Nadworny, 1955, Chapters 5 and 7; Stark, 1980; Whitaker, 1979).

*   *   *   *   *

It can be seen that as an ideological formation, Taylorism was in fact far more complex than is usually thought. Although the dominant perspectives in his later works were derived from classical economics and liberal individualism on the one hand, in combination with a powerful emphasis on the necessity for managerial control over work organization on the other, there also emerged a sub-theme of voluntary cooperation between worker and employer. If this rested *ultimately* on mutual economic interests arising from productivity growth, it became clear in Taylor's later years that it was by no means an automatic consequence of such interests.

One interpretation of these differing views would set them out as undesirably inconsistent, the inevitable product of a poorly educated engineer creating a system of theory and practice in the face of conflicting public reactions. Undoubtedly inconsistencies exist within and between Taylor's works, but a more fundamental interpretation of them is available. The apparent inconsistencies in Taylorism reflect the actual contradictions in the social relations of capitalist production itself. On the one hand, capitalist production engenders and requires relations of exploitation and thus of antagonism in which labour *is* a commodity whose value is determined in the same way as any other. Within the process of production, the aim of capitalists is, and must be, the reduction of the cost of labour to the minimum point consistent with its long term productivity and with capital's long-term profit maximization. On the other hand, *both* parties have an interest in the continuation of their particular branch of industry, and therefore in its remaining competitive and profitable. Historically, employers had come to realize that there were serious limits to authoritarian, coercive management, and that to some degree it was in their interests to secure a measure of consent to their rule, not least because of the rise of working class organizations both within and outside production, that is, trade unions and political parties.

Insofar as it expressed (even if it failed to grasp) these contradictions Taylorism marked a tremendous advance in understanding of employment and division of labour partly because of the wider political and ideological climate within which Taylorism was produced. As Bendix (1956) and others have shown, American industrial relations were undergoing a radical transformation in the first decades of this century because of the dramatic growth in the size and influence, during the War, of organized labour and because of the almost simultaneous expansion of the social stratum of enterprise managers and engineers (Merkle, 1968; Stark, 1980). The legitimation of the functions of the latter, through their abilities and special conceptual functions, went hand in hand with several forms of opposition to trade unionism. One form, influential in the 1920s, was an insistence on 'partnership' and cooperation as 'the American way', which meant in practice company 'unions'. Within this conception, the worker was seen as an active, if ultimately compliant subject, whose welfare was again, ultimately, the concern of a paternalist management.

Given these developments, it becomes clear that Taylor's emphasis in his later years on 'the mental revolution' that would usher in cooperation in industry, and the early industrial psychologists' concerns with 'the human factor' (See Myers, 1929; Travis, 1970) were closely related elements of the same general ideological trend. This conclusion contrasts with conventional one-sided views that emphasize the discontinuity between Taylorism and early industrial psychology because of their differing views of motivation and of workers' needs.

2.4 Taylorism and division of labour

Scientific management, according to many writers, constitutes almost a qualitative transformation in the division of labour, as a result of which the worker is reduced to a condition in which he exercises little skill, and then, only at the discretion of the management. Such a view is held by writers such as Drucker (1968), Guest (1957), Jessup (1974) and Lindholm and Norstedt (1975), and has also been advanced by radical critics of Taylorism, such as Braverman (1974).

The notion that Taylorism entails or necessitates detailed division of labour rests on three different arguments:
  (i) that Taylor did, in *practice*, subdivide three groups of workers— bricklayers, machinists, and supervisors;
 (ii) that he sought to demarcate conception and execution; and
(iii) that in his account of time and motion study, Taylor insisted on the need to break down work into its smallest components.
The principal defect of the first argument is a logical one: the fact that Taylor carried out subdivision of labour does not tell us whether such division is an integral or a necessary feature of scientific management. It does not tell us, in other words, whether Taylorism is the *cause* of this subdivision, or whether there might be *other* causes that lie outside of, or that pre-date, Taylorism (*cf.* Savall, 1981). Indeed Taylor's response to the House 1912 Committee Hearing presented precisely this argument (Taylor, 1912):

> THE CHAIRMAN. Is not one of the elements of scientific management this possibility to divide it up so that the workmen will have the same operation to perform over and over again?
> MR TAYLOR. That is just the same under scientific management as it is under the other types of management; neither more nor less. Under scientific management precisely the same principles of work are used in that respect as under the other types of management . . . under scientific management, or any other management, the manufacture of shoes is

divided into very, very, many minute parts . . . each one performed by a
different man in a well-run shop. . . . this is what takes place under the
older types of management, and that undoubtedly would continue under
scientific management . . .

THE CHAIRMAN. Does not scientific management undertake to show
that a change from one part of the work to another . . ., if they involve
different operations, is a loss of time and consequently it is better, if
possible, to have one man perform each of the operations?

MR TAYLOR. . . . what is true under scientific management in this
respect is also true under all types of management. I think this tendency
to training toward specialising the work is true of all managements, for
the reason that a man becomes more productive when working at his
speciality . . .   (pp. 203–5)

Taylor thus dissociated increased division of labour from scientific
management, in particular by pointing to the existence of subdivision
elsewhere, and to the benefits already reaped from the principle (as
adumbrated by Smith).

The second point to notice about the empirical argument on Taylorism and subdivision is that it actually overlooks significant features of
the cases on which it is supposedly based. In the example of the
machinists, it is true that Taylor removed certain parts of their job,
such as fetching supplies and removing finished goods, and assigned
them to other workers, thus leaving the machinists free to continue with
the most skilled parts of their work (Taylor, 1893, pp. 188–9; 1903, pp.
125–6). In addition he also codified the knowledge of the machinists
and attempted to regulate their work in accordance with the principles
thus discovered. Equally, in the case of the bricklayers (who were
actually studied by Gilbreth and Gilbreth, 1953, although Taylor
thoroughly approved of the work done) the preparatory work of mixing
the appropriate grade of mortar, and of laying out the bricks ready for
immediate use by the bricklayer, were both separated off and assigned
to the skilled worker's assistants (Taylor, 1911, pp. 78–9). In both cases
this process was conceptualized by contemporaries, as well as by more
recent writers, as one of subdivision or fragmentation of labour: the
range and level of skills exercised by a worker were reduced.

It is important to notice, however, that this conclusion is one that
reflects a particular view of the process that took place, namely that of
the skilled workers. From their standpoint, skills and activities were
removed from their jobs and transferred either to un/semi-skilled workers, or to new technical and managerial staff. And the public debate

about scientific management that occurred in the USA in the early part of this century also reflected this concern with the job of the skilled worker, involving, as it did, the American Federation of Labor, a largely craft-based union federation (Hoxie, 1915; Nadworny, 1955).

Yet although the perspective, and fate, of the skilled worker is of historical and political importance, one must recognize that other workers were involved in the processes described as fragmentation; and from their point of view, the processes, in fact, looked rather different. In the brick-laying example, ordinary labourers were assigned the task of sorting out the bricks, and of laying them out, ready for use. Mortar mixers were given the responsibility of tempering the mortar so that bricks could be laid with the minimum effort (Taylor, 1911, pp. 78–9). And in the machinists' example, Taylor noted the benefits that accrued from separating off the tasks of minor repair and maintenance and assigning them to day labourers (1903, p. 96). In both these cases, we can see that a process of subdivision or fragmentation viewed from one standpoint, appears as combination of roles viewed from another. Of course we cannot say that one view is 'true' as against the other, for these two views merely represent two aspects, or phases, of a single process, the transfer of work from one group of workers to another. But the revelation of this dual aspect of the process shows up the one-sidedness of the empirical evidence linking scientific management with subdivision of labour.

Thirdly, let us consider the case of foremen, for in this instance Taylor clearly and unambiguously recommended the division of their labour into a series of segmented roles—gang boss, speed boss, route clerk, time and cost clerk, etc. Although Taylor was aware that by so doing he could obtain the same work with cheaper labour (1903, p. 105), the extensiveness of subdivision in this case was tied to a specific, and peculiar, feature of their work. This was the tremendous increase in the number and range of duties that Taylor assigned to management and that arose out of his analysis of the need for planning, regulation and measurement of all aspects of production (1903, p. 94ff). Partly because of this, he argued that suitably qualified labour would be almost impossible to obtain, and only subdivision of the foreman's role would allow companies to find, and to hire, suitable employees. That this process of subdivision would permit the hiring of cheaper labour, or the payment of lower wages, had been shown previously by Babbage.

Finally, it should be pointed out that in two cases in which he was involved, those of ball-bearing inspection, and pig-iron shovelling, Taylor did *not* introduce any further subdivision of labour, even though this would have been possible, for example along product lines (1911, pp. 64–72, 86–89). This throws further doubt, therefore, on the notion that labour subdivision was an integral or a necessary feature of Taylorism.

The second argument introduced earlier as sometimes being made in favour of this proposition is that Taylor sought to demarcate conception and execution, or 'planning' and 'doing'. The truth of this proposition hardly requires documentation, and it was given its most pointed expression in *The Art of Cutting Metals* (1906), which articulated very clearly a control-centred view of the employment relationship. In addition, the accounts of scientific management in practice, reproduced in *Shop Management, Principles of Scientific Management* and the *House Testimony*, were used to show, among other things, the benefits arising out of the separation between planning and doing. This indeed is one of the features for which Taylorism has become so well known.

It is pertinent to observe here, as was done elsewhere in a different context, that much of the conceptual labour that was to be divided from executive work was in fact new work, previously not carried out by any group of workers. Time-and-motion study, and systematic planning and routing of materials are the best examples here. A considerable body of work remained however, and much of this had to do with the codification and systemization of work already performed within the shop. In the case of machinists, Taylor studied machine speeds and feed rates for over 20 years in order to try and elucidate a set of clear relationships between the dozen or so parameters of the raw materials and machinery, and to specify the precise way in which any job was to be done. This knowledge was gathered up and, as Taylor put it 'placed in the hands of management, in the form of charts and slide rules thus facilitating their control over production'.

But there is a fallacy involved in the argument that this codification of knowledge and its placement in the hands of management entails subdivision of labour, the decline of workshop power and the strengthening of management. It rests on the assumption that knowledge is a commodity that can be 'taken' from workers and 'given' to management, but in fact the position is quite different. Even if management, through scientific investigation, accumulates knowledge of production that enables it to revise work norms and methods, the workers in production still possess the knowledge they have accumulated through training and experience. What changes in the situation is not the *possession* of knowledge, but its *monopoly* (see also Burawoy, 1978).

According to the final argument, introduced earlier, on Taylorism and subdivision of labour, one of Taylor's mistakes was to confuse a principle of analysis with a principle of action, in that as well as subdividing jobs for analysis, he also did this in practice (Drucker, 1968). We have examined already the evidence on Taylor's own practices, so we shall focus here on his analysis of jobs. The most complete description of the method of conducting time and motion studies is to be found in *Shop Management*. Work was to be subdivided into elementary units for two reasons. First, by timing very short and quick movements Taylor thought that possible sources of error and interruption would be minimized, and the whole procedure rendered more efficient (1903, p. 169); second, an analysis of work methods would show that some of the motions made were superfluous, and these could be discarded in the calculation of the final time for the job (1911, pp. 117–8). That Taylor did not intend these elementary motions of work to be the bases of new, fragmented jobs is clear from the example which he uses, that of shovelling. Time study, he said, should measure separately the actions of filling the shovel, and of throwing off the contents (1903, pp. 168–9). Presumably these elementary motions were *not* to be performed by two different workers! It is not Taylor then who has confused a principle of analysis with a principle of action, but a number of his critics.

Taylor himself did discuss the limits of subdivision of labour and acknowledged the possibility that jobs might be recombined under his system of management (1903):

> ... When a number of miscellaneous jobs have to be done day after day, none of which can occupy the entire time of a man throughout the whole of a day ... In this case a number of these jobs can be grouped into a daily task which should be assigned, if practicable, to one man ... (p. 71)

This possibility was in fact realized as early as 1923 (see Reilly, 1923) but of more importance than specific instances is the fundamental principle that determined them (1903):

> The task should call for a large day's work, and the man should be paid more than the usual day's pay (p. 82)

Faced with a choice between subdividing labour, and assigning a 'large day's work', Taylor preferred the latter. What this indicates about the status of subdivision of labour within Taylorism is that it was conceived as a means, and not as an end in its own right. Furthermore, as a means for achieving the objective of maximum labour productivity Taylor was clear it was not always appropriate (de Montmollin, 1974; Haber, 1964, p. 26).

2.5 Taylorism and Ford's moving assembly line

Beyond Taylor's own limited applications however matters were different, and nowhere more so than in the expanding consumer goods sector. Gartman (1979) has shown that the introduction of moving assembly lines in the Highland Park plant of the Ford motor company in 1914 was in fact the culmination of a long process of work reorganization. Starting at the turn of the century, management began to remove from the skilled car assemblers some of the ancillary duties, particularly fetching of parts and tools. Over a period of years, more and more of their duties were removed and reallocated to cheaper labour, a process facilitated by increased standardization of parts that undercut the skill and power of the craft workers grounded in product variability and uncertainty.

This permitted an augmentation of management control over production, since they were able more effectively to deploy the pressure of the army of unemployed against a growing proportion of their own workforce. And it also allowed a more or less continual *intensification* of labour in order to meet the growing market for cars. But while the degree of division of labour was taken very much further than under Taylorism, the process can be analysed as an extension of Taylorism *insofar* as it deployed no fresh means of control. The Highland Park 'experiment' altered this situation entirely by substituting for the authority of foremen, the incentive of the pay system, and the pressure of the unemployed, a qualitatively new mode of control embodied in machinery itself (Aglietta, 1979; Fridenson, 1978; Palloix, 1976). The moving assembly line itself appeared to dictate the pace and intensity of work, notwithstanding the fact that its design and implementation reflected management objectives. The introduction of *technical* regulation clearly marks off 'Fordism' from Taylorism (Edwards, 1978).

The two formations are also distinguished by the kinds of industry in which they emerged. Taylor's work was centred principally around batch engineering production in machine shops employing skilled craftworkers. By contrast, Ford pioneered the production line in the *assembly* of consumer goods: cars, bicycles, typewriters and domestic appliances principally (Branson and Heinemann, 1971). And whereas under Taylorism the control exercised by foremen was invariably increased, under Fordism it was arguably less significant than that embodied in the machinery itself. On the other hand *both* were endeavours to create high productivity – high wage movements, and thus stood counterposed to managerial practices centred on the extraction of greater surplus from a stable or stagnant production system and volume. Integral to this productivity increase was an intensification of labour (Gartmann, 1979). Not the least of Taylor's achievements was his implicit recognition that capitalism not only required high rates of exploitation of labour in order to produce profits, but that it also required markets for its realization. The emphasis on *high* wages thus served simultaneously to cater for problems of distribution as well as production (Clegg and Dunkerley, 1980).

2.6 An appraisal of Taylorism

How far did Taylorism influence managerial practice, or was it largely a failure in this respect? And even if it did not directly or necessarily entail enhanced division of labour, did it nevertheless embody a 'dynamic of deskilling' as some have argued (Littler, 1978)?

As a strategy of management, Taylor's own work covered an extraordinarily wide range of topics including machine maintenance, work flow, work planning, pay systems, division of labour, accounting, etc. Much of Taylor's practice was current at the time, but was raised by him to a new level of rigour, as for instance in his work on motor belts and pulleys (Taylor, 1893). Equally, as Aitken (1960) makes clear, many of Taylor's detailed recommendations have become standard practice, certainly throughout manufacturing industry, and to an increasing extent, in the services sector. It is these practices, such as job descriptions, planned flow of work, systematic stock control, detailed unit cost accounting, etc., which we may describe as the 'bedrock' of contemporary management, and to the extent that they are universal features of management they no longer exist as strategic choices, or options, in decision-making terms. What is important for our present purpose is to identify the unique features of Taylorism under the headings of the employment relationship, motivation, techniques and objectives.

(i) The employment relationship

At the level of general orientation to work organization, Taylor retained throughout his three views of the employment relationship an emphasis on *individualism*. This was not, as some commentators have suggested, because he was unaware of workers' social 'needs' and thereby paved the way for the correctives of the 'human relations' school. On the contrary, Taylor's individualism arose from an acute recognition of the *strength* of social bonds and social organization among shopfloor workers and of their capacity to frustrate and obstruct managerial initiatives. It was further evidenced in his often repeated accounts of collective output regulation, not only in the US but throughout Europe. In this context, the conventional view that output regulation was discovered in the Hawthorne studies is quite erroneous.

(ii) Motivation

Taylor's individualism then was partly strategic, but it also rested on a philosophy of hedonism derived from his early classical economics approach to employment. This view resurfaced in Taylor's 'third period' as the material basis for the mental revolution among workers and employers, and brings us to the second crucial component of Taylorism, *financial incentives*. Taylor referred at different stages of his development to slightly differing patterns of motivational forces and techniques. In *A Piece Rate System* (1895) the provision of higher wages for higher productivity was conceptualized in terms of equity, as part of an economic exchange. *Shop Management* (1903) witnessed the elaboration of goal-setting (in the 'task idea') and the importance of rhythm in repetitive work, anticipating Baldamus (1961) (see also Kakar, 1970, p. 98). In addition, the role of foremen was both specialized and extended. Finally, Taylor also wrote of the promotion prospects created through the Planning Department and through his attempts to remove duties from skilled workers and assign them to upgraded labourers (Farquahar, 1924; Hoxie, 1915, p. 93; Taylor, 1912, pp. 245–6).

Nevertheless, this complex structure of mechanisms overlay a simple and fundamental insistence on the centrality of financial incentives, and in that sense the idea that Taylorism rested on a concept of economic rationality is more or less accurate even if it does not quite do justice to the complexity of Taylorism.

(iii) Techniques

If financial incentives were the principal means for augmenting and securing work performance, decisions about the volume of work required by the employer and the methods to be used were to be derived from *time-and-motion studies* of actual work performances. Taylor was not the first to use this method, and both Midvale Steel and Bethlehem Steel held records of such studies. Equally Taylor's own work focused on job *times*, although he also made recommendations on methods, but it was Gilbreth and Gilbreth (1953) who principally developed the use of film to record actual physical motions. But Taylor's time-and-motion study was not, like some contemporary practice, merely a process of *recording*, at best for purposes of collective or individual bargaining. Rather it was a process of *regulation* of work performance, to be carried out systematically and to be tied closely to pay levels. Moreover best work methods were to be determined and prescribed.

(iv) Objectives

The objectives of these endeavours were twofold and interconnected: control of labour and raised productivity. Taylor's observations on 'soldiering' have already been discussed, dating back to his first experiences of industrial work in the late 1870s. But it was not until his 'second period' views began to crystallize after 1900 that *control* came to be seen as the essential precondition both for the increase of productivity and for the maintenance of the new levels of productivity. In his 'third period', control and co-operation coexisted somewhat uneasily, but the *mechanisms* of control, payment systems and time-and-motion study remained.

This complex of strategy (employment relationship and motivation), techniques and objectives can be said to constitute the specificity of Taylorism as a management practice. Its insertion into industrial capitalism at the turn of the century may well have accelerated the pace at which extended division of labour was being introduced, as some writers have suggested, although the evidence on this point is by no means clear. Littler (1978) argues for such a connection, partly on the basis of a post-World War Two empirical survey of management practice which found, not unexpectedly, continued adherence to subdivision of labour and cost minimization as criteria for designing jobs. Yet in the absence of a *theoretical* justification for the Taylorism – fragmentation link, such empirical work actually tells us very little about Taylorism.

Brown's (1977) study suggests that Taylorism was used very selectively in Britain before 1914. Although the techniques—time-and-motion study and incentive-payment systems—spread throughout sectors of British industry as part of a drive to raise labour productivity, there is little evidence of enhanced division of labour connected with this phenomenon, and some evidence of strong, and effective resistance (Brown, 1977, Chapter 7; Phelps-Brown, 1959).

The fourfold differentiation of Taylorism along these lines also permits a more refined analysis of its implementation in different contexts. Even in the USA in the 1920s, significant sections of the American Federation of Labor came to support the *techniques* of Taylorism, and to a lesser degree the *objectives* within a strategic framework that was at variance with Taylorism. Union – management cooperation, as espoused by the AFL, was much closer in concept to the 'industrial democracy' advocated by the more progressive, pluralist Taylorites such as Cooke and Valentine (Nadworny, 1955; Nelson, 1975). In Japan the uptake of Taylorism was both rapid and extensive, despite the absence of strong craft unions, as Taylorism harmonized neatly with the paternalistic and welfare-oriented larger Japanese companies (Wood and Kelly, 1982).

2.7 Conclusions

One of the most important points to emerge from this analysis of Taylorism is the conclusion that Taylorism is not synonymous with increased fragmentation of labour. It is therefore possible for Taylorism to be applied without further extension of the division of labour, a point that will be vital in understanding job redesign in flowline production (Chapters 4 and 5). Second, many writers have misunderstood Taylorism because they failed either to understand its development over time, or its complexity. It was shown that Taylor's view of the employment relationship shifted from an emphasis on economic exchange through to an emphasis on control and finally to an appreciation of the crucial need for cooperation in industry. Taylorism was differentiated into a set of ideas and practices based on an overall strategy, a set of techniques, and a set of objectives. This analysis makes it easier to understand the differential implementation of Taylorism, and to see, for instance, that it differs significantly from Ford's assembly-line principles. In the next chapter some of the ideas of Taylor are used to produce a new theory of job redesign.

3   Origins and assumptions of classical job redesign: a critique and a new theory

3.1   Social science in industry in the interwar period

Braverman's (1974) assessment of the content, role and impact of industrial social science following the First World War is schematic, simplistic and unflattering—but also, very accurate:

> The later schools of Hugo Münsterberg, Elton Mayo, and others of this type dealt primarily with the adjustment of the worker to the on going production process as that process was designed by the industrial engineer . . . personnel departments and academics have busied themselves with the selection, training, manipulation, pacification, and adjustment of 'manpower' to suit the work processes so organised. Taylorism dominates the world of production; the practitioners of 'human relations' and 'industrial psychology' are the maintenance crew for the human machinery.   (p. 87)

However, as Chapter 2 has shown, the relationship between Taylorism and early industrial psychology was rather more complex than Braverman suggests. Baritz (1960), author of the most detailed historical study of US industrial psychology, has argued that Taylorism served to demarcate a terrain, or set of problems, based on the assessment and regulation of worker *abilities* and *motivation* in order to improve their job *performance*. The American successors to Taylor worked within this set of problems for a considerable period although initially their focus was on aptitude measurement and employee selection. These subjects had been brought to prominence following American entry into the first World War, and the mobilization of psychologists to test rapidly large numbers of army recruits. American industrial psychology continued to expand throughout the 1920s and 1930s on the basis of aptitude tests, in line with the growth of the US labour force, from 37 millions in 1910 to 50 millions by 1935 (Braverman, 1974, p. 379).

The readiness with which industrial psychologists offered their services to employers reflected a strategy of legitimation, according to Baritz, but given the middle class origins and values of many psychologists it is doubtful whether this process caused them much anguish, moral or otherwise. Even with the expansion into counselling and attitude measurement in the 1930s, the dominant view remained 'that psychology should be used to adjust the worker to his job' (Baritz, 1960, p. 135).

Although human-relations theory challenged the mechanistic views inherent in the testing movement through its conception of informal groups, social needs and social structures, it reinforced the dominant tendency to take the detail division of labour as given.

British industrial psychology arrived at a similar position, albeit somewhat later and by a very different route. When the extension of working hours in the World War One munitions factories failed to raise productivity sufficiently (indeed, in some cases it resulted in a reduction in productivity) the Health of Munitions Workers' Committee began investigations into fatigue. The committee, quickly redesignated the Industrial Fatigue Research Board, soon advanced from a physiological to a psychological concept of fatigue (Rose, 1975). Postwar industrial studies led to observations on the effects of repetitive work conceptualized in terms of boredom and monotony. These studies (which continued up to the 1940s) were often concerned directly therefore with the effects of, and responses to, the division of labour (see Myers, 1929; Wyatt and Fraser, 1928). One of the leading sponsors of this work was the National Institute for Industrial Psychology, but its precarious financial position served to curtail both the scope and the diffusion of the work. It has also been suggested that the Depression extinguished any lingering necessity for industrial psychology in Britain because of the vast expansion in the reserve army of labour (not to mention the political defeat of the working class in the 1926 General Strike). This suggestion should be treated with caution, if not scepticism, since the effect of the Depression in America was apparently the reverse, and the expansion of industrial psychology continued unabated.

If US industrial psychology in this period was largely a *technology*, its transition to a *discipline* made considerable progress with the publication of Hoppock's study of 'job satisfaction' in 1935 (See Baritz, 1960).

The terrain of satisfaction – motivation – performance was now mapped out on the basis of existing assumptions about work. The emphasis on 'adjusting' the worker to his job in the interests of job performance underlined the managerial view of industrial conflict as a problem in need of a solution. One possible solution had emerged from the Hawthorne studies: friendly supervision and 'good' communications could ease conflicts and tensions that might otherwise escalate into major confrontations.

The growth of industrial psychology away from the study of division of labour and of the conflicts structured into the employment relationship; its assignment of privilege to 'social' over 'economic' needs; and its production of supervisory and communications recommendations might all have suggested that industrial psychology was destined for a marginal position in the armoury of management techniques, though for a more significant role as ideology (Bendix, 1956).

Yet by 1960 industrial psychology was beginning to enjoy a new vogue and to feel its approaches had been vindicated. How had this transformation come about? The answers provided by industrial psychologists themselves were complex and varied, but all of them focused on a growing contradiction between the types of jobs provided in manufacturing industry and the psychological characteristics of job holders.

3.2 Beginnings of job redesign

Empirically, several studies conducted in the late 1940s pointed to the dissatisfactions engendered by work on vehicle assembly lines, the most famous being the study by Walker and Guest (1952). They reported, in particular, that workers complained of lack of variety in their jobs and objected to the constant pacing by the moving line. The suggestion, towards the end of the book, that a moderate reversal of the detail division of labour would improve worker satisfaction arose in part from precisely such an exercise carried out a few years earlier at IBM. Walker's classic paper 'The problem of the repetitive job' (1950) described a machine shop in which the discrete work roles of operator, set-up man and checker had been reintegrated into a single enlarged job, resulting in labour cost savings for IBM and increased satisfaction and regrading for some of their employees. A few years later the other author, Guest (1957) was able to write about 'job enlargement' as 'a revolution in job design' and describe four case studies of mass production and clerical work, where flowline organization had been reduced or abolished.

These studies seemed to vindicate the psychological emphasis on job satisfaction as against a vulgar economics concern with 'rational-economic' man. This distinction was conceptualized in terms of jobs by Herzberg *et al.* (1959) and for individuals by Maslow (1943), and forms a crucial theoretical underpinning for one section of the job-redesign movement. Herzberg was in fact more interested in *motivation* than satisfaction, and argued that the determinants of motivation fell into two classes: those extrinsic to the individual—pay, supervision, company policy—that could alleviate dissatisfaction, and those intrinsic to the individual—such as feelings of responsibility, recognition—that promoted satisfaction. He went on to argue that the latter were associated with effective job performance and were highly motivating.

Herzberg claimed in the Introduction to *The Motivation to Work* (1959), that the issue of motivation had arisen because the growth of affluence in the capitalist economies had satisfied men's basic needs and undercut the motive power of 'carrot and stick methods'. He referred briefly and with reservations to the work of Maslow in this context. In 1943, Maslow published an account of his 'need hierarchy theory', according to which human needs were ordered in an ascending scale embracing physiological, safety, social, self-esteem and self-actualizing needs. As one level was satisfied, the next was thought to come into effect. Although many employees' lower level needs had been satisfied, Herzberg (1966) later argued that the design of industrial (and service) jobs was failing to satisfy their higher needs (see Chapter 7).

Not all writers in the job-redesign school based themselves on Maslow. Some argued for job redesign on the basis of social changes. Rising levels of education, and falling levels of unemployment, were said to have generated rising aspirations, especially among younger people (Berg, 1970; Blauner, 1964; Kornhauser, 1965; see Halsey, 1972, for UK data). Equally, moves towards less authoritarian teaching methods in schools were seen as having underwritten the

increasing trend for employees not to submit automatically to authority, an argument that took on force after 1968 (Report of Committee of
Enquiry, 1977). These higher demands of work were thought to be
reflected in such diverse phenomena as calls for participation in enterprise decision-making and, when frustrated, in job quitting, absenteeism, sabotage and strikes (see Kelly, 1981, for more details).

Arguments of this type were frequently produced by sociotechnical
theorists in America such as Davis and Trist. The contribution of
sociotechnical theory to this overall movement was threefold: the early
(1950s) studies located their work as a reaction against both human-
relations theory, with its emphasis on the social aspects of work organization, and against technological determinism, which emphasized
the constraints on job design emanating from technology. It was argued
instead that these two components of an enterprise were aspects of a
single sociotechnical system. Pursuit of either technology or social
organization alone would not bring about maximum or optimum 'effectiveness'. This could only be achieved by 'joint optimization' of both
aspects of the system (see Chapter 6).

Secondly, writers such as Davis (1957), Emery (1959) and Emery
and Thorsrud (1964) developed criteria for job redesign that would
engender motivation and satisfaction. In particular they identified
variety, discretion (or autonomy), task wholeness, and responsibility as
crucial features.

Thirdly, it was in the 1960s that some sociotechnical theorists began
to argue for a 'Second Industrial Revolution' thesis. With the growth of
automated and semi-automated technologies, the dissatisfying, repetitive jobs engineered by 'scientific managers' were being gradually
eliminated, and replaced by more challenging tasks, such as machine
maintenance and process control (Trist, 1976). For some theorists,
these processes of upgrading were seen as more or less inevitable,
whereas others argued they were contingent on managerial choices that
themselves reflected either traditional, scientific management values,
or the more enlightened neo-human relations values of trust and
cooperation (Theories X and Y in MacGregor's, 1960, terms).

MacGregor was one of a group of writers—the others were Argyris
and Likert—sometimes known as the 'neo-human relations' theorists
because of their emphasis on social relations at the workplace. Despite
their differences, each produced models of opposed organizational
structures and supporting values. Argyris (1957) examined the ways in

which organizational control systems reproduced patterns of dependency and stunted individual growth; Likert (1961) emphasized more flexible and participative organizational structures as crucial to the release of employees' abilities and commitments, previously suppressed by authoritarian structures. These writers played an important role in educating managements to think in terms of harnessing and exploiting employee resources rather than trying to suppress them or minimize their effects (*cf.* Davis *et al.*, 1955).

Davis (1971) did reintroduce strong elements of technological determinism into sociotechnical systems theory by arguing for a fairly straightforward link between technology and social values. Where the mass-production technologies of the Industrial Revolution were associated with competition and conflicting objectives, the new technologies were more likely to be associated with collaboration around linked objectives, i.e., with increased social integration.

These arguments on the *origins* of job redesign are closely linked, as we shall see, with theories of the *mechanisms* of job redesign, and they certainly 'captured', however obliquely, significant socioeconomic trends in the post-war period.

Productivity growth in the USA and UK was undoubtedly slower than in its major competitors, France, West Germany and Japan, despite extensive automation in several branches of industry in the late 1950s and early 1960s. This combination of factors was one possible determinant of a concern with 'human resources' and labour productivity and was reflected in the UK, for instance, in widespread promotion of productivity bargaining in the 1960s (Clegg, 1969). Evidence on job attitudes is notoriously ambiguous and difficult to interpret, but it was certainly true in the UK that public sector expansion provided new opportunities for upward social mobility by working class children. At the same time there occurred a sharper degree of labour market segmentation in many of the advanced capitalist countries as many lower-paid and lower-status jobs came to be occupied by social minorities: women and blacks in the US and UK; Yugoslavian and Turkish 'guest-workers' in West Germany; Finns in Sweden; Algerians in France; Belgians in the Netherlands (Castles and Kosack, 1980). Low rates of unemployment, economic expansion, and improved social security provisions allowed many young indigenous workers to avoid lower-status occupations. The same factors also resulted in a characteristic increase in labour turnover as labour markets tightened, and, although the evidence is ambiguous, absenteeism does seem to have risen in certain branches of industry, especially in the 1960s (Berg *et al.*, 1978).

Job-redesign theory was also selectively reinforced by events and case studies. The construction of the Volvo Kalmar car assembly plant was widely hailed as a radical blow at the assembly line. The fact that all the major *principles* of flowlines were embodied in the Kalmar plant was overlooked (Emery, 1975). In 1972 a long strike at the new General Motor's Lordstown, Ohio, car plant highlighted the Swedish – American contrast (Gainor, 1975). Young workers with 'blue-collar blues' were said to have revolted against monotonous and controlled jobs. The fact that their actual grievances were the traditional ones of the speed of the production line and its control, as well as other working conditions, received less publicity. As Brooks (1972) wryly commented:

> . . . It was another strike in the long struggle of auto workers to improve their lot. A similar strike over like issues in Norwood, Ohio, received zero attention because it did not fit into the new conventional wisdom. The Norwood workers, you see, are older.

Again, job-redesign projects conducted by a few big multinationals—Philips, ICI, Texas Instruments, Cummins Engine—received extensive coverage in the popular media, and were used as demonstrations of the validity and possibility of job redesign.

If we combine all these arguments on the origins of job redesign with their emphasis on individual characteristics and job content, we would come up with a model of the kind set out in Fig. 3.1.

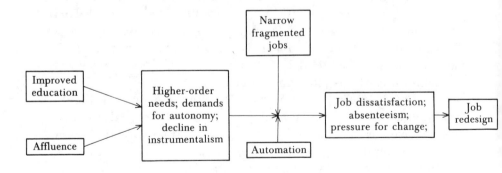

Fig. 3.1 The origins of job design according to the classical theory

In the late 1950s and in the 1960s, a series of studies suggested one substantial modification to the general view of the origins of job redesign portrayed so far. According to these studies, there was a section of the industrial workforce that was either disinterested in job redesign (Hulin and Blood, 1968; Kennedy and O'Neill, 1958; Kilbridge, 1960a; MacKinney *et al.*, 1962), or was attached, or adapted, to repetitive work (Smith, 1955; Smith and Lem, 1955; Turner and Miclette, 1962).

Explanation of these differences in work attitudes centred initially on urban – rural differences in background or factory location (Susman, 1973; Turner and Lawrence, 1965), and description was based on attachment to middle-class work values, especially the Protestant ethic (Blood and Hulin, 1967; Stone, 1975, 1976). Surveys of worker attitudes from the 1950s to the 1970s showed that in response to a general question on job satisfaction approximately 75–90% respondents declared themselves satisfied (Quinn and de Mandilovitch, 1974; *Work in America*, 1972). Appreciation of individual differences in work attitudes has been differentially incorporated into job redesign theories and practices as we shall see below.

3.3 The general perspective of classical job redesign

The term perspective will be used here to designate a set of assumptions and objectives, as well as significant absences, which together constitute the ideological – theoretical terrain occupied by several theories and practices of job redesign. No single theory is likely to embrace all of the components of this terrain: some indeed explicitly reject particular assumptions, and there have of course been significant developments within the theories.

The purpose of describing this general perspective is twofold: first the assumptions underlying job redesign are not always made explicit and their revelation will assist their critical appraisal; second, against the conventional account, which portrays 'progressive' changes in 'models of man at work' from Taylorism onwards, it is important to show the affinities and continuities that exist at a deeper level (*cf.* Schein, 1978). These assumptions can be located in four areas: social values, individual needs, relations between workers and employers and organizational change.

(i) Social values: anti-materialism

This is one of the most pervasive and significant features of job-redesign theory and manifests itself in three principal ways.

(a) Work and employment

The economic character of the employment relationship features in job-redesign writings either as a background feature or not at all. The early 'job enlargement' writers were principally concerned with the relationship between division of labour and job attitudes and behaviour. Wages, and the wage – effort bargain (Baldamus, 1961; Behrend, 1957) central to the employment relationship, were hardly mentioned. Although Herzberg *et al.* (1959) partly corrected this oversight it was only to argue that these features of the employment relationship were relevant factors, but were less significant for performance improvements than were motivators intrinsic to the work itself. This implicit distinction between work and employment has been widely used in connection with the assumption that job attitudes and behaviour are increasingly a response to the challenge, variety and other intrinsic properties of a job irrespective of its context in employment. The problems of implementation of job redesign have forced some writers to recognize that job content can often only be altered in conjunction with other organizational features (e.g., Hackman, 1977; Herrick and Maccoby, 1975). Wage adjustments, however, are often treated as a necessary precondition for job redesign, for example to satisfy requirements of equity, but continue to be denied *motivational* significance (e.g., Herrick and Maccoby, 1975; Hill, 1971, p. 144; Walton, 1974).

(b) Division of labour as a personnel problem

Anti-materialism also manifests itself in the diagnosis of the limits to division of labour, which are seen to centre around personnel problems (Hackman and Lawler, 1972):

> . . . it has been shown that simple, routine non-challenging jobs often lead to high employee dissatisfaction, to increased absenteeism and turnover, and to substantial difficulties in effectively managing employees who work on simplified jobs. The expected increases in profitability from work simplification have not materialised as had been hoped, and the reasons apparently have very much to do with the human problems encountered when jobs are standardised and simplified.

Little attention has been paid to the strains placed on division of labour because of changes in product and labour markets outside the enterprise.

(c) New bases of conflict

Implicit in the view that material needs have largely been satisfied, or that material factors, even if manipulated, can produce relatively little change in job performance is a radically new theory of industrial conflict. The conflicts between workers (or unions) and employers once fuelled by wages are seen as less significant than the new conflict between 'the individual' and 'the organization'. The individual is assumed by Argyris (1957), MacGregor (1960), Likert (1961) and Maslow (1943), to have various needs for independent thought and action, stimulation and challenge, which are frustrated by the monolithic organization that regiments and regulates the most minute details of job performance.

This area shows more clearly than any other the influence of the intellectual climate of the 1950s, particularly as reflected in American sociology. The economic expansion of this period was providing a progressive increase in living standards for millions of ordinary people, and by transforming their life styles was thought to be lifting them out of the proletariat and into the ranks of the middle class. This 'embourgeoisement' implied that the industrial class conflict fuelled by economic problems would decline, as indeed Ross and Hartmann (1960) suggested. Accompanying the decline of class conflict would be the decline of class ideology, a thesis expounded by Bell (1960). What sort of society was emerging in place of the old industrial capitalism? On this question theorists were divided, but the dominant response in the 1950s foresaw the development of a 'mass society' populated by privatized and isolated individuals sharing a common culture, but paradoxically lacking social integration. The same society was dominated by large, powerful, bureaucratic organizations which further stultified individual aspirations (cf. Riesman, 1953).

Job-redesign theory grew and matured in this intellectual climate and its early formulations were stamped with the anti-materialism, and a concern for 'the individual' characteristic of this climate.

(ii) The active, complex subject

MacGregor (1960) drew an important distinction between two managerial views of the worker, which he labelled Theories X and Y. According to the traditional, Theory X, popularized by scientific management, 'man' had an inherent dislike of work, had to be directed and controlled, craving little apart from security. Workers lacked ambition and they were resistant to change. By contrast, Theory Y stated that 'man' had a hierarchy of needs—physiological, safety, social, self-esteem and self-actualization (Maslow's hierarchy)—that work was natural, that man would perform well in the service of objectives to which he was committed, commitment being a function of rewards, and that he learns and seeks responsibility.

The assumptions of Theory Y have informed, in different ways the most significant work in job redesign. Herzberg (1966) explicitly deployed a higher-order versus lower-order needs model in describing 'the nature of man':

> ... man has two basic sets of needs – his animal needs, which relate to the environment, and his distinctive human needs, which relate to the tasks with which he is uniquely involved   (p. 12)

In relating to these tasks man is:

> . . . impelled to determine, to discover, to achieve, to actualise, to progress and to add to his existence.   (p. 168)

Hackman and Lawler (1972) and Hackman and Oldham (1976), proponents of the job-characteristics model of job redesign (see later), argue that higher-order needs are becoming more salient as motivators, and that these include needs for personal growth, and for feelings of worthwhile accomplishment.

Within sociotechnical systems theory, Rice originally argued simply that man has a need 'to get on with the job' (1958, p. 34; 1963, p. 256ff). Later work in this tradition posited human 'requirements' of work consisting in opportunities for learning, for satisfaction of social needs, for involvement in decision-making, and for the creation of links to the outside world and of a desirable future (Thorsrud, 1967, 1972).

In short, the subject of enquiry was no longer conceived purely as a passive commodity, as a potentially recalcitrant element of production, or as a rational-economic man, but as an active and complex subject whose abilities could be harnessed to the goals of the organization.

(iii) Reconciliation of interests and social integration

The third element within the perspective of classical job redesign is an optimistic assessment of the possibilities of reconciling employer and worker interests. According to Herzberg *et al.* (1959):

> To industry, the pay off for a study of job attitudes would be increased productivity, decreased turnover, decreased absenteeism, and smoother working relations . . . To the individual, an understanding of the forces that lead to improved morale would bring greater happiness and greater self-realization.   (p. ix)

Whereas Hackman and Lawler (1972) were even more precise, if more cautious:

> . . . it may be possible under specifiable conditions simultaneously to achieve high employee satisfaction and high employee effort toward organizational goals.   (p. 147)

By building into jobs variety, autonomy, responsibility and other desirable characteristics, it is suggested that the motivation of job holders will be increased, thus resulting in higher performance levels for the employer. At the same time the performance of such a redesigned job will be a source of greater satisfaction for the job incumbent, and the interests of both parties will thus be catered for.

However, this mutual-benefits thesis rests on an implicit, asymmetrical analysis of worker and employer interests. Although employers continue to be concerned with economic matters such as productivity, costs, and profitability, workers' needs (or interests—the terms are rarely delineated clearly) are said to centre almost exclusively in the psychological sphere because *their* material needs have been largely satisfied (see above). By advancing a new conception of worker interests, job-redesign writers have been able theoretically to circumvent the obstacles to interest reconciliation and social integration arising from the employment relationship, and provide the foundation for a very much greater degree of unity of purpose within organizations (Davis, 1971a).

The other crucial component of this view is that attitudes and behaviour are, or can be, brought into alignment: job satisfaction *and* job performance can both be increased. The weight of evidence from correlational studies of attitudes and behaviour suggests a rather different and more complex conclusion. Herzberg *et al.* (1959) simply comment that the conventional view at the time of there being *no* significant relationship rests on a degree of scepticism they happen not to share. A more sophisticated approach was taken by Hackman and his colleagues who argue on the basis of Vroom's (1964) expectancy theory of motivation that satisfaction and performance will be correlated *only* where employees have higher-order needs and where they perceive a close link between need satisfaction and job performance.

(iv) Theory and practice: committed pragmatism

Like the earlier human-relations movement, the job-redesign perspective is both optimistic and normative (Strauss, 1970). Its proponents believe that given sufficient support and encouragement by top management, lower-level managers can successfully embark on radical reorganization of division of labour (e.g., Klein, 1976; Wilkinson, 1971). Job redesign is both theory and technique, and the link between them is predicated on the close ties between job-redesign theorists and their designated principal change agents, managers. Many of the well-known job-redesign writers are in fact managers themselves: P. Gyllenhammar (Volvo), T. Persson (Saab-Scania), L. Ketchum (General Foods), I. McDavid (BOC), Sorcher (GEC), R. Ford (AT&T), E. J. Bryan (Cummins Engine), or prominent ex-managers, e.g., O. Tynan (ex-BL, now Head of the Work Research Unit), and P. Hill (ex-Shell, now a consultant). Many are consultants who work closely with managements; D. Burden, C. Jacobs, R. Janson, F. Herzberg, R. Walters, L.K. Taylor, W. Paul, K. Robertson, L. Klein, F. den Hertog. Others, particularly in Sweden, work for employers' organizations: R. Lindholm, J.P. Norstedt, A. Noren, H. Lindestad, S. Aguren, T. Edgren. Finally, there are academics who have written explicitly for managements and managerial specialists: D. Birchall, A. Wilkinson, K. Carby, F. Foulkes. Links with trade unions and trade unionists are, by contrast, few and far between.

As Berg *et al.* (1978) have pointed out, job-redesign theory presupposes the manager of an organization to hold almost unlimited power to change an existing division of labour, notwithstanding market, finance, corporate or other constraints. Obstacles to change are invariably located *within* the organization, e.g., in particular social groups, such as supervisors, or trade union representatives, or are thought to be embodied in outmoded values or philosophies such as Theory X. The implication of the latter analysis is that education and enlightenment by intellectuals is a significant element in the process of social change: structural contradictions or wider social forces are rarely discussed (*cf.* Goldthorpe, 1974, on similar solutions to British industrial relations problems).

It is also assumed that work in employment ought to be a major source of need satisfaction and fulfillment for individuals. In part, this assumption derives from a universal theory of human needs coupled with the premiss that lower-order, material needs have been satisfied. The analysis would seem to preclude the notion of relative, rather than absolute deprivation, according to which 'needs' are socially defined using specific significant reference groups (Runciman, 1966). It does nevertheless entail the possibility of individual differences in attitudes to work, even if, as with Herzberg, those continuing to display an instrumental orientation are considered to be suffering from an 'illness of motivation' (1966, p. 81).

3.4 Shortcomings of the classical perspective

(i) Neglect of organizational environments

The definition, in this stylized account, of organizational problems as principally *psychological* in character undoubtedly captures part of the 'reality' of post-war industrial and service organizations. Full employment allowed many people an unprecedented degree of choice in the labour market. At the same time it is crucial to recognize that the problems of employing organizations do not derive simply from their labour force (*cf.* Heckscher, 1980): an industrial organization in a capitalist economy normally competes with other firms and may be faced with a series of problems stemming from its product market (Channon, 1973). Companies may also have to update their products, or even to introduce new designs (Packard, 1960); they may have to reorganize their management structure along product and/or geographical (particularly international) lines (Burns and Stalker, 1961); they may face difficulties in investment programmes; complex technologies, e.g., new computer systems, strain the existing organizational structure (Mumford and Banks, 1967). In short, even where company managements identify their problems in terms of labour productivity or labour costs, it does not follow that the solution lies in a reorganization of labour, even less in a strategy aimed specifically at morale or motivation. Labour productivity is contingent on a range of factors—psychological, social, technical—of which motivation is but one.

These comments apply less to sociotechnical-systems theorists, who as we shall see in Chapter 6, have sought to conceptualize the organization as an 'open' system, exchanging inputs and outputs with its environment, and hence as being amenable to environmental pressure and constraint (Emery and Trist, 1965).

(ii) Overemphasis on personnel problems

If job redesign was primarily an organizational response to 'personnel' problems, one would expect such problems to feature prominently in the reasons given by companies for embarking on their respective initiatives. Table 3.1 is a 'survey of surveys' and presents the frequency with which two broad classes of reason—economic and personnel—were advanced by companies that had undertaken a programme or an exercise in job redesign. The data are taken from questionnaires, or interviews, completed by managers whose specialism is normally not stated.

Economic reasons—productivity, costs or quality problems—were cited by 35–67% of respondents, whereas personnel reasons—absenteeism, turnover, or morale—were cited by the slightly lower number of 26–51%. It appears therefore that personnel considerations predominated in probably less than half the companies using job redesign, and that more traditional problems stood to the fore (cf. Heckscher, 1980). Caution needs to be exercised in the interpretation of such results, since the criteria for selection in the secondary source surveys are unclear. Equally, it is not always clear how the terms 'job enrichment', etc., were used either by the investigators or the respondents. Finally, it is rarely stated which managerial specialist actually completed the questionnaires or interview schedules, and since the perceptions of say, personnel and production managers could differ appreciably (see Appendix) this is an important omission.

(iii) Overemphasis on job dissatisfaction

Evidence in support of other elements of the perspective of job redesign is equally unconvincing. Studies of job dissatisfaction and collective

Table 3.1 Reasons for using job redesign
(% age respondents citing) *

	Productivity, costs or quality problems	Personnel problems —absenteeism, turnover or morale
Reif and Schoderbeck (1966)	52%	35%
Wilkinson (1971)**	38%	43%
Work in America (1972)	62%	42%
Birchall and Wild (1973)	45%	26%
Butteriss and Murdoch (1975)	44%	36%
Birchall and Hammond (1978)	35%	51%
Alber (1979a)**	49%	51%
Lupton *et al.* (1979)	67%	39%

* Reif and Schoderbeck (1966) sampled 276 of Fortune's top 500 industrial concerns, plus 50 each of the largest life insurance, transport and utility companies in the USA. Wilkinson (1971) visited 24 companies in Scandinavia, Belgium, Holland and the UK. *Work in America* (1972) reported on 34 case studies, 24 in the USA, the rest in Europe. Birchall and Wild (1973) reported on 91 applications, mainly in the USA, but also in Europe. Butteriss and Murdoch (1975) reported on 109 applications among manufacturing and service industries in the UK. Birchall and Hammond (1978) surveyed 32, mainly service organizations in the UK, focusing on clerical work. Lupton *et al.* (1979) surveyed European manufacturers who had used job redesign. Alber (1979a) surveyed 58 American organizations using job redesign, both manufacturing and service.

** % *reasons* given, not cases

industrial action have produced ambiguous results, but it appears that demographic variables offer the best predictions of attitudinal or behavioural 'militancy' (Kelly and Nicholson, 1980). If we consider statistical analyses of causes of industrial conflict, we discover not a declining concern with material issues, as job-redesign theorists posit, but a continuing and recently an increasing concern. In statistics collected by the UK Department of Employment, some two-thirds of officially recorded industrial stoppages were assigned a principal cause either of wages or workloads throughout the period 1950–76 (Smith *et al.*, 1978). Economic or material needs are likely to continue to play a prominent role in industrial conflict, especially under conditions of high inflation. Such conditions, particularly since the late 1960s in the USA and the UK, have served to slow down, and for short periods actually reverse, increases in living standards, and with inflation running at between 10% and 20% per annum over the past few years, there seems good reason to be sceptical of claims that the motive power of material needs is being eroded by affluence.

Again, reviews of the relationship between job satisfaction and absenteeism have yielded mixed conclusions, with the predicted negative correlation obtaining in some studies but not others (Nicholson *et al.*, 1976). The relationship between these variables appears to be mediated by organizational features, such as size, or technology. Likewise, analyses of labour turnover have identified the phenomenon as a response to 'pull' from the environment, e.g., alternative jobs, changes in domestic circumstances, as well as to 'push' from dissatisfying work (Lyons, 1972; Mobley, 1977).

(iv) Neglect of variations in the incidence of job redesign

The focus on personnel problems also leaves open the question of variations in the incidence of job redesign. The impression produced by the literature on the subject is that of a growing *movement,* spreading throughout the industrial world, and manifested in the growth of national centres, or institutes (as in Norway, Sweden, Britain, USA), allocation of greater resources for relevant research (West Germany), and the expansion of published case studies from a wide range of industries and countries (see for instance, Butteriss, 1975). We can consider temporal trends by simply plotting the starting dates of all known, i.e., published, cases of job redesign, whatever their form, their industrial or their national location, and we find the pattern shown in Fig. 3.2.

Although there was a substantial growth in the number of published job-redesign exercises started between 1950 and 1976, the general upward trend has been punctuated by a series of troughs, in 1951/52, 1958/59, 1961/62 and from 1972 onwards. The significance of these dates is that each represents a downturn, or recession in the advanced capitalist economies as a whole, when economic activity fell (or its rate of growth slowed down) and unemployment rose (Halsey, 1972, for the UK; Boff, 1977, for the USA). Indeed MacGregor, writing in 1960, observed that the American recession of 1957/58 put an end to a decade of experimentation with 'democracy' in industry as employers resorted to more traditional methods of control over labour. The overall, tem-

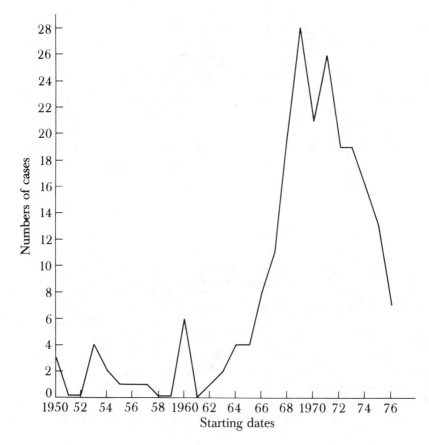

Fig. 3.2 Incidence of job-redesign cases 1950–1976[1]

poral trends could suggest that job redesign is a tactical alternative for more traditional methods of labour control that have been undercut by full employment. It may also be the case that recession introduces a conservative ethos that militates against *any* innovation.

(v) Neglect of the wage – effort bargain

Despite the emphasis on intrinsic motivation and higher-order needs, many job-redesign exercises *have* involved increases in basic rates of pay and/or earnings. And the insistence that job redesign satisfies the mutual interests of the parties concerned is difficult to reconcile with the finding that many cases of redesign have involved the displacement of labour (see also Carby, 1976). These data are taken from all published cases of job redesign in which information was provided on the provision of pay rises, the elimination of labour or the type of payment system in use, and the results are summarized in Table 3.2. The Table shows, for instance, that labour was eliminated in 121 cases of job redesign, which was 68% of the cases where information on labour was available. Clearly these mechanisms are sufficiently widespread to be of some significance for job performance. They are also interrelated, as Table 3.3 shows.

*Table 3.2 Incidence of extrinsic and structural mechanisms
for raising job performance in cases of job redesign
(as percentage of total number of cases)[2]*

Item	Incidence	Number of cases
Pay rises	65%	93
Incentive pay systems	63%	45
Labour elimination	68%	121

*Table 3.3 Relationship between the incidence of pay rises and
labour elimination in cases of job redesign[3]*

| | Labour eliminated | | |
	Yes	No	Total
Pay raised	35	12	47
Pay not raised	11	24	35
Total	46	36	82

$\chi^2 = 12.2, p < .001$

These changes in pay and manning levels are more commonly examined as the outcomes of collective bargaining, i.e., as adjustments in the exchange relationship between labour and capital. The process does not preclude analysis in terms of motivation, but the emphasis in studies of bargaining in one crucial respect *reverses* the typical sequence postulated by job-redesign theory. Where the latter sees motivation to be under the control of rewards emanating from job performance which then reinforce that performance, collective bargaining is a process where rewards and performance levels are settled *in advance* of any desired changes in work organization. Subsequent changes in job performance then represent the fulfillment of obligations by employees within the terms of an exchange relationship.

There is indeed some weak evidence to show there exists a relationship between plant unionization and two key elements in the wage — effort bargain and provision of pay rises and job displacement (see Table 3.4). It appears, then, that in all plants labour is more likely to be eliminated than not, and that there is a marginally higher chance of elimination in non-unionized plants. Table 3.4 also suggests that unions *may* have more successfully influenced wage levels than job levels (although the difference is again not significant).

Table 3.4 Labour elimination, pay rises and trade unions (number of cases)[4]

	Labour eliminated?*		Pay increased?**	
	Yes	No	Yes	No
Unionized plant	23	15	32	12
Non-unionized plant	8	4	5	6

* χ^2 not significant
** $\chi^2 = 1.86$ (not significant)

Studies of the operation of financial incentives (which were reported in 63% of cases of job redesign) have produced evidence that further underlines the importance of looking at the wage — effort bargain in the study of job redesign. The introduction to a collection of readings entitled *Management and Motivation* (Vroom and Deci, 1970) observed that:

> This approach to motivation rests on a rather substantial foundation of psychological research and theory   (p. 13)

A similar point was reiterated in two reviews of the literature on pay incentives, written by psychologists. Acording to Lawler (1971):

> ... individual (incentive) plans typically lead to substantial increases in productivity   (p. 128)

Whereas Marriott (1968) noted that despite its many deficiencies the available evidence served to:

> ... reinforce the large body of opinion that human beings, given the right conditions, are stimulated to produce more if a pecuniary inducement is directly linked to the effort they make   (p. 174)

And a study of changes in payment systems in Sweden found similar, and predictable, effects in a survey of 73 plants (Lindholm, 1972). Of those that replaced piecework with flat rates, i.e., abolished financial incentives, productivity fell on average by 15–25%. Those companies that *introduced* an incentive where none had previously existed experienced productivity increases averaging 25–35%. On the other hand, small increases in productivity (5–10%) were also elicited by the transition from piecework to flat rates plus incentives. A study of industrial relations in the British car industry by Turner *et al.*, (1967) reported a widespread difference of approximately 10% in the performance levels of time workers and pieceworkers. A recent study (Locke *et al.*, 1980) compared the performance effects of job redesign with participation, goal setting and financial incentives. The results were carefully checked for artefacts, and showed a median performance improvement of 17% in 13 cases of job redesign, but 30% in ten cases where financial incentives were used.

More pervasive effects have been documented by writers such as Cunnison (1966), Klein (1964), Lupton (1963) and Roy (1952) in their studies of output regulation and worker attitudes. The significance of changes in pay levels and systems in cases of job redesign for changes in performance level has been seriously neglected by writers in this field, largely because of their emphasis on *intrinsic* motivation. The only exceptions to this stricture are the important works by Parke and Tausky (1975) and Tausky and Parke (1976), which do argue, on the basis of a few cases, for the importance of extrinsic rewards in explaining job-redesign outcomes.

(vi) Overemphasis on individual motivation

All theories of job redesign turn on the manipulation of the employee's motivation to perform, itself analysed as a function of job content. The limits of this conception can be discerned on both empirical and theoretical grounds. Empirically, it is predicted that an association exists between changes in job performance, motivation and job satisfaction; in the Hackman and Oldham (1974) model all of these changes are themselves contingent on changes in employee perceptions of their jobs. There are many cases, however, that have reported *no* associations between different combinations of these variables.

Studies by Ford (1969), Kuriloff (1963), Locke *et al.* (1976), Paul and Robertson (1970) have all reported conventional initiatives in job redesign that resulted in improvements in job performance measured usually in terms of productivity, i.e., physical output per man-hour. But the studies failed to report corresponding changes in job satisfaction, and in several cases, motivation. There are possible methodological explanations that would suggest that the measuring instruments were inadequate, or that insufficient time elapsed to detect attitudinal changes. But these arguments are essentially *ad hoc*, since they cannot explain why other studies using equally poor measuring instruments or equally short-time periods *have* detected attitudinal changes. Their function (which is not to deny their validity in all cases) is to sustain hypotheses contradicted by pertinent facts. Conversely, there are cases where job redesign has culminated in attitudinal improvement but performance has been unaffected, e.g., Emery and Thorsrud (1975) and Rush (1971). Although there may, of course, have been technical or social barriers to increased performance in these cases, such factors seem unpromising in the particular cases cited.

It has been argued that such findings could merely signify the inappropriateness of a *universalistic* theory of job redesign which imputes similar motives to all employees. Some employees may be reconciled or adapted to short-cycle, repetitive work, and hence resist job redesign because it is not perceived as rewarding, or may indeed be considered psychologically threatening (Turner and Miclette, 1962). The individual-difference hypothesis is, in principle, quite plausible, and correlational studies have suggested that responses to job characteristics are mediated by several individual psychological characteristics. But in both correlational and experimental studies it has proved difficult to discover general psychological correlates of responses to job redesign, and the attempts centred around the Protestant work ethic, growth need strength, and urban – rural differences have all encountered empirical objections in the form of contradictory evidence (Stone, 1976).

Theoretically the individualist conception of motivation is open to the objection that it overlooks the social determinants of motivation and performance that have been extensively documented among primary work groups particularly those employed under piecework or incentive pay schemes in manufacturing industry (Coch and French, 1948; Dalton, 1948; Roy, 1952, 1954; Lupton, 1963; Gowler, 1970; Salancik and Pfeffer, 1978).

The existence and enforcement of group norms of performance varies both with the nature of the production system and its degree of required interdependence, as well as with the stability of the firm's product market (Lupton, 1963). Again, such norms may serve various purposes—protection against rate-cutting, maintenance of job security, or maintenance of group cohesion, among others (Guest and Fatchett, 1974). In short, manipulation of the determinants of individual motivation *may* be a necessary condition, but it is certainly not a sufficient condition for improved job performance, especially in manufacturing industry.

3.5 A new theory of job redesign

In examining cases of job redesign, I have drawn on two major theoretical traditions. The first is the analysis of the employment relationship as a locus of conflicts of economic interest, which runs from Marx, through Taylor's scientific management, and up to the work of Baldamus (1961) on the wage – effort bargain. The second is the work of 'contingency theorists', and in particular the 'Manchester School' of Cunnison (1966), Lupton (1963) and Lupton and Gowler (1969), whose major postulate is that organizational structures and processes will vary according to their environments, both external and internal. For example, Lupton's (1963) study of incentive-payment systems showed that output regulation by workers was more pronounced in the more stable firm where collectivist values were more firmly entrenched.

For Marx, the employment relationship under capitalism was an economic exchange between the owners of means of production—factories, mines, machinery, etc.—on the one hand, and sellers of the capacity to labour on the other (1867). The necessity for the exchange arose from the workers' standpoint, because, owning no means for producing the goods and services required for their own existence, they were compelled to place their capacity for work at the disposal of an employer. From the employer's standpoint, the employment of workers was vital to the production of goods that could be sold in product markets and thereby realize a profit, a determinate rate of return on capital invested. For *both* parties, the act of producing goods was fundamentally instrumental in character, and subordinate to the production of wages and profits, respectively. According to Marx, profits derive from unpaid labour within the working day. Workers receive, directly and indirectly, only *part* of the value of the goods they produce: the remaining portion—surplus value—is expropriated by the employer and appears in various forms among different sections of the capitalist class, such as profit, rent or interest. The expropriation of this surplus value is based on the legal and economic power of the employer as owner of means of production.

It follows from this analysis (and indeed from non-Marxist approaches) that the employer has a direct economic interest in reducing the price of labour in order to maintain or increase the rate or volume of profits, whereas conversely, the worker has an equally direct interest in raising the price of labour but thereby eating into profits. The employment relationship therefore contains an inherent structural antagonism derived from the exploitation of labour which is central to the capitalist mode of production. This is not to deny that both parties have an interest in cooperating to produce the goods whose sale is essential for their economic gains; and this distinction between spheres of conflict and cooperation has been reproduced in, for example, surveys of employee attitudes towards participation (Ramsay, 1976). Nor does it follow that this structural, economic antagonism will necessarily be expressed in overt conflict: the relation between structure and behaviour is considerably more complex and mediated by many factors.

More generally, the analysis suggests that employers are inevitably confronted with two problems in the achievement of their goals (Braverman, 1974). First, because in the employment relationship (always nowadays embodied legally in a contract) workers agree to sell their *capacity* to work for so many hours daily and not a fixed quantity of labour, the employer is faced with the task of securing and maintaining particular levels of performance. This problem appears variously as the problem of *control* and/or *motivation*. Second, the employer is faced with the necessity to minimize the cost of labour in order to maintain or increase profitability, an imperative that, in Braverman's (1974) view, issues in a tendency to deskilling.

The instrumental character of employment points to the manipulation of wage levels and systems as likely to constitute the most powerful levers for influencing worker performance, and ultimately reducing labour costs.

Such indeed (although for different reasons) was the conclusion reached by Frederick Taylor, whose model of job performance has been described in previous chapters. Where job-redesign theory locates job-performance determinants within the worker – task nexus (narrowly defined), the mature Taylorism located this same nexus within a much wider context comprising extrinsic rewards (principally pay), organizational controls, such as performance standards, or supervision, and job structure. This latter was described as *efficient* according to the proportion of 'unnecessary and superfluous' motions that had been eliminated from the prescribed method of job performance.

Taylor's analysis of output regulation and economic antagonism was adopted in part by Baldamus (1961). The indeterminancy within the employment relationship provides ample scope for bargaining between the parties over the constitution of an appropriate amount of labour in return for any given sum of wages or earnings, and it is this bargaining (in the broad sense of the word) that occupies the centrepiece of Baldamus's analysis of the employment relationship, or the wage – effort bargain. Indeed 'the organization of industry . . .', according to Baldamus, '. . . ultimately revolves on a single process: the administrative process through which the employee's effort is controlled by the employer' (1961, p. 1). According to this perspective, worker – employer conflict is an enduring feature of employment since each party constantly strives to optimise the wage – effort ratio in their own favour.

Baldamus's analysis is certainly consistent with Marx's, as Eldridge (1975) has observed, although like Taylor he does not locate his conclusions in the context of a mode of production driven by profit. By analysing the determinants of boom – slump cycles within capitalist economies, Marx's view allows us to recognize and analyse concomitant variations in managerial and worker behaviour. It is more difficult to see how, within their respective frameworks, one avoids the 'stoic pessimistic' vision of unending conflict painted by Baldamus, or the tempered optimism of Taylor based on the prospect of continuous economic growth.

It should also be noted that each of these theorists endeavoured in different ways, to describe and analyse worker responses to jobs. Marx in this context wrote of *alienated* labour. Taylor's early view of work was close to that of Marx insofar as he concentrated on the cash nexus and considered work itself to possess little intrinsic value, but later in his career his view gradually shifted to embrace elements of satisfaction derived from work performance and cooperation with employers in a 'joint venture'. The tension between these positions was never successfully resolved, or indeed acknowledged. For Baldamus, the satisfactions available in work were strictly relative: industrial work itself was fundamentally instrumental and unsatisfying in character.

For each of these writers economic and structural analysis of work was the most powerful entry point for examining work performance, and psychological considerations were strictly secondary (*cf.* Ackroyd, 1974; Kelly, 1978). However simplistic this view may appear, it is in fact consistent with much of the evidence on phenomena, such as strikes and wage incentives (see above), widely interpreted by job-redesign theorists as vindicating their own analyses. It is also consistent with the reasons given for using job redesign reported earlier.

Contingency theory is considered by some writers not to be a theory at all, but only a statement of an anti-universal principle (Wood, 1979). Contingency *theorists* reject two 'extreme' assumptions which state either that organizations are unique, and defy general principles, or the obverse, that they share the same features and can be analysed by a single set of specific concepts or categories (Warmington *et al.*, 1977, Chapter 1). The 'middle ground' assertion that organizational processes and features vary with environments only becomes useful when the content of the variation is described. The 'Manchester School' has focused on the variables of *production systems, product markets, labour markets,* and *worker values.* Cases in job redesign almost always provide information on production systems, often on worker values (or attitudes—the terms are used rather loosely), *sometimes* on product markets, and rarely on labour markets.

We are now in a position to combine these approaches into a new

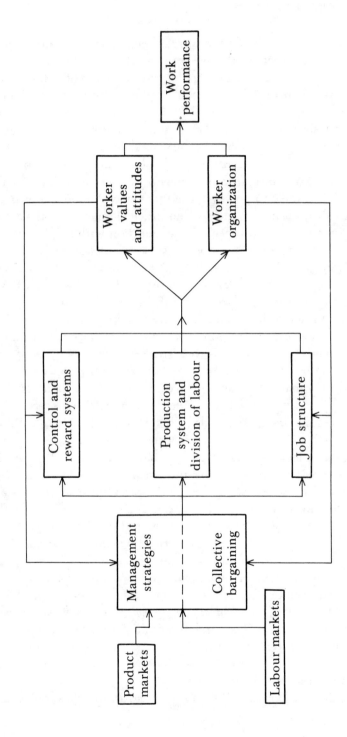

Fig. 3.3 New theory of the origins, mechanisms and outcomes of job redesign

theoretical framework that will explain the origins, mechanisms and outcomes of job redesign. The new theory is shown in outline in Fig. 3.3.

Broadly this theory suggests the following: managerial behaviour in respect of division of labour may be seen as a response to external variables, principally changes in product and labour markets, and/or internal variables, conceptualized as feedback on the functioning of current systems of production, control and reward, and job structure, and worker responses to each of these elements.

Three features of the theory distinguish it, by emphasis at the very least, from conventional models of the origins and mechanisms of job redesign. First, managerial behaviour is seen here as a response to *markets* as well as to allegedly long-run changes in the composition and characteristics of the labour force (*cf.* Fig. 3.1). 'Pressures for change' are likely to fluctuate as patterns of competition and monopoly change, as products are modified, become obsolete or are superseded. Second, pressures for change whether internal *or* external are 'filtered' through managerial 'decisions', which is to say that several options (which need not be of equal availability, utility or appeal) are available to managements, of which job redesign is only one. Third, changes in work performance arising from job redesign need to be analysed as the outcomes of bargained changes in controls, rewards and task performance in the context of particular sets of worker values and modes of social organization. Again, in general terms, this statement would not be contested by job-redesign theorists, but they would emphasize changes in intrinsic motivation as the key variable. In the present theory, changes in motivation are explained as the result of changes in reward and control systems, and in job structure (following Taylor). The emphasis in the new theory is therefore on *extrinsic* motivation as crucial to the explanation of changes in job performance.

The foregoing discussion of classical job-redesign theory and my alternative theory have emphasized the importance of explaining *both* the origins *and* the outcomes of job redesign, on the grounds that these are likely to be interconnectd. And on the basis of the new theory we can advance the following hypotheses:

(1) that insofar as the factors prompting the use of job redesign do involve personnel problems, i.e., poor morale, absenteeism or turnover, then the mechanisms of performance improvement posited by classical job-redesign theory will explain performance improvements.

(2) insofar as the factors prompting the use of job redesign derive from other sources, i.e., either product markets and/or the production system itself, then more conventional reward and control systems, i.e., job structure, supervision, pay and other controls, will explain performance improvements.

In the following chapters we concentrate on detailed analyses of case studies and exercises in job redesign, to compare the validity of the classical and the new theories.

3.6 The job-redesign literature

Any comprehensive analysis and review of the job-redesign literature is confronted at the outset with two problems: first, there may be many more cases of job redesign that have gone unreported and whose omission from the published literature creates unknown distortions and biases.[5] Non-reporting may, for instance, occur because exercises failed (Hackman, 1975b); or because companies are anxious to avoid publicity. In the present review, it will be assumed that all known *forms* of job redesign are represented in the literature. It will not be assumed that the literary distribution of these forms corresponds to their actual distribution, except for the USA and the UK, where information is available about many cases.

The second problem is that case studies of job redesign are often written within the classical theoretical framework and present information mainly on changes in job content, productivity and job attitudes. It is not often that detailed information is available on traditional reward and control systems, or on job structure, and such omissions do place obstacles in the path of an explicitly comparative theoretical review, since all of the data required for such a task are often not available.

The spirit of the present analysis and review will be very much that of Cummings and Molloy (1976) and Cummings *et al.* (1977), insofar as it entails the belief that the numerous limitations of the job-redesign literature need to be taken into account, while at the same time avoiding the 'trap' of rejecting almost the whole literature as methodologically unsound (*cf.* Hulin and Blood, 1968). The review will concentrate (though not exclusively so) on the methodologically more rigorous studies, but it should be stressed that the level of rigour in this field as a whole is far from high. Consequently, any conclusions that are drawn from this review can only be tentative and must be subjected to further and more critical test.

Two issues remain to be considered before we can start the review proper: the first is the type of outcome criteria that will be examined, and the second concerns the way in which the literature will be divided.

(i) Outcome criteria

Adequate data are available only for the outcome of 'productivity', and it will not be possible to examine in detail changes in product quality, absenteeism or labour turnover, although it has been pointed out above that the links between these phenomena and job satisfaction are tenuous and often exaggerated. At the most general level, productivity is a measure of the ratio of outputs to inputs for a production system (Dunlop and Diatchenko, 1964; Faraday, 1971). Job redesign however is concerned with the organization of *labour,* and although it *may* also involve the increased utilization of machinery there are many situations where this is not the case. The input of labour can be measured either in terms of time, or of money, or of both, but in view of the relative poverty of the data on wages, salaries and costs, the time measure will be used here. In other words I shall use as my unit of labour the man-hour, which is the conventional measure in this field, and is the term used for the labour input of one man working for one hour. Productivity will be deemed to have increased where the ratio of output to man-hours has increased, which it may do in several ways. According to Owen-Smith (1971) productivity may be raised in four ways:

> ... (1) working longer hours; (2) working more intensively; (3) working in better organised ways; (4) increasing, or introducing, capital equipment.   (p. 11)

Job redesign has not involved (1), and only on very few occasions has it been associated with (4), which leaves us with (2) and (3) to consider. More intensive working may take the form either of *faster* working, i.e., an increased *rate* of effort expenditure in the same time, or of more prolonged working within the working day. Where productivity is raised in this way, we can speak of *intensification* of labour. Better organization of work may involve training or the elimination of inefficient or non-productive movements. The productivity results reported in case studies will be assumed to be accurate and to be based on the man-hour, unless stated otherwise.

It will also be assumed that productivity changes have been calculated by reference to those workers whose jobs have been redesigned *unless* other workers and/or jobs have also been displaced, in which case the latter will be included in the measure.

(ii) Categories of job redesign

The conventional distinctions between job 'enlargement', job 'enrichment' and autonomous group working are inadequate on several counts. There are difficulties in distinguishing the addition of similar tasks (job 'enlargement') from different tasks (job 'enrichment') related to problems of measuring job content. The distinction between horizontal and vertical forms of job 'enrichment' can also be objected to, on the grounds that the horizontal dimension (addition of similar, production tasks) can often entail the vertical dimension (addition of decision-making).

There are, of course, other possible bases for distinctions: origins of the redesign, mechanisms involved, whether the change creates individual or group jobs. Each of these criteria can separate case studies into several groups, but they all have problems. For example, an individual-versus-group working distinction would assign to different categories, assembly-line reorganizations that in one case reduced a flowline to only two persons, and which in another case created individual units. But it is far from clear that these two changes involve radically different mechanisms (although their psychological outcomes may differ).

The distinction to be used in the present review employs the category of work *roles,* and rests on the following assumption. In a service or production organization, the main products and materials flow sequentially through a series of (more or less) interdependent work roles for processing. Attached to this *horizontal* organization of roles are several offshoots, of *vertically* organized roles responsible for occasional interventions in, or receipts from, the major flow of work. These vertically organized sections are responsible for such functions as maintenance, repair, materials supply and collection, cleaning, inspection and supervision. Some of these functions may be designed into the main flow of work, such as brief quality checks, and the distinction between the two sets of roles is not absolute. The vertically organized (or ancillary) roles typically enjoy *either* lower *or* higher rewards and status than the horizontally organized roles.

We can now draw a more rigorous distinction between different types of job redesign, all of which entail the amalgamation of different, hitherto separate, work roles. The first category involves the addition of *horizontal* roles to an existing role. The second category involves the addition of *horizontal and vertical* roles to an existing role. The third category involves the addition of vertical roles to an existing role.

There are three points to be noted about these distinctions: firstly, although, as will be seen, they approximately correspond to the three traditional categories of job redesign, the correspondence is by no means an exact one. In any case the distinctions are based on a more clear-cut criterion than hitherto. Secondly, the use of work role as the principal criterion entails no judgement as to whether this role will 'enrich' its incumbent or in any other way contribute to his/her satisfaction. It also entails no judgement about the nature of the additional role(s) as it/they may be *either* higher *or* lower in prestige, status, rewards, etc., than the role currently occupied. Thirdly, this set of distinctions can be applied to any *part* of an organization in which there are products or materials being processed in some way by workers, and where there may also be vertically organized roles. Thus, cleaners may experience job redesign through the addition of supervisory duties, although in a larger context, the cleaning role may itself be considered as part of a vertical organization.

The first type of redesign invariably affects a flow-line system of work, and may be called *reorganization of flowlines*. Typically, a sequential, or horizontal series of work roles in product manufacture or assembly, or in document processing, is contracted or abolished, and replaced either by a shorter chain of work roles, or by individual work stations.

The second type of redesign involves the combined amalgamation of horizontal and vertical roles, and typically creates *flexible work groups,* in which labour is allocated between jobs as and when required.

The third type of job redesign, which we may call *vertical role integration*, can be illustrated in offices, by the amalgamation of the roles of clerk and quality controller, and in factories, by the combination of roles such as production, machine set-up and simple maintenance.

It is possible to use Woodward's (1958) classification of types of production technology—batch production, mass production and continuous process production—to be rather more precise about the industrial distribution of one form of job redesign—flowline reorganization. This would be expected to occur most commonly in mass-production industries, and within those industries to be the most common form of job redesign. The importance of differentiating job redesign in this way is further underlined by data that show that the three categories have been unevenly applied to blue-and white-collar workers, as Table 3.5 shows. The primary distinction between categories is predicated on the notion of work *roles*, but as we shall see in this and the ensuing chapters, these categories also involve different *mechanisms* for increasing performance. In addition they will be seen to enjoy differing relationships with scientific management; to entail different consequences for the workers involved; and to be differentially distributed between industrial sectors.

Table 3.5 Distribution of cases of job redesign
by status of worker[6]

	Blue collar	White collar	White collar as % total
Vertical role integration	31	26	48%
Flowline reorganization	48	15	23%
Flexible work groups	64	11	14%

Notes

1. Fig. 3.2 is based on the following cases: Anon, (1972, 1974a, b; 1975 a–e) Agersnap *et al.* (1974), Aguren *et al.* (1976), Alderfer (1976), Andreatta, A. (1974), Andreatta, H. (1974), Aquilano (1977), Archer (1975), Armstrong (1977), Biggane and Stewart (1963), Birchall and Wild (1974), Bjork (1978), Blair (1974), Brekelmans and Jonsson (1976), Bryan (1975), Butteriss and Murdoch (1975), Champagne and Tausky (1978), Conant and Kilbridge (1965), Coriat (1980), Cotgrove *et al.* (1971), Cox and Sharp (1951), Cummings and Srivastva (1977), Daniel (1970), Davis and Valfer (1965), Davis and Werling (1960), De (1979), Delamotte (1979), den Hertog(1974), Dunn (1974), Dyson (1973), Emery and Thorsrud (1975), Engelstad (1972), Fantoli (1979), Ford (1969, 1973), Foulkes (1969),

Frank and Hackman (1975), Gallegos and Phelan (1977), Glaser (1976), Gooding (1970 a, b), Gorman and Molloy (1972), Greenblatt (1973), Guest (1957), Hackman (1975 a,b), Hackman *et al.* (1976), Hallam (1976), Harding (1931), Harvey (1973), Hepworth and Osbaldeston (1979), Herzberg and Rafalko (1975), Hill (1971), Incomes Data Services (1979), Jacobs (1975), Janson (1971,1974), Jenkins (1974), Kenton (1973), Kraft (1971), Kraft and Williams (1975), Kuriloff (1963), Larsen (1979), Lawler *et al.* (1973), Leigh (1969), Lindholm (1973), Lindestad and Kvist (1975), Lindholm and Norstedt (1975), Locke *et al.* (1976), McBeath (1974), McDavid (1975), Maher (1971b), Maher and Overbagh (1971), Mills (1976), Moors (1977), Morse and Reimer (1970), Mukherjee (1975), Nichols (1975), Noren and Norstedt (1975), Norstedt and Aguren (1974), Novara (1973), Orpen (1979), Paul and Robertson (1970), Peacock (1979), Penzer (1973), Pocock (1973), Powell and Schlacter (1971), Powers (1972), Poza and Markus (1980), Prestat (1972), Randall (1973), Rice (1953), Robey (1974), Roeber (1975), Ross and Screeton (1979), Rush (1971), Sirota (1973a, b), Sirota and Wolfson (1972), Smith (1968), Staehle (1979), Takezawa (1976), Taylor (1977a), Taylor (1973), Terisse (1975), Torner (1976), Trist *et al.* (1963), Tuggle (1969), van Beek (1964), van Gils (1969), van Vliet and Vrenken (n.d.), Waldman (1974), Waldman *et al.* (1976), Walker (1950), Wall and Clegg (1981), Walton (1972), Webdill (1976), Weir (1976), Wild (1975), Wyatt and Fraser (1928).

2. Table 3.2 is based on the cases used in Fig. 3.2 but *excluding* the following: Anon (1974b, 1975a, b, d), Andreatta, H. (1974), Brekelmans and Jonsson (1976), Cox and Sharp (1951), Davis and Valfer (1965), Ford (1973), Hackman (1975a), Harding (1931), Herzberg and Rafalko (1975), Jacobs (1975), McBeath (1974), Norstedt and Aguren (1974), Penzer (1973), Sirota and Wolfson (1972), Smith (1968), Takezawa (1976), Taylor (1973), Terisse (1975), van Gils (1969).

3. Table 3.3 is based on the following cases: Agersnap *et al.* (1974), Anon (1975c, e), Archer (1975), Armstrong (1977), Bjork (1978), Bryan (1975), Butera (1975), Butteriss and Murdoch (1975), Conant and Kilbridge (1965), Cotgrove *et al.* (1971), Cummings and Srivastva (1977), Daniel (1970), Davis and Werling (1960), den Hertog (1974), Dyson (1973), Emery and Thorsrud (1975), Engelstad (1972), Ford (1969), Gooding (1970b), Gorman and Molloy (1972), Guest (1957), Hallam (1976), Hartel (1977), Harvey (1973), Hepworth and Osbaldeston (1979), Hill (1971), Hull (1978), Incomes Data Services (1979), Kuriloff (1963, 1977), Lawler *et al.* (1973), Lindestad and Kvist (1975), McDavid (1975), Maher (1971b), Mills (1976), Moors (1977), Mukherjee (1975), Nichols (1975), Novara (1973), Orpen (1979), Paul and Robertson (1970), Pocock (1973), Powell and Schlacter (1971), Powers (1972), Rice (1953, 1958, 1963), Roberts and Wood (1981), Roeber (1975), Ross and Screeton (1979), Rush (1971), Staehle (1979), Taylor (1973), Torner (1976), Trist *et al.* (1963, 1977), Tuggle (1969, 1979), van Vliet and Vrenken (n.d.), Waldman (1974), Walton (1972, 1974, 1975, 1977), Weed (1971), Weir (1976).

4. The labour-elimination part of Table 3.4 is based on the following cases: Anon (1975c), Agersnap *et al.* (1974), Andreatta, A. (1974), Archer (1975), Biggane and Stewart (1963), Bjork (1978), Bryan (1975), Coriat (1980), Cotgrove *et al.* (1971), Cummings and Srivastva (1977), Daniel (1970), Davis and Werling (1960), Emery and Thorsrud (1975), Engelstad (1972), Ford (1969), Hallam (1976), Harvey (1973), Hepworth and Osbaldeston (1979), Hill(1971), Hull (1978), Incomes Data Services (1979), Lindestad and Kvist (1975), Macy (1979), Maher (1971b), Mukherjee (1975), Nichols (1975), Novara (1973), Powers (1972), Poza and Markus (1980), Rice (1958), Roberts and Wood (1981), Ross and Screeton (1979), Rush (1971), Staehle (1979), Trist *et al.* (1963, 1977), Wall and Clegg (1981), Walton (1972, 1974), Weed (1971). The pay-increase part of Table 3.4 is based on the above cases, but *excluding* Andreatta (1974), Biggane and Stewart (1963), Coriat (1980), Hepworth and Osbaldeston (1979), Macy (1979) and including in *addition:* Butteriss and Murdoch (1975), Delamotte (1979), Fantoli (1980), Locke *et al.* (1976), Morse and Reimer (1970), Pocock (1973).
5. This is so despite the existence of substantial bibliographies: Birchall and Wild (1973), Newton *et al.* (1979), Pierce and Dunham (1976), Taylor (1977b, c), Taylor *et al.* (1973), Walters and Associates (1975).
6. Table 3.5 is based on the cases used in Fig. 3.2 but *excluding* the following: Aguren *et al.* (1976), Anon (1975), Birchall and Wild (1974), Champagne and Tausky (1978), den Hertog (1974), Dyson (1973), Ford (1969), Hackman *et al.* (1975), Hepworth and Osbaldeston (1979), Maher (1971b), Novara (1973), Orpen (1979), Robey (1974), Sirota (1973b), Sirota and Wolfson (1972).

4 Flowline reorganization and mass production

The previous chapter delineated the beginnings of job-redesign theory in the 1950s, and referred to the seminal work by Walker (1950). The present chapter is based on developments within the mass-production sector of industry which uses flowline work organization, usually, though not always, in the assembly of finished or semi-finished products. A flowline is defined, following Wild (1975), as a linked series of work stations through which products are passed sequentially by a series of operators. Flowlines are used where products consist of discrete parts (unlike say, chemicals) and where both parts and products are standardized. Consequently, flowlines are often used for mass production, but they are also found among large batch producers. The difference here is only one of degree (Woodward, 1958), and is difficult to determine with precision. Suffice to say that flowline refers to the system of production, mass or batch production to the typical or average size of batches of a given product.

Psychological theory of task design emerged around flowline production; all of the cases reported in the paper by Guest (1957) are of this type. The designation 'task-design theory' is a composite product, comprising several strands of theory, whose later work does not enjoy an unambiguous location in a particular type of production system, although there is a close relationship to flowlines. The work of Hackman and his collegues was derived largely from the study by Turner and Lawrence (1965), which in turn was heavily influenced by the 1950s studies of flowlines. Apart from this genealogical unity, there exists a more substantial thematic unity among the writers to be discussed below. All have focused primarily on the actual *structure and content* of jobs and the ways in which these can be dimensionalized. By contrast, the initial work of Herzberg *et al.* (1959) concentrated on the *psychological structure* of the jobs, that is, on the factors such as achievement, recognition and responsibility associated with performance, satisfaction and motivation. Sociotechnical-systems theory arose from a study of the inter-relations between jobs, although its proponents subsequently developed a set of hypotheses on job content and job performance (see Chapter 7).

The chapter will begin with a brief account of the content and development of task-design theory, and a review of some of the major criticisms of the theory advanced by psychologists. These criticisms are internal to the theory, in the sense that they share its assumptions; Section 4.1 will trace the development of flowlines and their contradictions, and develop the new theory of job redesign outlined in Chapter 3. There then follows a review of the major innovations in this area, which will attempt to demonstrate the role of work-method improvements and changes in pay levels and systems in generating productivity increases.

4.1 Task-design theory

Between 1950 and 1956 a series of studies of job redesign were conducted, in offices and factories, on a somewhat *ad hoc* basis. At that time, no consistent redesign principles had been developed, although the 1957 review by Guest did indicate a few of these, albeit indirectly. All of the changes that were reported involved the addition of *different* tasks to the existing job, in other words *variety* was increased. Some also attempted to create *whole* jobs by allowing workers to perform all of the operations on a particular product, and increased *autonomy* by allowing workers more freedom to control their own pace of work. For example, one group of workers, previously subdivided into nine subgroups on different phases of product assembly, was disbanded, and individual workers were each allowed to assemble the whole product. The studies also involved the allocation of preparatory duties, e.g., machine set-up, mail reception and inspection duties. Subsequent studies have been conducted in similar ways: assembly lines have been shortened or abolished, and workers allowed to assemble a larger number of components and sometimes to check the quality of their own work. In offices, a division of labour between processes, such as mail reception, letter writing and filing, etc., has been replaced by a division between groups of customers, so that each worker now performs all of the relevant operations for a particular group. These pragmatic changes are in fact the norm, and innovations consciously based on a particular theoretical orientation, as in certain Norwegian companies and in ICI, Texas Instruments, etc., are very much the minority. (For details of these cases, see Chapters 6 and 7.)

However, some recent attempts have been made to put both these and 'job enrichment' type innovations onto a firmer, conceptual basis, most notably in the work of Hackman, Lawler and Oldham (Hackman, 1975a, b; Hackman and Lawler, 1972; Hackman and Oldham, 1974, 1975, 1976; Hackman et al., 1976, 1978; Lawler, 1970). Their work is based largely on the study by Turner and Lawrence (1965) in which the authors developed and tested a checklist of job attributes (The Requisite Task Attributes Index, RTA). These attributes were drawn, according to the authors, from a survey of the literature, and from their own empirical studies in various organizations; and six of them were adapted by Hackman et al. into their Job Characteristics Model, these being: variety, autonomy, task identity (wholeness), feedback, dealing with others and friendship opportunities. The latter two dimensions were added for specific purposes in a particular study, and the more elaborated model of the early 1970s has dropped them, adding instead an attribute labelled task significance—the extent to which a task contributes 'to the lives of other people'. These dimensions were then hypothesized to lead to such outcomes as high quality work, low absenteeism and turnover, and higher job satisfaction, via what were called 'critical psychological states'. There are three of these: experienced meaningfulness of the work, experienced responsibility for work outcomes, and knowledge of results. Finally, the theory states that these critical states will be generated, and result in the outcomes indicated, only for those employees with stronger 'higher-order needs'.

The link between this work and the early job-enlargement studies can easily be seen, with the inclusion in the former of the dimensions of variety, autonomy, and task identity. The concept of variety, however, was used by Hackman and Oldham (1974), in connection with *skills*, not simply tasks, and that of autonomy was used to denote control over all aspects of a job, and not simply its pace (as was intended by Walker and Guest, 1952). The specification of employees with strong higher-order needs as the 'target population' was a response both to the work of Turner and Lawrence (1965) and to that of Blood and Hulin (1967;

Blood, 1968; Hulin, 1971; Hulin and Blood, 1968). These researchers claimed to have shown the existence of significant differences in job attitudes between urban and rural-origin workers, in urban and rural plants, with rural workers expressing stronger 'higher-order needs' —for job variety, challenge, etc., than their urban counterparts. And, interestingly enough, the original, and now classic, assembly-line study by Walker and Guest (1952) involved many workers who had no previous industrial experience but had come from rural environments.

The Hackman *et al.* model has generated a considerable volume of work, although characteristically much of it consists of rigorous methodological studies of the validity, reliability and internal structure of the Job Diagnostic Inventory and other measuring instruments developed by Hackman and his colleagues (Armenakis *et al.*, 1982; Arnold and House, 1980; Dunham, 1976; Dunham *et al.*, 1977; Oldham *et al.*, 1976; Wall *et al.*,1978). Theoretically, three major developments have occurred within this school of job redesign throughout the late 1970s. First, there has been an increased emphasis on the problems of implementation of job redesign, since, as Oldham and Hackman (1980) admit:

> We underestimated both the difficulties of carrying out significant changes in the work itself, and the degree to which changes in tasks wind up being altered by surrounding organizational systems, rather than vice versa.   (p. 250)

The same paper then proceeded to a discussion of technology, control systems, training and other organizational practices.

Second, there has occurred a shift towards the discussion of redesigning inter-dependent jobs, as in team work; and third, because of these two developments, a process of rapprochment has begun with sociotechnical systems theory (see also Wall, 1980). One response to the difficulties of implementation has been a renewed interest in 'greenfield' sites, and conversely, in labour – management committees, both of which will be examined later.

4.2 Criticisms and limitations of task-design theory

The Hackman, Oldham and Lawler model has been used to inform several job changes, and in reviewing the existing case studies an attempt will be made to evaluate its predictive value. For the moment, some shortcomings of their work should be mentioned. The most substantial criticism of the model is that it embraces a very narrow range of variables, and excludes, in particular, organizational characteristics. This omission, as we shall see, places serious limits on the explanatory power of the model; offers no guidance on the interaction between psychological and organizational variables; and provides no guidelines for the implementation of job redesign. Secondly, insofar as it hypothesizes higher motivation and performance to be contingent on job changes only for employees with 'higher-order need strength' it has a built-in conservative bias. The study by Cotgrove *et al.* (1971), for instance, found that certain employees who had been very guarded in their response to redesigned jobs were subsequently delighted on discovering that they could take more responsibility. The process of implementation and the experience of redesigned jobs may in themselves help to foster the predicted psychological reactions. In any case, the job motivation – performance link may be mediated by factors other than 'need strength'. Agersnap *et al.* (1974) showed that two groups of workers on similar jobs had very different reactions to job redesign according to their degree of hostility towards, and suspicion of, management.

Hackman and Oldham (1976) have themselves accepted that too much stress was placed on higher-order need strength, and claim now that although employees with stronger needs of this kind do show positive responses to 'job enrichment', so too do other employees, although the responses are weaker, and the correlations between job change and behaviour outcomes are lower (Oldham *et al.*, 1976).

Second, it should be noted that even employees with stronger 'growth' needs may not respond positively to job redesign because their needs are satisfied by other means. Third, the Hackman *et al.* work is entirely lacking in any dimension of time: jobs perceived as motivating at one point in time, may not be seen that way after several months or years because of employee expectations of career advancement, as Penzer (1973) and Kelly (1978a) have found. And conversely, jobs perceived to be relatively low on 'core dimensions' may be tolerated and performed well because they are seen as necessary steps on the path to more interesting work in the future, through career advancement. Fourth, the Hackman *et al.* work is ambivalent, or perhaps we should say silent, on the question of whether 'lower-order needs' must be satisfied before 'higher-order needs' can come into play.

Finally, the emphasis on need as a key means for differentiating individual responses to jobs has been called into question by several studies, and it has been argued that employee responses to jobs are considerably more complex. Kennedy and O'Neill (1958) found no systematic differences between the job attitudes of assembly workers and utility men in a US car plant. More interestingly, Conant and Kilbridge (1965) found that bench and line work were liked or disliked for *different* sets of reasons: 48 (out of 61) workers preferred individual bench assembly because of the autonomy, although reduced social interaction was disliked by 28, whereas 32 workers said they liked line work because of the specialization. The study as a whole *suggests* that workers' appreciation of benefits in specialization, e.g., low effort and mental requirements, in no way eliminates their capacity to appreciate enhanced autonomy and variety when it is available.

In conclusion, the task-design 'school' of job redesign can count to its credit two major achievements: the first is an attempt to describe systematically those features of jobs that need to be altered to improve job performance (as well as other outcomes). Second, task-design theorists have endeavoured (with rather less success) to identify factors that differentiate between individuals' responses to jobs. The practical applications of task-design theory are to be found mainly in the mass-production industries, which make extensive use of flowlines for product assembly, e.g., vehicles, electrical appliances. In these sectors employees and manufacturers were facing problems rather different from those identified by task design theorists. These problems will next be examined under the broad headings of structural and behavioural problems, before I return to look at job dissatisfaction.

4.3 Flowlines and mass production in the post-war period

From the employers' point of view, long flowlines offer several advantages: they allow the employment of cheaper, less-skilled labour (according to the Babbage principle); training time and cost are reduced; workers are more easily interchangeable; and labour productivity is higher by comparison with previous systems of production. The final point is certainly undisputed and was demonstrated clearly with the introduction of the moving assembly line by Henry Ford (Gartman, 1979). Walker and Guest (1952) note in the introduction to their study of the car-assembly line that such methods of production doubled US labour productivity between 1919 and 1939.

In all probability it was this potential to increase productivity (or to establish high levels in the case of new industries) that simultaneously dictated the massive spread of flowlines throughout industry after 1914 and obscured the structural inefficiencies of the system. Flowlines were in widespread use after World War Two in the assembly of domestic electrical appliances, a relatively new sector of industry with probably less well-established norms or standards of production. It was therefore not surprising that the first major statement of 'the assembly line balancing problem' was produced by an industrial engineer working for the General Electric Corporation, a major manufacturer of such appliances (Salveson, 1955). He stated the problem as follows: in order for the flow of production to be continuous, it is necessary that work-loads at the work stations comprising the line should be equivalent, i.e., equal having regard to operator abilities and motivation. In practice, such a state, which amounts to a high intensity of labour, is extremely difficult to achieve, and since 1955 a series of reports on this problem have appeared (e.g., Kilbridge and Webster, 1961). It has now been conceptualized in terms of three classes of 'idle time' the first being *balance-delay time* proper, which arises for the reasons just given. Second, there is *non-productive time* consumed in handling materials and products and passing them along the line, and in checking and rectifying errors and defects (Kilbridge and Webster, 1961). Third, there is *waiting time* due to interruptions in supplies, or to machine breakdown. Each of these problems is magnified in its effect by the work-role inter-dependencies on which the assembly line is constructed.

In his examination of assembly-line organization, van Beek (1964) estimated that on average as much as 20% of the average cycle time was spent by the operator waiting for parts and supplies. This was on a line of 104 stations with an average operation time of 90 seconds, as determined by work study. Kilbridge (1961) estimated lower proportions of *non*-productive time on powered and manual assembly lines, for jobs requiring 62–69 minutes for completion. On powered lines, non-productive time varied between 4.8 and 5.6% of total production time, according to the number of work stations. For manual, i.e., unpaced lines, the figures were 4.8 to 13.6%.

The figures in the Kilbridge cases presuppose no change in the employee's *rate* of working, that is in the proportion of the working day spent productively, or in the rate of effort expenditure. They show nevertheless that the maximum division of labour is not necessarily the most efficient, and that indeed the reverse is true on manually paced lines, and there exists an *optimum* division of labour on powered assembly lines. *In other words, there was an economic argument, internal to assembly-line structure and functioning, for increases in worker cycle times.*

(i)   Product-market pressures

This argument took on added force as manufacturers found themselves faced with a growing contradiction between production and distribution. The original car-assembly line was created to produce the Model T Ford—and nothing else. Once the line was set up with tools, parts and labour, no major changes in production volume, pace or scheduling were necessary, at least not in theory. The domestic electrical appliances sector operated quite differently, and from the end of the second World War manufacturers of domestic irons, heaters, record players, washing machines and so on, increased their *range* of products enormously. By catering for a variety of consumer 'preferences' they were able to secure higher levels of sales than with smaller product ranges. Nevertheless Corley (1966) records:

> The year 1955 marks a dividing line in the post-war history of the appliances industry. The earlier sellers market had disappeared and there were signs of increasing consumer resistance.   (p. 49)

This 'resistance' dictated increased expenditure on advertising, which consumed 1.2% of the value of UK home sales in 1950, but 5.5% in 1963 (Corley, 1966, p. 85). It also resulted in efforts to rationalize production. Some companies *reduced* their product ranges from the mid-1950s; others, e.g., Hotpoint, concentrated on building up their sales of *particular* appliances, such as washing machines; there were even discussions between big producers on the possibility of product specialization by factory (a practice that was spreading among multinational manufacturers). Under these proposed arrangements, English Electric would make washing machines in Liverpool for itself and EMI, while the latter would produce refrigerators in Scotland for the two companies, thus enabling them to maintain a wide product range as well as long production runs. But by 1963, British manufacturers were still producing over 3000 models of 40 basic appliances

(Corley, 1966, p. 68). The effects of such product variety on *production* were deleterious.

With a small range of products, production runs of a single product can be as long as several months, but as product range grows, the average length of production runs is likely to fall, other things being equal (such as numbers and length of flowlines). With increased frequency of product changeovers, there arises a higher proportion of waiting time—in this case waiting for the old parts to be cleared away and the new parts to be brought and distributed between the work stations. There will also then be a higher proportion of working time spent by operators working up to their normal work rates as they accustom themselves to the new products. Under incentive pay systems, this in turn will lead to reduced earnings and labour turnover, and therefore to higher costs and a weaker competitive position (Gowler, 1970; and Figure 4.1) The net result in short, is that labour productivity, measured as output per paid man-hour is likely to rise more slowly, and may indeed stagnate or decline, as product range increases.

In short the *inflexibility* of the assembly line was increasingly coming into contradiction with the requirements of the market; the *realization* of profit was limited by constraints on its *extraction*.

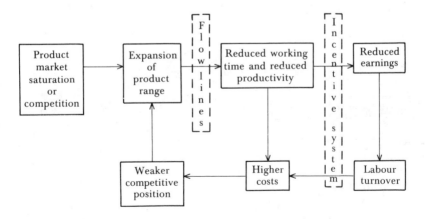

Fig. 4.1 The origins of flowline reorganization

(ii) Behavioural origins: the role of conflict and class struggle

Several writers have suggested that the reorganization of flowlines has been a managerial response to worker militancy. Friedman (1977a, b) has pointed to the upsurge of militancy in the Italian FIAT plants as evidence in support of this argument, and Coriat (1980) has suggested:

> The motor industry provides the best example of the widespread growth of this type of fragmented and repetitive work, together with the most overt and manifest forms of workers' resistance . . . what has been applied there can also be applied in other mass production industries.   (p. 35)

The category 'mass production' is useful for certain purposes but it is extremely misleading to overlook the differences within this sector, between say vehicles and electrical engineering. The British car industry has a high union density (over 90%) and is one of the most strike prone of all British industries (Smith *et al.*, 1978). Electrical engineering, by contrast, has a lower union density, a very much higher proportion of women, and a lower strike record, a fact that is significant when we consider the industrial distribution of known cases of flowline reorganization (*Social Trends*, 1973; Smith *et al.*, 1978); see Table 4.1.

UK strike statistics for the period 1966–73 show that electrical engineering was ranked 7th among industrial groups I–XXII for stoppages per 100 000 employees, and 6th for working days lost per 1000 employees. Within this sector, the domestic electrical appliances area has an above-average strike record, both by frequency and days lost.

Table 4.1 Incidence of flowline reorganization
by industrial group[1]

Industrial group	Number of cases
Electrical engineering	31
Insurance etc.	10
Vehicles	5
All other manufacturing	12
Don't know	6
Total cases	64

Nevertheless, there is little in the case studies of job redesign to suggest that such innovations have been introduced to 'quell worker resistance' (Gorz, 1976, a, b, c).

It is also worth noting that most of these innovations have involved women. Of 22 cases in which data are available, 16 involved women, four involved men, with two groups being mixed.[2] In view of the lower strike record of women *in general* (notwithstanding particular struggles as at Trico or Ford; see Friedman and Meredeen, 1980) this sex distribution of 'recipients' of flowline reorganization again suggests that such innovations may have been responses to structural problems rather than to conflict and struggle. It does need to be borne in mind, however, that some of the 'inefficiencies' in assembly line production may themselves be the result of worker organization and reflect their preferences for work breaks and lower rates of effort expenditure over managements' preference for production.

(iii) The significance of job dissatisfaction

As we have seen, industrial psychologists have represented the 'problem' of the assembly line as being one of low job satisfaction. Diminishing returns are experienced because of rising levels of turnover, absenteeism and dissatisfaction, themselves a product of growing aspirations and abilities being constrained by manufacturing procedures.

Evidence on the origins of assembly-line reorganization is extremely difficult to obtain and equally difficult to interpret. Case studies often cite various reasons for undertaking work reorganization, and it is hard to know if these represent motives (and if so, whose) or *post hoc* rationalizations. Peripheral motives may be inflated in significance by journalists or academics keyed into a particular theoretical framework, and major motives pushed to the background. Nevertheless the available evidence is all we have, and whatever their validity, many case studies have been described as responses to a principal problem. These fall under the three headings outlined above, namely assembly-line inefficiencies; production – distribution contradictions; and personnel problems of turnover, absenteeism and morale. Table 4.2 shows the principal reasons given for undertaking flowline reorganizations in 40 cases implemented between 1950 and 1976 in ten countries.

Thirty of these cases (75%) were described as responses primarily to

*Table 4.2 Principal problems determining the
reorganization of flowlines 1950–76*[3]

	Production – distribution contradiction	Flowline inefficiencies	Personnel problems	Totals
Principal problems	16	14	10	40
Cases cited	16	32	23	71

structural rather than personnel problems. Clearly, some cases cited
other problems as well: the authors of ten initiatives undertaken to
overcome production inefficiencies *also* cited problems of worker
'morale' (Kraft and Williams, 1975; Larsen, 1979; McDavid, 1975; van
Beek, 1964). Equally, the three categories are not entirely distinct and
each type of problem may exacerbate or cause the other two. It is also
worth noting that there is no significant trend in the pattern of principal
problems over time. For instance, there was no tendency for authors to
cite personnel problems more frequently during the upsurge of 'job
enrichment' in the 1970s than in earlier periods. This might suggest
that social desirability was not particularly significant in the citation of
humanitarian, 'personnel' motives as distinct from classical or structural problems. One might have expected the expansion of behavioural-
science training for managers in the 1960s coupled with the upsurge in
job enrichment would have produced a more personnel-oriented
vocabulary of motives.

The significance of structural problems is further highlighted when
we examine problems cited according to whether the products of the
flowline are commodities for sale in markets (as with manufacturing) or
are simply items such as documents for internal company use.

The figures in Table 4.3 show that structural problems (productivity, markets, etc.) predominate where employers exploit labour to produce profit. Where no profit is produced, as with clerical labour,
'structural' problems are *less* likely to be cited than problems of morale
and turnover. It would be dangerous to overemphasize this dichotomy,
as many innovations in division of labour are likely to arise from a
confluence of differing motivations (Donaldson, 1975; see also the

Table 4.3 Problems determining the reorganization of flowlines in manufacturing and clerical work[4]

	Structural problems	Personnel problems
Manufacturing	27	5
Clerical work	3	5

Fisher's $p = 0.001$

Appendix). It is likely, on balance, that, however problematic the state of employee morale (and there is evidence as far back as Adam Smith on that problem; see Heisler, 1977), it is likely to generate employer action *only* in conjunction with production problems as here defined. Turnover and absenteeism *may* be dysfunctional, depending on their level, on the ease and cost of recruitment, on their degree of concentration or diffusion among the workforce and so on, but a threat to production or realization of profit will invariably be taken seriously, since it hits at the very raison d'être of the capitalist system. It is also worth noting that the effects of changing product markets on production systems have been noted by researchers in the field of wage-payment systems. Reduced batch sizes and increased frequency of line changeovers, have led to changes in manning levels, and increased internal labour mobility, thereby straining existing incentive payment systems (Gowler, 1970; Lupton, 1963).

The general incidence of flowline reorganization in the post-war period is shown in Fig. 4.2. It should be noted that the data used in its construction represent only the published accounts of job redesign, and there are probably many other similar initiatives that have never been written up. This fact, coupled with the small numbers of reports in earlier years, should engender caution in the interpretation of trends. It does appear, however, that the general upward swing in flowline reorganization from 1950 to the present day has been thrown into reverse at periods that coincide with international recessions, as noted in Chapter 3.

Finally, it is significant that Salveson's (1955) paper on the assembly-line balancing problem was published during the first 'wave' of job-redesign exercises, in the early 1950s, and during a turning point in the production – distribution strategies of British (and to a lesser extent American) manufacturers of domestic appliances, a contiguity that reinforces the argument that these sets of phenomena are connected.

In line with the theoretical outlook of the present analysis, it is plausible therefore to suggest that the psychological emphasis on job dissatisfaction on flowlines is an over-generalization of a theme predominantly found among clerical workers, and a serious distortion of the structural problems faced by capitalist manufacturers of electrical appliances (and other commodities made using flowline principles). This is not to suggest that reports of job dissatisfaction on flowlines are invalid (*cf.* Beynon, 1973; Chinoy, 1955; Walker and Guest, 1952), but only that job dissatisfaction does not in practice constitute the typical determinant of flowline reorganization.

Job redesign on flowlines may thus be viewed as one of a series of strategies evolved to secure high rates of exploitation of labour and to overcome the contradiction between mass production and a diversified and fluctuating product market. Reduction or abolition of assembly

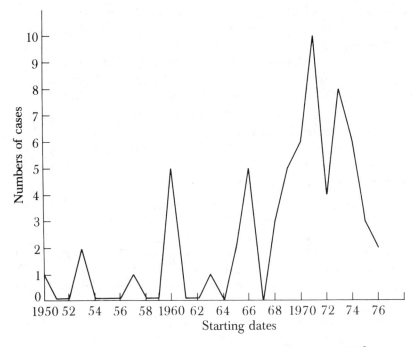

Fig. 4.2 Incidence of flowline reorganization 1950–1976[5]

lines should yield a greater degree of flexibility in production sufficient to match the requirements of the market. But in order to examine the *mechanisms* by which flowline reorganization is effective we must consider several possible determinants of performance improvements: changes in job content and intrinsic motivation as posited by classical job-redesign theory; and changes in flowline structure and work methods, financial incentives, labour elimination and control systems as posited by the new theory.

4.4 Case studies and experiments

It should be said in advance that many of the published case studies and experiments on flowline reorganization are, by scientific standards, extremely poor. As Hulin and Blood (1968) have observed, many employed no control groups, failed to use statistics and improperly inferred causes from correlations. Although these and other methodological criticisms (e.g., Cummings and Molloy, 1976) are valid, they often presuppose an experimental paradigm, whose attainment in manufacturing organizations is a near impossibility. The only proper procedure in such circumstances is to evaluate the varied available evidence as rigorously as possible.

One of the most detailed studies in this category was reported by Conant and Kilbridge (1965) who took a six-man line, assembling domestic appliances, and transformed it into five individual work stations at which each operator performed the task previously divided between himself and his five co-workers. Unit production time was said to be 1.77 min. and this time was divided as shown in Table 4.4. In

Table 4.4 Production times on flowlines and individual work stations

	Six-man line	Individual assembly
Actual unit production time	1.39	1.39
Non-productive time	0.30	0.10
Balance-delay time	0.08	0.00
Average total production time	1.77 min	1.49 min

other words, 21.5% of 'working time' or non-break time (0.38 min), was being spent 'idly', or on tasks (such as product handling and tool setting) that were not strictly necessary. The effect of the switch to individual assembly was to eliminate entirely the small amount of balance-delay time, since worker interdependencies had been removed, and to cut by two-thirds non-productive time. Total production time was therefore cut by 15.8%, and labour costs were reduced from $19 900 to $16 762; one of the six workers was eliminated, so the six-man line was replaced by five individual work stations (Kilbridge, 1960b).

What happened to production volume? Assuming for the moment, a continuous working day of 8 hours, i.e., 480 min, output per man per day = 480/1.77 = 271 units, and output per line = 271 × 6 = *1626* units. On individual assembly, output per man per day = 480/1.49 = *322,* and output for five men = 322 × 5 = *1610* units. Total production with the five work stations was, therefore, almost the same as with the six-man flowline, and this increase in productivity of 20% was achieved in two ways. Non-productive time was replaced by productive time, and balance-delay time, previously spent 'idly' was also consumed productively. The first change need involve no increase in effort on the part of the workers, since it merely substitutes one set of activities for another, but the second change involves a direct increase in effort expenditure. On the figures given, the former change accounted for some 70% of the productivity increase, the latter 30%, i.e., 14% and 6% productivity increases, respectively. The former change requires no further explanation, but what of the latter? No pay increase was given in this case, and the report by Conant and Kilbridge merely states that management was able to capitalize on the extra time 'liberated' by the job changes. Nor do the attitude data give us much clue either, for a substantial minority of workers liked *both* bench *and* line work, although most of the grievances about bench work focused on changes in the wage – effort bargain. It should be recalled, however, that the workers were paid by incentive, and the removal of constraints inherent in the assembly line may have allowed employees to achieve more easily desired levels of earnings.

Product quality also improved in this case, with rejects falling from 2.9 to 1.4% of the total production. Job-redesign theorists might argue this reflects the increased responsibility that the employees took for their work, but it could also be explained by reference to the fact that on the assembly line (which was mechanically paced) operators frequently had little time to correct defects, and the control inspectors were few in number. Individual working allowed the precise assignment of responsibility for defects, i.e., accountability was individualized and augmented.

In a similar case reported by Biggane and Stewart (1963) quality testing was originally carried out by one member of a five-man assembly line, and feedback of results would therefore have been fairly quick, and, to that extent, arguably effective. Under job redesign, the flowline was replaced by individual assembly stations at which operators (fewer in number) assembled and tested the whole product. Cycle time increased from 0.33 to approximately 1.5 min. The individualizaton of work made accountability much easier to operate, and it was reinforced by requiring each operator to stamp his product with a personal identification mark. Rejects fell from 5% of total production to 0.5%, a much greater fall than in the Conant and Kilbridge study, where accountability was high, but not reinforced by personal stigmata. The same volume of production was achieved with three individual stations as had been obtained from a five-man line (including one relief man), and workers continued to be paid incentives.

Wild (1975) reported two cases that also illustrate the two mechanisms of method improvements and intensification of labour referred to above. In the first case, involving the assembly of floor sweepers, an eight-station flowline was replaced by two-station lines, as a result of which balancing losses fell from 9% to 2% of total work time, and cycle time rose from 35–45 sec to 2–4 min. There would also have been a reduction in non-productive motions, such as product handling in this case, but no figures were given. Again by reducing worker interdependencies, certain barriers to higher performance were removed. More recently Coriat (1980) described a series of initiatives by the French car manufacturer, Renault. One of these involved the replacement of a 13-station assembly line making suspensions by two four-man modules, as a result of which assembly time fell considerably. Where the assembly line yielded 26.5 suspensions per worker per day, the modular system gave an increase in production of 26.4%, which Coriat accounts for in terms of the elimination of the time losses inherent in assembly-line work.

Effects of pay levels and incentives were revealed in a study by Champagne and Tausky (1978). Potential loss of earnings arising from transfer to a job-enrichment scheme led only 28% of eligible employees to volunteer, but the figure rose to 55% when compensation for loss of bonuses was agreed upon. Although employees were given additional tasks and responsibilities, their jobs were not regraded or retimed, and consequently they had 'to work harder and faster than they had before in order to stay within the wage incentive standards' (p. 33). Although an attitude survey showed that 82% of the 28 participants found the new job 'more interesting and enjoyable', 79% also thought they should be paid more and 71% that bonus-making was a major problem. Not surprisingly, therefore, productivity results were mixed and showed no clear trend.

Another study was reported by van Gils (1969), this time in the white-collar sector. The job in question was the preparation of material for computer processing, and the material passed through a flowline organization made up of clerical groups, punching groups, control punching group, tabulating group, clerical group, correcting group and final tabulating group. After reorganization, each worker performed many operations, instead of just one. An attitude survey administered after the changes had been introduced found that 88% of the 60 employees preferred the new organization of work and that they scored significantly higher than a control group on both intrinsic and general job satisfaction. An index of productivity showed an increase from 110 to 122 for the experimental group, and from 100 to only 104 for the control group, measured over a three-month period.

Similar findings were obtained in a case by Kraft and Williams (1975) in the Deposit Accounting Division of a New York bank. Both of these cases, in particular that described by van Gils (1969), appear to reinforce the view of classical job-redesign theory that improved job attitudes and job satisfaction are necessarily connected with improvements in job performance, but one can find studies where job performance changed while attitudes remained constant. Gallegos and Phelan (1977) studied blue-collar workers in the Pacific Telephone Company. In the first study, the experimental group of wire-connectors was allowed to perform a 'whole' job, and was provided with appropriate training. After eight months, the output of the 26 experimental workers had increased by 50% compared with that of the control group, but job satisfaction (measured by the Job Description Index) showed no significant change. In a second experiment, using a test − retest design, similar job changes with nine workers also failed to elicit any increase in job satisfaction. Customer complaints—a crude measure of performance quality—did however decline.

It is possible then for job performance to improve while attitudes remain constant, so that it is difficult to explain the above-described performance changes solely in terms of attitude changes.

Conversely, there are cases where attitudes changed while performance effects were insignificant or mixed. A study by Orpen (1979) of South African clerical workers (whose race was not mentioned!) found that a programme of 'job enrichment' in which the clerks performed an increased variety of tasks, and exercised increased discretion over their work, yielded significant effects on job attitudes. Job satisfaction, job involvement and intrinsic motivation all showed significant increases compared with a control group, and absenteeism and turnover fell over a six month period. Measures of performance and productivity showed no effect of job enrichment (see also Champagne and Tausky, 1978).

4.5 Questions arising from the cases

(i) Mechanisms of productivity increases

In each of the cases described, a certain portion of the increased productivity (70% in the Conant and Kilbridge study) can be attributed to the substitution of productive time and productive labour for time and labour previously consumed in product handling, etc. Yet there remains a portion of the increase that is not due to such methods improvements, and there also remains to be explained those improvements in product quality that are typically reported.

(a) Removal of barriers to higher performance

In discussing flowline reorganization, it should be borne in mind that duties are not taken from workers of higher grades, and that the changes made are, by some standards, far from momentous. In the Biggane and Stewart study, cycle time was increased from 0.33 min to 1.5 min; in the Conant and Kilbridge study, from 0.78 to 3.15 min; in the Wild study, from 35–45 sec to 2.4 min; in a study by Staehle (1979) from 1 min to a maximum of 6.5 min. Assuming an effective daily working time of 6 hours, the same operation will still be repeated with considerable frequency.

We also know that in several cases the workers involved were paid some form of incentive or pay rise, either in addition to a flat rate, or as a straight piecework payment. To be precise, in 13 cases whose payment systems are known, three involved individual bonuses, four were based on a group bonus, and two were individual piecework schemes, after jobs had been redesigned.[6] The median productivity increase in these cases was 37%, but in the two remaining cases with flat (time) rate pay systems, productivity increases of 2% and 0%, respectively, were recorded, (although the basis of payment changed in only two of them). Nevertheless, the shortening or abolition of assembly lines would establish a closer link between individual performance and reward.

We also know that flowline reorganization has been undertaken in many cases to reduce balancing losses and increase labour utilization. If these points are combined, it could be argued that under flowline organization workers are sometimes obstructed in their efforts to earn money by balancing losses and waiting time (due to poor materials supply for instance). Under individual assembly, materials supply must be considerably improved, for there is now a whole series of individual benches to be supplied with parts, rather than the starting point of one flowline, as previously. It could therefore be argued that the elimination of balancing losses, and the improvement in materials supply, in conjunction with the existence of pay incentives, *enable* workers to increase their output in pursuit of earnings. Recombination of work roles could thus be seen as a facilitating mechanism, rather than the cause, *per se*, of output increases.

Some indirect evidence that this may be the case is provided by the findings from several studies. Thornely and Valentine (1969) investigated worker perceptions of their jobs, pre- and post-change, and found, for instance, no significant difference between unit assembly and flowline operatives, in perceptions of learning opportunities on the job, scope for pace control, involvement with the product, feeling that one could take wider responsibility or that the job 'could lead somewhere'. On the other hand, the two groups did differ in their perceptions of variety, and use of abilities on the job. This pattern of responses suggests only the most qualified support for task-design theory.

By contrast, the two groups differed significantly in their appreciation of the effects of others' mistakes on their own work (seen to be less in unit assembly), and of the existence of 'starting and finishing in the job' (again there was seen to be less in unit assembly). These perceptions are as one would expect in a situation where balance – delay time was eliminated, along with worker interdependencies.

(b) Non-task sources of motivation

If we consider the work of Tuggle (1969), a similar argument can be made. On the flowline, balancing losses and worker interdependencies necessarily inhibit some workers from functioning at their optimum, or preferred pace. In the situation described by Tuggle, the workers on unit assembly were not only released from such inhibitions, but also had before them the incentive provided by a job-and-finish system. Once standard output had been attained, they were free to leave off work and spend the remainder of the day in the recreation room.

In the Conant and Kilbridge study, there were some complaints by operators about the tightness of piece rates on the bench system (*cf.* Champagne and Tausky, 1978), a fact that suggests that the rates were probably changed in the transition from flowline to individual assembly. Evidence in support of this view was provided by Kilbridge, who noted that although wages remained static output rose by 6%, over and above methods improvements. In other words, workers may have had to put out more effort in order to acquire the same level of earnings as previously. Equally, in the study by Delamotte (1979), revised work norms were set unilaterally by management on the basis of time-and-motion study.

Finally, in the Biggane and Stewart case, even before job enlargement workers were performing at 135% of standard performance, under a system of pay incentives (whether bonuses or piece rates, we were not told). In this situation there appeared to have been no significant lack of motivation before job redesign.

(c) Traction

In addition to the removal of barriers to higher performance, and the incentive provided by a job-and-finish system, we also need to consider the psychological effect of reduced or eliminated balance delay and waiting time. We saw from the Thornely and Valentine survey that workers in that situation recognized the reduction of 'starting and finishing in the job'. In other words, uninterrupted production runs were presumably longer, though cycle times *after* redesign were often less than 4 min, and operations were repeated at least 100 times daily. According to Baldamus (1961) such long periods of uninterrupted, repetitive work generate traction, a feeling of being pulled along by the job in a steady rhythm. Insofar as flowline reorganization increased long production runs, (at least for blue-collar work—the argument has less force for white collar work) it will increase traction, which is associated, according to Baldamus, with higher production.

(d) Labour elimination
Let us finally consider the role of labour elimination, the incidence of which is shown in Tables 4.5 and 4.6.

*Table 4.5 Incidence of labour elimination in cases of
flowline reorganization[7]*

	Yes	No	Total
Cases	20	8	28

*Table 4.6 Numbers of jobs redesigned and eliminated in
cases of flowline reorganization[8]*

Number of jobs redesigned	Number of jobs eliminated	Total cases*
250	39	18

* The number of cases here is only 18% because those were the only ones that reported actual numbers of jobs redesigned and eliminated.

Although the clear majority of cases of flowline reorganization have involved the elimination of labour, the ratio of jobs lost to jobs redesigned is small by comparison with the two other forms of job redesign (i.e., flexible work groups and vertical role integration), with an average of only 2.2 workers eliminated per case (see Chapters 6 and 7).

The explanation for this result can be traced to the detailed mechanisms of productivity increase under flowline reorganization. A considerable increase in labour productivity can be, and has been, secured by substituting productive activity for the non-productive time consumed on assembly lines by product handling and quality checking. The corresponding attempt to reduce balance-delay and waiting time constitutes an intensification of labour. Whatever combination of these mechanisms is employed, the net effect is that greater output can be achieved with the same volume of labour, or indeed with less labour. The volume of labour eliminated from the production process depends to some degree on the state of the product market and on whether overall production is stagnant or expanding. But the fact that productivity *can* be increased here in the absence of labour elimination explains the reduced significance of labour elimination in flowline reorganization by comparison with other forms of job redesign.

(ii) Quality improvements

In the reorganization of flowlines, workers have often been required to assume a degree of responsibility for the products or services in whose production they are engaged. This responsibility has sometimes taken a purely 'formal' character, with workers carrying out no quality tests as such, but only being held accountable for the results of the tests carried out by other personnel. Alternatively, simple quality testing previously performed by one or more specialist members of a flowline work team has been assigned to all individuals. In terms of Hackman and Lawler's dimensions, the absence or the assignment of purely 'formal' responsibilities for product quality should result in a much lower score on the job dimension of feedback, as well as slightly reducing the skill variety

Table 4.7 Median percentage reduction in errors or defects after reorganization of flowlines[9]

	Reduction	N	
Where workers are responsible for quality testing	75.0%	8	
			$U = 9$ ns
Where workers are not responsible for quality testing	50.0%	4	

score, and they would therefore predict a lower degree of quality improvement in such cases. Equally, Herzberg has argued that holding employees accountable for their work is essential to enable them to experience responsibility and a sense of achievement, as well as recognition. Table 4.7 shows the reduction in errors and defects consequent in flowline reorganization.

The difference predicted by Hackman and Herzberg is not borne out by these figures, but more striking than the (non-significant) 25% difference in product quality is the 50% improvement found even in the absence of worker responsibility for testing. How are we to explain this improvement? Sirota (1973a) has clearly specified the advantages of individual working, in this respect:

> First, management found it was much easier to identify the source of quality problems when they occurred because they knew which employee had built which mechanism. It is interesting that while job enrichment is often seen as an aspect of 'soft' management, the fact is that traditional 'hard' management practitioners have so designed work that it is often impossible to find out who did what, and who is responsible for what. In other words, the extreme fragmentation of jobs has served to violate basic and sound management principles regarding responsibility and accountability.   (p. 13)

Similar points regarding the greater ease of accountability have also been made by Biggane and Stewart (1963), Delamotte (1979), Guest (1957) and Larsen (1979), and worker accountability was accentuated in the first case by means of a personal stamp used to mark finished products. It does not necessarily follow of course that managements have been able to exercise greater control since their ability to do so is constrained by worker organization.

4.6 Conclusions

The available evidence from the electrical engineering industry, a major site of flowline reorganization, shows that the industry was, in the 1950s and 1960s, beset by a growing contradiction between the long production runs required for the efficient operation of mass-production systems and the widening product range required to satisfy customer 'demand'. The shortening of production runs revealed some of the inefficiencies inherent in long flowlines. This pattern of problems generated various management responses—rationalization of ordering, product-range restriction, plant specialization—of which flowline reorganization was but one. The role of personnel problems in dictating the adoption of job redesign seems in general not to have been particularly significant.

This argument on the *origins* of job redesign also has implications for its *mechanisms*. For if personnel dissatisfaction has not been the driving force behind flowline reorganization, then it becomes that much less probable that such schemes rely for their effectiveness on the alleviation of discontent and the activation of 'intrinsic' motivation.

The evidence available in the case studies of flowline reorganization is not the easiest to interpret. However, it has been shown that some portion of reported productivity improvements can be accounted for by reference to the changed structure of activity, i.e., to the substitution of productive for non-productive time. It was also suggested, more tentatively, that the productive use of 'idle time' was made possible by the removal of barriers inherent in flowline organization, thereby permitting the establishment of a closer connection between pay and performance, where incentives were in operation. Finally, the elimination of labour would also make possible a greater rise in output per man-hour. Product-quality improvements were attributed to the greater ease with which line management could hold smaller groups or individuals to account for particular batches of products.

The fact remains, however, that the data are not only consistent with these interpretations, but are also consistent with some form of psychological interpretation based on job content and intrinsic motivation. There is certainly evidence to show that workers often preferred individual work stations to flowlines (see Conant and Kilbridge, 1965; Thornely and Valentine, 1969) and to that extent experienced increased job satisfaction. But in the absence of any substantive grounds for believing that there is a firm link between job satisfaction and job performance, this evidence has little bearing on the determinants of productivity increases. There are suggestions that at least some of these cases involved highly 'instrumental' employees, based on their major expressed concerns at work (Staehle, 1979); or on pay demands issued during or after job redesign (den Hertog, 1974), or on their already high level of job performance under a regime of financial incentives (Biggane and Stewart, 1963). Accordingly, the next chapter provides a detailed account of a case study of flowline reorganization that enabled a direct comparison to be made between the various potential determinants of improved productivity.

Notes

1. Table 4.1. is based on the following cases: Anon (1979), Agersnap *et al.* (1974), Andreatta (1974), Biggane and Stewart (1963), Bjork (1978), Blair (1974), Brekelmans and Jonsson (1976), Butteriss and Murdoch (1975), Conant and Kilbridge (1965), Coriat (1980), Cox and Sharp (1951), Delamotte (1979), den Hertog (1974), Dunn (1974), Ford (1973), Foulkes (1969), Gallegos and Phelan (1977), Glaser (1976), Guest (1957), Harding (1931), Harvey (1973), Janson (1971), Kraft and Williams (1975), Larsen (1979), Leigh (1969), Lindholm and Norstedt (1975), McDavid (1975), Maher (1971b), Moors (1977), Novara (1973), Penzer (1973), Pocock (1973), Sirota (1973a), Sirota and Wolfson (1972), Smith (1968), Staehle (1979), Takezawa (1976), Thornely and Valentine (1968), Tuggle (1969, 1977), van Beek (1964), van Gils (1969), van Vliet and Vrenken (n.d.), Webdill (1976), Weir (1976), Wild (1975), Wood (1976).
2. The 16 cases with women were: Agersnap *et al.* (1974), Butteriss and Murdoch (1975), Delamotte (1979), Dunn (1974), Ford (1973), Foulkes (1969), Glaser (1976), Guest (1957), Harding (1931), Harvey (1973), Janson (1971), Pocock (1973), van Gils (1969), Weir (1976), Wild (1975). The four cases with men only were in: Pocock (1973), Tuggle (1969), Weir (1976) and Wild (1975), and the mixed-gender cases were: Maher (1971b), Staehle (1979), van Beek (1964).
3. Table 4.2 is based on the cases cited in Table 4.1 but *excluding:* Anon (1979), Blair (1974), Cox and Sharp (1951), Coriat (1980), Foulkes (1969), Glaser (1976), Kraft and Williams (1975), Leigh (1969), Maher (1971b), Novara (1973), Penzer (1973), Pocock (1973), Sirota (1973a), Sirota and Wolfson (1972), Takezawa (1976), van Gils (1979).
4. Table 4.3. is based on the same cases as Table 4.2.
5. Fig. 4.2 is based on the same cases used in Table 4.1.
6. The cases are as follows: Agersnap *et al.* (1974), Biggane and Stewart (1963), Conant and Kilbridge (1965), Dunn (1974), Harvey (1973), Larsen (1979), Maher (1971b), Novara (1973), Pocock (1973), Tuggle (1969), Wild (1975).
7. Table 4.5 is based on the following cases: Agersnap *et al.* (1974), Anon (1979), Biggane and Stewart (1963), Bjork (1978), Blair (1974), Butteriss and Murdoch (1975), Conant and Kilbridge (1965), Coriat (1980), Foulkes (1969), Glaser (1976), Guest (1957), Harvey (1973), Janson (1971), Kraft and Williams (1975), Leigh (1969), McDavid (1975), Maher (1971b), Novara (1973), Staehle (1979), Tuggle (1969), van Vliet and Vrenken (n.d.), Wild (1975).
8. Table 4.6 is based on the following cases: Biggane and Stewart (1963), Bjork (1978), Blair (1974), Conant and Kilbridge (1965), Coriat (1980),

den Hertog (1974), Foulkes (1969), Glaser (1976), Kraft and Williams (1975), McDavid (1975), Pocock (1973), Tuggle (1969), van Vliet and Vrenken (n.d.), Wild (1975).
9. Table 4.7. is based on the following cases: Biggane and Stewart (1963), Conant and Kilbridge (1965), Glaser (1976), Guest (1957), Harding (1931), Janson (1971), Kraft and Williams (1975), Leigh (1969), Sirota (1973a), Takezawa (1976), Tuggle (1969).

5 The introduction of unit assembly at Toysite

In this chapter, I will present a case study of flowline reorganization at Toysite Ltd, in order to illustrate in more detail the type of job redesign. In this case the unit-assembly method was one in which each worker assembled a whole product, or unit. The principal question to be answered is: how was labour productivity increased?

The data on which this case study is based are derived from three principal sources. Firstly, I have drawn heavily on three of the reports produced by the firm of consultants that recommended, and supervised, the introduction of unit assembly in 1971–72. The first report outlines their analysis of the assembly line and its deficiencies, and contains a list of recommendations for change. The second report describes the results of the first experimental trial of unit assembly, and the final report evaluates the unit assembly one year after its introduction into a whole shop. Secondly, I have consulted company records for data on performance and pay levels, absenteeism, and certain parameters of production. Thirdly, I conducted interviews with representatives of both management and unions, including three interviews with the Works Manager, and one interview each with the Training Manager, Work Study Officer, Unit Assembly Superintendent, Unit Assembly* Foreman, and the Chief GMWU (General and Municipal Workers Union) Shop Steward. In addition, I participated in a discussion about UA involving the Works and Training Managers and the Work Study Officer, and spent some time observing both the assembly line and UA in operation. Unfortunately, it proved impossible to conduct interviews with, or administer questionnaires to, the employees themselves. This means that direct statements about employee attitudes and motivation cannot be made, but we do have data on changes in employee behaviour in response to changes in their work situation. Since

---

* Hereafter abbreviated to UA.

the principal concern of this book has been with explanations of employee behaviour, i.e., job performance, the absence of attitudinal data is not critical, although it does weaken somewhat the conclusions drawn from the case. In addition I have also examined several independent reports of the Toysite exercise, which portray it as a typical initiative in job redesign, and, presumably therefore in principle, amenable to analysis in terms of changes in intrinsic motivation.

5.1 The Company and the plant

In 1971, when the work reorganization project began, Toysite Ltd was registered as an independent company, and existed as such, but the same problems that led the management to hire consultants to examine their production processes simultaneously resulted in the Company being taken over by Fastfix Ltd. Although the takeover affected the autonomy of Toysite management, the work reorganization continued without interference.

The plant itself is situated in an industrial complex which is itself located in a working-class suburb of Liverpool. In 1971 the plant employeed 1200 workers, but with the onset of the world economic recession, the Company saw its sales fall, and resorted therefore to job redundancies and non-recruitment of staff. By 1976 the workforce had fallen below 1000, and no recruitment had taken place for at least twelve months. During this period, a number of workers quit their jobs, or were dismissed for disciplinary reasons, thus contributing further (by so-called natural wastage) to the reduction of the labour force.

The company manufactures toy cars at its Liverpool plant, but Toysite construction sets themselves are produced elsewhere. The products are aimed at the upper end of the toy market, and in 1976, a single toy could cost between £2 and £5. The market itself is both competitive and unstable, and the two features are interlinked. Although there are few other producers of scale model cars, etc., selling in the British market, there are numerous companies producing cheaper toys made, for instance, from thermoplastic. The company has learned from experience that during economic recessions, sales of its own products slump as consumers divert their spending to cheaper products. During certain periods, therefore, the company does compete with manufacturers at the lower (price) end of the market. In addition to this competition and instability enforced by the business cycle, there also exists an instability intimately connected with the product itself. It has been found that sales of a new model are very high during the first months of its life, but fall off rapidly thereafter, eventually stabilizing at a much lower level. This phenomenon is, in all probability, both cause and effect of the way toys are marketed by most world manufacturers. They are intended to sell over a relatively short period, thereafter to be replaced by a new model, and as sales of the new model rise, those of older models fall. By means of this continuous replacement of models, the manufacturers are able to maintain their sales at a higher level than would otherwise be the case. This continual transformation of the product is a feature that has considerable repercussions on the production process within the plant, as we shall now see.

5.2 The production process

The process of producing toy cars comprises, from the standpoint of labour, a series of quite simple processes. The final product typically contains no more than about 10–12 separate pieces, and of these only the major ones are actually produced at the Liverpool plant. The base of the cars is made from an aluminium alloy that, after melting, is run into a mould and rapidly cooled, before being released into a hopper. This process is repeated at (a maximum of) sixteen machines arranged in a row along one side of a rectangular room, with an aisle on the other. The body of the vehicle is made from thermoplastic: tiny pellets are melted down, run into moulds, and released into hoppers, and again each process is repeated on a series of identical machines. These two operations are paid at a higher rate than the final assembly work, and are conducted almost entirely by men.

The remaining parts that go to make up the complete model are manufactured elsewhere, and delivered to the Liverpool plant for final assembly. Before reorganization, the assembly work was divided into major assembly and sub-assembly, and, in addition, there were several ancillary operations performed at individual workplaces. The assembly operation before reorganization was carried out by two teams, each of 10–12 female workers, seated either side of a moving conveyor. Service workers would feed parts, such as the metal chassis, onto one end of the conveyor, and each worker in turn would pick it off the moving conveyor, add his (her) piece, and replace the product on the conveyor, whence it would pass to the next worker. In general there were between nine and twelve workers on each side of the belt, and each one would be kept supplied with their particular piece of the model by one of the service workers. Again, as with the individual ancillary operations, cycle times are short, between 5 and 10 sec on average, with a complete product usually taking just over a minute to be fully assembled.

The ancillary operations include tasks such as punching holes in the metal base of the car using a simple hand press, or placing pictorial symbols onto the body of the car. Each of these ancillary operations is performed by individuals arranged in rows of tables and chairs. At each workplace there would be a tray into which parts were placed by a service worker, and a tray into which the parts were dropped after whatever operation had been performed on them. The work does not require the development of any fresh skills, but simply the co-ordination of hands and eyes in order to maintain a high rate of production. The cycle time is often less than 5 sec, so that the same operation may be repeated as often as 500–600 times each hour. Typically, the workers on these ancillary jobs are young, unmarried girls, and the rate of pay is lower than most jobs in the factory.

In addition to the workers described so far, there were numerous other workers engaged in internal and external transport, in storage and loading, maintenance, repair, catering, clerical and administrative work, management and its specialisms, such as finance, sales, personnel, work study and supervision, and in general labouring throughout the plant. When asked about industrial relations in the plant, most of those interviewed claimed that in general they were very good, with the exception of one or two 'black spots'. At the time of this study, and indeed, for the past few years, management had been engaged in negotiations with some of the 'skilled' workmen over grading and regrading, but there seemed no reason to disbelieve the general assertion that industrial relations were generally quite peaceful. Most assembly, and ancillary workers belonged to the General and Municipal Workers Union (GMWU), whereas the 'skilled' workers, such as the repair and maintenance workers, and the toolroom workers, belonged to the engineering section of the Amalgamated Union of Engineering Workers (AUEW).

The workers with whom this case study will be concerned, namely the assembly workers, were paid according to a mixed time rate and output incentive scheme. All received a basic rate of pay for 40 hours (or 30 hours in the case of the 9–3 shift, of whom more later) which amounted in the early 1970s to approximately 67% of earnings for 100% standard performance.

5.3 Background to the work reorganization

Production was expanding in the late 1960s and early '70s, and at the lower end of the labour market there were a considerable number of jobs. Demand for Toysite products was rising, and production was sufficiently profitable to justify expansion, so in the late 1960s the labour force was swelled by the recruitment of almost 100 married women. Because most had children, they were employed for six hours each day, instead of eight, from 9 o'clock until 3 pm. Although a necessary response to rising demand, this expansion of production nevertheless served to expose several deficiencies in the production process, viewed from the standpoint of distribution in the market.

I have already explained the basis on which the production and distribution of toys is maintained at a high level, that is, through rapid model changes. In the late 1960s and '70s, this process was intensified, and the number of new models produced each year increased. This increased turnover of models placed considerable strains on a production system that was designed primarily for medium- and long-term mass production. Although an assembly line can quite easily cope with infrequent product changes, it does have the drawback that during the changeover all of its workers are idle unless they can be employed elsewhere (see Chapter 4). The increased frequency of new products thus had the effect of increasing the proportion of working time during which the workers were 'idle', waiting for fresh supplies of parts in order to begin the assembly of a new product. But there is also a cumulative effect to be considered. As the range of the company's products grew in size, the number of products that could be re-ordered by a wholesaler or retailer grew likewise. The production system had to bear an increased number of product changeovers, producing an increased amount of waiting time, and thereby raising product costs. To some degree these greater demands could be, and indeed were, handled by rationalization of incoming orders. The Production Manager would hold up orders for a particular product until he had a sufficient number to provide a production run of at least one day's duration or more. But however satisfactory this may have proved as an interim measure, it failed to tackle the root of the problem, which was the inflexibility of the production system itself.

There were, of course, a range of alternative solutions open to the company: it might, for instance, have attemped to standardize its products. Or it might have tried to reorganize the system of distribution to wholesalers so that they held both a greater volume and a greater range of products in stock. The decision to tackle the organization of production was taken because of a conjuncture of problems and circumstances, as a result of which it appeared at the time that such a decision might help to solve several problems simultaneously. First, with the continued expansion of local production throughout the late 1960s the turnover of labour increased substantially, reaching an annual rate of 50–60% in one year. Although this turnover was confined to approximately one-third of the workforce, the other two-thirds being more long term employees, it nevertheless represented a substantial disruption to assembly-line working. Workers who quit did not always give the required notice (usually one week) or indeed give any notice at all, and their departure, as well as entailing recruitment and training costs had an effect on production similar to that of absenteeism. The effect of absenteeism, the second problem confronting management, was altogether more serious, for two reasons: firstly, it was, by definition, unpredictable. Although the management knew that it generally experienced a weekly absenteeism rate of 10–15%, it was difficult, if not impossible to tell with any accuracy which section of the workforce, and hence of the production process, would be affected. But absenteeism was particularly costly where production was so organized that the workers were highly interdependent, as is the case with assembly lines.

The third reason for management's decision derived from the composition of the capital invested in production. The amount of machinery was small compared to the volume of labour employed, and the assembly lines in particular were highly labour intensive. With labour comprising such a high proportion of the costs of production, it was not surprising that management's thoughts turned to labour when it seriously began to consider the necessity for improvements in efficiency. A firm of consultants was therefore invited to study the production system and prepare an initial report outlining possible ways of reducing costs and/or improving efficiency.

5.4 The consultants' report

The report, produced in 1971, made two chief proposals: firstly, that assembly-line working should be abolished and replaced by individual assembly; and secondly, that the requisite re-assessment of payment schemes, standard performances etc., should be carried out on the basis of MTM2 (Methods Time Measurement) analyses of the production process (see below). It was suggested that the results of implementing the proposals would be method improvements and a reduction in labour and overhead costs per unit of output. As it was anticipated that earnings per operator would rise under the new work scheme, what the consultants were in fact proposing was a significant increase in the productivity of labour. The current assembly lines were seen as being subject to two major problems: it was difficult to balance out the total workload, so that some operations took longer (or shorter) to perform than others, with the result that some of the total labour time went unused. And secondly, because some operators had occasionally to work faster than others, and also because there were times when all the operators had to work fast, there was a tendency for product quality to be rather low. Consequently, a not inconsiderable number of workers had to be engaged on checking and adjusting the assembled products as they came off the line. These and other considerations led the consultants to propose eight criteria that ought to be satisfied by any proposed changes in the organization of work, and they were as follows:

i. provision of facilities for identification and quantification of methods improvements and for ways of 'making these acceptable to labour'.

ii. provision of means for more accurate assembly balancing and for reducing the frequency of component handling.

iii. provision of simple work data for use in preliminary costing of operations.

iv. simplification of wage calculations.

v. provision of a basis for sound labour cost control which allows supervision to take remedial action.

vi. an increase in the proportion of operations covered by measured standards.

vii. reduction in the effect of lateness and absenteeism by increasing flexibility while minimising the need for standby operatives.

viii. 'Give employees a wider responsibility, thus providing JOB ENRICHMENT'.

(Capitals in original)

Of course not all of these objectives were attained in practice: for instance, the payment system was left substantially unaltered. And indeed some objectives, such as the first one, may best be regarded as selling points, as there seems no *a priori* reason why the progressive assembly system could not result in methods improvements.

But before turning to examine the recommendations in practice, it is worth dwelling on some of the theoretical assumptions underlying them, for it then will become clearer that the use of the term 'job enrichment', is to say the least, somewhat ambiguous. One of the chief proposals was that the production process should be reorganized with the aid of MTM2, a technique of work measurement. The series of MTM techniques—Methods Time Measurement—differs from more conventional work study in one crucial respect. Whereas in the latter, a particular operation is assessed by first analysing it into its constituent elementary motions and then timing each motion in turn, with MTM one already has a series of elementary motion times ready to hand. For MTM assumes (Currie, 1972):

> . . . that manual work in industrial conditions can be regarded as consisting of different combinations of a relatively small number of basic motions.   (p. 179)

MTM practitioners have therefore spent a considerable amount of time and energy in developing catalogues of the times required to perform these 'basic motions'. In theory, one can then provide an accurate assessment of the time that would be required for any piece of work, regardless of whether it has ever been performed. The members of work-study departments, again in theory, are thus relieved of the necessity ever to appear on the shop floor, watch in hand. MTM2, a development of MTM1, is a system in which times are produced and recorded not only for 'basic motions' but also for combinations of these motions. That MTM2 bears a striking resemblance to some of the ideas of 'scientific management' is confirmed by a scrutiny of Taylor's *Piece Rate System* (1919b) or *Shop Management* (1947a). On pages 177–8 of the latter, Taylor expressed his long-felt wish to see the compilation of a book in which the times for all the elementary motions in a number of trades would be clearly set out, for use by employers. Although Taylor recognized that people worked at different *rates,* he eventually came to deny that variability in working *methods* was compatible with the demand for efficiency. For this goal to be attained, it was essential to combine those elementary motions that together constituted 'the one best way' of performing a particular operation. This 'one best way' was to be determined by scientific analysis of elementary motions and by synthesis of 'the quickest and the best movements . . .'. It was then the task of the management to train workers in the 'one best way' of working, and to transfer, or otherwise eliminate, workers who were revealed as other than first-class in this particular 'trade'.

MTM2 (and work study more widely) is based on a similar philosophy. The numerous critiques by psychologists of the idea that there is 'one best way' of working for all workers, and their assertions that patterns of movements must be allowed to vary in order for efficiency to be achieved, have apparently made little impact on the consultants in our present study. But we then come to the curious contradiction; for, having advocated the use of MTM2, the consultants also advocated 'job enrichment', a concept that is generally taken to refer, at the most abstract level, to the maximum development of the individual through his/her work. And at a more concrete level, as we have already seen, it involves the redesign of jobs to provide variety, autonomy, feedback and 'wholeness'.

The use of MTM2 would seem therefore to conflict with at least one of the prescriptions generally featured in a programme of job redesign, i.e., choice of work method, as well as with the principle of individual development. It is of course true that employees in this case study were to be given control over their work pace, to be assigned more responsibility for product quality, and were to assemble a whole product instead of only part of the product, all of which are prescriptions strongly recommended by job-redesign practitioners. But the use of MTM2 does not merely violate a particular job-redesign prescription, but more importantly, it signifies a profound contradiction in the way job redesign was understood in this context. Having pointed out some of these contradictions in theory, let us see how they manifested themselves in practice, and how they were ultimately resolved.

5.5 The changeover to unit assembly

Both consultants and management were confident that their scheme would be accepted by the unions and the workforce, not only because it promised more interesting work and relief from the continual grind of the assembly line, but because of the extra pay. The transition to unit assembly (UA) began in late 1971 with a series of observations on an assembly-line team. These were carried out to establish a baseline against which changes in work methods and organization could be assessed, and they included measures of total output, number of hours actually worked, the amount of time spent on rectification and in waiting, and the total payroll for the operation. It was then possible to calculate the total time taken to produce a toy, and the labour cost per toy. This team of workers, in addition to several foremen and supervisors was then transferred to a unit assembly area where they were trained for two months on the new operation. Each worker on main assembly now sat at a specially designed work station, which consisted of a work surface and a series of trays, stacked on top of one another, in which were laid out the various pieces to be assembled. The operator sat facing this cluster of trays, assembled the product on the work surface and then placed it on the conveyor line beside her. Each operator was now responsible for the quality of her product, as well as for booking her total daily output.

Table 5.1 Results of trial application of unit assembly

	Assembly line	Unit assembly	Reduction	As a percentage of total reduction
Clock minutes on measured work*	4.44	4.13	0.31	17.6%
Waiting time*	0.43	0.27	0.16	8.9%
Rectification time*	1.46	0.39	1.07	60.8%
Packing time*	0.51	0.29	0.22	12.7%
Total clock minutes per unit	6.84	5.08	1.76	100.0%
Labour cost per unit	3.85p	3.05p		
Actual performance as a percentage of standard performance	18.0%	54.5%		
Standard performance (standard minutes per unit)	2.59	2.25		

* These figures have all been calculated from those in the consultants' report.

At the end of this time observations were made, on the criteria mentioned above, for a period of nine days, and the figures for unit production time and labour cost recalculated. Both sets of figures are shown in Table 5.1. It thus appeared from the results that several objectives of UA had been achieved. Both unit production time and unit labour costs had been reduced, and this under conditions in which no financial incentives had been paid. Operators were however remunerated according to their average earnings over the few months before the trial. At the same time the amount of time spent on product inspection and rectification showed a dramatic decline. The changeover then seemed successful, although the overall performance of the operators was still below 60% of standard performance.

The question posed at the beginning of this chapter was how one should explain these findings, and it is to this question we now turn. As we saw in the analysis of the consultants' report there was a certain ambiguity in the way future changes were described, and the languages of both work study and job redesign were employed.

If we turn back to Table 5.1 we can see that unit production time was reduced by an average of 1.76 min. Of this reduction, 1.07 min (or 60.8%) was due to the savings made in rectification and inspection of the product. With the pacing effect of the line removed, operators were thus able to devote more time to the quality of their work, and since product quality was now their responsibility, they were compelled to devote this time to it. It should also be pointed out that on UA it was much easier for supervision to trace faults in the product to the operator responsible than was the case on the assembly line, and in this enhancement of social control one can see yet another tendency pushing in the direction of better quality work. A further 0.31 min (17.6%) was saved on each product through a simple reduction in the amount of time actually spent working on it. If we turn to the consultants' report we find a ready explanation of this occurrence. First, in moving from the line to UA, a certain amount of unproductive time inherent in assembly-line work, such as handling time, was automatically eliminated. Second, during the two months of training that they received before the experimental results being recorded, operators were taught systematically to work with two hands. Trainee operators had been taught two-handed work in preparation for assembly-line work, but on UA this method of working was enforced much more rigorously than on the line. Third, a certain reduction in work time had been achieved by the simple expedient of designing the individual work station in such a way as to make it both easier and quicker for operators to reach out and pick up their parts, and so a further source of 'non-productive' time had been eliminated.

In view of the 'inefficiencies' eliminated by the abolition of the assembly line, it was perhaps surprising that unit production time did not fall even more dramatically. And in view of the elements of variety, autonomy, responsibility and task wholeness that were introduced, it is surprising that worker performance did not rise above the unusually low level of 60% of standard performance. Management too was surprised at these findings, if not actually disappointed. How might this relatively small improvement be explained?

The creation of a production system in which various forms of non-productive movements are actually eliminated means that with an approximately constant rate of performance, output will be higher as these movements are replaced by 'productive' movements, as happened in this case. But it does not mean that the free time now made available, stemming from balance–delay, and waiting time, will also be used 'productively'. Having released this free time from the constraints of the assembly line, management was now faced with the problem of ensuring that it was used 'productively' and not merely consumed by the workers in relaxation, conversation, etc. It was faced, in fact, with the necessity to intensify the production process precisely because it had succeeded in raising its productivity. The restructuring of tasks, in accordance with job-redesign theory and the provision of a guaranteed wage, had failed to achieve the required degree of intensification. Instead of there being more production, and more working time, management found that the workers were turning out more production, but in the same time. Output then was increased, as was productivity, but these increases were due to methods improvements that cut unit time. However, the consultants pointed out that the results had been obtained without financial incentives, and predicted that with their re-introduction, once the new payment system and payment levels had been devised, unit production time would fall further and total output would rise.

It has already been observed that the first report of the consultants contained a contradiction between its advocacy of job redesign and its stress on the use of MTM2 in order to raise productivity. I pointed out that MTM2 reflected a Taylorist theory of work organization in which methods of working are predetermined and specified for the worker. By contrast, job-redesign theories have emphasized the importance of such job characteristics as autonomy, variety and task identity. With the suggestion that worker performance could be raised by the use of financial incentives, the consultants apparently took a further step towards scientific management and away from job-redesign theory.

In discussing flowline reorganization in the previous chapter, it was suggested that productivity was generally increased by the operation of two mechanisms: methods improvements and pay rises and incentives. In the cases on which data were available, these mechanisms were empirically conflated, but in the present case they were temporally separated. In the experimental trial, the performance of the workers remained below 60% of standard performance, but output rose because of methods improvements. With the extension of UA to the whole shop, the second mechanism, pay incentives, was brought into operation.

5.6 The extension of unit assembly

When UA was transferred into the body of the shop, out of its experimental area, it was accompanied by revised payment levels. Basic rates were raised by an average of approximately 8%, and the incentive component was increased from 33% to 40% of the total wage, at 100% of standard performance. This upward revision of the incentive component was designed to ensure that high performance was attained in the absence of machine pacing. At the same time, the potential productivity increases arising out of the improved work methods, and the elimination of unproductive time were consolidated by management through an upward revision of the output required to achieve standard performance. Since the incentive component of the wage was tied to output, this meant in effect that the operators had to turn out more goods for the same earnings. It was anticipated by the consultants that once the scheme was fully operational, productivity could be increased by 75% and unit labour costs reduced by 32%, whereas earnings would rise only 18%. The results for the period December 1972 to April 1973 were remarkably close to these predictions. With the extension of UA, and the introduction of the revised payment levels, productivity was increased by 70%, unit labour costs reduced by 40%, and earnings increased by 15%. Operator performance, which averaged 54.5% of standard during the trial period, reached an average of 81% during these five months, an improvement attributed to the better supply of materials and to the use of incentives.

The various features of job redesign present in the UA trials, namely control of pace, responsibility for product quality, task variety and task identity had apparently failed to result in any significant increase in motivation, as judged by time spent working. The increased productivity resulted almost wholly from methods improvements, such as the elimination of excess checking and of handling time. Yet the same task, when performed under a regime of financial incentives, and with improved materials supply, yielded an increase in performance from 54.5% to 81% of standard performance.

The transition from flat-rate payment to incentives was experienced only by those who had participated in the experimental trial. There were other workers in the shop, apart from these 12, whose first contact with unit assembly involved no such dramatic change in payment system. They continued to receive financial incentives, as they moved over to unit assembly. Can we therefore say that the improved performance of these workers was due to financial incentives, or might it perhaps owe something to enhanced motivation derived from improved job content? Perhaps the significant factor in helping to raise the performance levels of these workers was not so much the provision of incentives *per se*, as their transformation from a group to an individual basis, thus linking individual rewards much more closely to performance. This experience was common to both the experimental group, and to those who later switched to UA. It should also be remembered that the improved job content did not raise performance levels of the experimental group, and it is therefore not very likely that it would have acted in a radically different manner when extended beyond this group.

The fact remained however that the performance level of 81% had often been exceeded on the assembly lines, particularly the 9 am – 3 pm shift of married women. Several years later, in early 1976, when UA had been in existence for almost four years, and many of the 'teething troubles' had supposedly been overcome, management remained dissatisfied with the results. The scheme itself, they argued was successful insofar as it created surplus time within the working day, but they themselves had yet to succeed in taking full advantage of this. The use of traditional rewards—financial incentives—had apparently not worked entirely; and the use of job redesign to enhance employee motivation appeared to have been even less effective, except perhaps insofar as it may have resulted in a slight improvement in product quality. Understandably, in this situation, the 'problem' was reconceptualized: it was not the workers who required motivation, but the supervisors. The raising of output was now seen to revolve not so much around the activity of the workers, but around that of their superiors. Supervisors and foremen, it was said, needed to play a more active role in stimulating performance. Furthermore, incentives—both material and psychological—had to be described and explained to the workforce, those who lacked sufficient motivation to perform well had to be 'encouraged', slacking had to be eliminated, and the pacing effects of the conveyor replaced, in part, by the actions of the supervisor; finally, materials supply had to be more effectively managed.

This perspective was echoed by the supervisors themselves. One of them suggested that the absence of pacing on UA rendered the supervisors' job more difficult, as the workers were able, and did, take more time off to go for a chat or a smoke. Since the base rate for wages was higher than on the assembly line, the incentive of bonus earnings was less compelling for some of the workforce. And finally, since part of the 'self-control' on UA involved booking one's own output, it was suggested there was a tendency to overbook. The general idea that UA was 'harder to control' was also supported by the foreman in charge of the assembly section, who pointed to the necessity to compensate for the absence of the conveyor's pacing effect. What was significant about this new 'perspective' was that it marked a complete break with the traditional job-redesign ideas of worker autonomy, self-control, etc., as integral to increasing productivity. In their place was substituted a further component of the Taylorist theory of management. We have already observed the way in which the disappointing results obtained during the UA trials were attributed to an absence of financial incentives, and it was remarked that this stress on financial rewards, as opposed to those inherent in task performance was a characteristic feature of Taylorism. With the shift to an emphasis on the necessity for supervisory control, yet another feature of Taylorism made its appearance. The significance of these moves is an issue we shall take up in the concluding section of the chapter.

5.7 Workers, management and Taylorism

(i) The labour force and work output

It was claimed on the basis of weekly performance figures that, although a proportion of UA workers produced a high level of output, rather more workers used their new-found freedom to engage in conversation. The group that performed well on UA tended to be mostly married women in their late 20s and 30s. It was noted earlier that the most productive shift in the factory—the 9 am – 3 pm shift—was mainly composed of these women. Although the husbands of the majority were also working, their motivation to perform at a high level chiefly reflected their economic situation; with a house and children, in a period of rising prices, their need for money was strong. Women in this category were said by all interviewees to work hard whatever their work, whether it was sub-assembly, assembly or unit assembly, and there is no advantage in having recourse to theories of job redesign and intrinsic motivation to account for their behaviour on UA.

The second group consisted of younger girls, some of whom were married, but many of whom were not. Although management, and supervisors, suggested their 'need' for money was that much less because of their domestic situation (that is, being without children and often living at home), the situation was not quite so simple. There was certainly no compulsion to earn money of the sort that resulted in the high performance levels among the married women, but there may well have been a desire to earn money in order to support an extensive social life. Performance levels among such girls on UA varied between 60% and 80% and management assumed this wage – effort trade-off was adequate so far as the girls themselves were concerned. What appeared to concern them far more than the intrinsic satisfaction to be derived from task performance were the satisfactions to be derived from social interaction. Unfortunately, for management, the unit assembly stations had been designed and located in such a way that it was difficult to talk and work simultaneously. In order to do the former, it was necessary to turn away from the assembly station, and away from one's work. Contrast this situation with the assembly line, where, as it was generally observed, the workers appeared to be part of a social group, and regularly talked among themselves at the same time as they worked.

It would appear therefore that the management had abandoned, or forgotten, not only some of the ideas of job redesign, but those of Mayo and the Hawthorne studies as well, and the 'social needs' of the workforce seem to have been subordinated to the demands of production. Does this mean that management's commitment to, and understanding of, job redesign was so limited that it would have been unreasonable to expect results other than those obtained?

(ii) Management and job redesign

It was undoubtedly true that the Toysite management did not elaborate their programme of job redesign into a 'new' managerial philosophy, as was done at Shell, Philips or ICI. But these cases are the exception rather than the rule, for the overwhelming majority of job-redesign changes have been initiated without benefit of a revised philosophy on the part of the organizational leaders. The cumulative experience of these cases, reviewed in Chapters 4, 6 and 7 lends no support to the view of writers such as Klein (1976) and Wilkinson (1971) that top management support for, and commitment to, job redesign is an integral and a necessary feature of a successful innovation of this type. In the present case, commitment to the ideas of job redesign *was* weak, and the managers who were interviewed considered in retrospect the redesign element of the work reorganization to have been only a minor feature. But the progressive introduction of scientific-management mechanisms, and the underfulfilment of management's expectations were not the results of a lack of commitment to the philosophy of job redesign. Rather, it was the relative ineffectiveness of job redesign compared to these other mechanisms that was responsible for the decline in commitment and for the introduction of further elements of scientific management.

(iii) Scientific management and reorganization of flow lines

Certain French writers, such as de Montmollin (1974), have attempted to characterize the practice of job redesign as a form of neo-Taylorism, a blanket conclusion that overlooks the very important differences in the *forms* of job redesign. The limitation of the present form of job redesign—characterized by the ambiguous term 'job enrichment'— was made clear at the very beginning of this chapter when we examined the consultants' first report to the company on work reorganization. Subsequent performance improvements materialized in response to the re-introduction of financial incentives, raising of the basic rate of pay and tightening of supervision.

These processes however did not mark a sudden break with the theory and practice of job redesign, but represented a consummation of tendencies inherent in the *form* of redesign and in the project from its inception. The initial report spoke both of work-study problems and techniques, and of 'job enrichment', a contradiction that might have allowed movement towards either of these poles. However, the productivity increases during the UA trial could in fact be accounted for in terms of method improvements arising out of the application of work study, when the absence of any change in performance level was attributed to the corresponding absence of financial incentives, and when incentives were reintroduced (in conjunction with improved materials supply) performance levels did rise. Finally, having individualized the work process, employed work and method study and utilized financial incentives, it was but a small step to complete the Taylorist trend and call for the tightening of supervisory control. It can be seen then that this final move was consistent both with the initial project, and with its subsequent development. Insofar as flowline reorganization achieves results through the use of individual pay incentives, individual work stations, increased managerial control, and work and method study it can be said to constitute a contemporary application of Taylorism, and is certainly not incompatible with Taylorist precepts.[1]

5.8 Conclusions

In Chapter 4 it was suggested that flowline reorganization was typically characterized by methods improvements as well as direct intensification of labour in order to raise productivity. Indeed, on the basis of several studies, methods improvements were seen as the major elements in this category of redesign, since they appeared to account for the greatest proportion of increased productivity, but more importantly because they derived directly from despecialization of labour, the hallmark of job redesign. Direct intensification was seen as a separate process, in no way connected with redesign *per se*, and attributed to the operation of financial incentives. In the present study we have been able to observe these processes separately, and it can be seen that they are indeed quite distinct. In the experimental phase of UA, productivity was raised by means of method improvements, some, though not all, of which derived from the abolition of progressive assembly, e.g., the elimination of handling time. At the end of this phase, productivity had been raised by 35%, although employee performance, measured against standard, remained unchanged.

The second attempt to increase output and productivity further had nothing to do with job enrichment, strictly speaking, but simply involved raising the basic rate of pay, and increasing the incentive component of earnings. As a result of this change productivity was increased by the same amount again, as in the UA trial. The total productivity increase, measured against performance was 70%. Compared with the more usual assembly-line levels of performance, of the order of 75–90% standard performance, the use of UA with incentives raised productivity by approximately 35–40%.

The Toysite case provides a comparison of psychological job-redesign theory with the theory offered in the present book (Chapter 3). A substantial part of the total productivity increase can be attributed to the operation of two mechanisms central to the present theory: pay rises and incentives, and work-method improvements. Whatever the role of 'intrinsic motivation' in particular cases, or with particular sections of the workforce, the cases and experiments in the last two chapters indicate that *in general* it appears to play at best a minor role in the genesis of productivity improvements. Its significance may well be greater for other work behaviours, such as absenteeism and employee turnover.

Notes

[1] The granting of quality-control and inspection duties to workers constitutes one possible ground for objecting to this analysis, but in no case have workers been assigned *final* responsibility for product quality, and they have invariably been held accountable for their work. There are, of course, cases that violate the principle of separating conception and execution, where for instance, workers may be assigned formal and final responsibility for their work. Such cases have been reported by Guest (1957) and by Janson (1975), for instance, but precisely because they have involved reorganization of both production and ancillary labour, I would regard them as mixtures of different forms of job redesign rather than deviant and pure forms of flowline reorganization.

6 Flexible work groups in the continuous-process industries

The first form of job redesign in the present classification—flowline reorganization—has a high degree of industrial specificity, being concentrated in mass-production industries, such as electrical engineering and vehicles. A similar degree of specificity manifests itself when we consider the creation of flexible, or 'autonomous' work groups. The classical studies in the application of sociotechnical systems theory conducted by the Tavistock Institute of Human Relations in Britain, and the Work Research Institute in Norway, covered a seemingly wide range of industries: coal mining, textiles, chemicals, paper, metal manufacture and electrical engineering. But with the exception of the last-mentioned, all of these industries are commonly regarded as continuous-process industries, on the basis of Woodward's (1958) definition: that is, they entail the production of 'chemicals in batches', or the 'flow production of liquids, gases or solid shapes'.

Flexible work groups have been designed and introduced almost exclusively with the aid of sociotechnical systems theory. The key propositions of the theory are simply stated even if their meaning is not so clear, but as with any wide-ranging theory that has evolved over a period of 30 years, it now exists in several variants. Hence the theory *in toto* is less easy to describe than one might at first think. The first section of this chapter will set out the main propositions of the theory in their simplest form; this will then be followed by a brief account of the major theoretical developments and divergencies that have arisen within the broad ambit of the theory (a fuller description can be found in Kelly, 1978b). Repeating the sequence used in Chapter 4, Section 6.1 will examine the external environment of the industries featured in the classical studies in order to try and elucidate the origins of problems presenting themselves *within* firms. The major section of the chapter then reviews the main case studies of flexible work groups and the competing explanations of their outcomes. The review will seek to demonstrate that the use of financial incentives and the elimination of labour have played a major role in generating productivity increases following the introduction of flexible work groups, and that flexibility, not autonomy, provides a key concept in understanding this form of job redesign.

6.1 The major concepts of sociotechnical systems theory

Sociotechnical theory was first presented by Trist and Bamforth (1951) shortly after the Second World War in a paper on the effects of mechanization in British coal mines. The authors argued that a production system could not be seen either as a technical system only—plant and machinery—or as a social system—social relations and work organization—but had to be seen in terms of *both* of these concepts. A production system, in other words, was a *sociotechnical system*. The argument was based on the fact that mechanization in the coal mines had disrupted the previous organization of work, through the 'hand got' system, in which a small team of two or three miners performed all of the tasks necessary for the extraction of coal. The disruption of what the researchers considered to be a psychologically effective mode of organization was said to arise from a view of the production system as purely technical in character, when in fact it ought to have been seen as sociotechnical.

From this analysis followed the proposition that effective performance, defined usually in terms of output, absenteeism or morale, was a function of matching, or *jointly optimizing* the social and the technical systems. If one system, for instance, the technical system, were maximized at the expense of the other, then the result would be, not maximum performance by the joint system, but suboptimum performance, as in the British mines.

This analysis of changes in the coal mines also suggested that the technical system, or the technology, need not determine in simple fashion the organization of work. Indeed, organizational choice was said to be possible and for a given technology several social systems were possible (Susman, 1976; Trist *et al.*, 1963).

The form of work organization employed in the coal mining, and in subsequent studies, was that of the *autonomous work group*. This was a group of multi-skilled workers that possessed all of the skills essential for the performance of a particular set of tasks and that decided on its own allocation of labour, and sometimes on other matters, such as internal leadership.

In view of the obvious prominence of the notions of social and technical systems, it is perhaps surprising to discover that only one attempt has been made to produce a detailed characterization of these terms (Emery, 1959, Pt.II; see also van der Zwaan, 1975). Most accounts adopt a rather crude working definition of the social system as comprising work or occupational roles, and worker inter-relations, and the technological system as the machinery and its spatio-temporal layout (e.g., Engelstad, 1972; Rice, 1958). There has been a suggestion, and some disagreement, as to whether a third dimension—the economic system—should also be included, on the grounds that a production system must also satisfy financial, as well as social and technical, requirements if it is to be effective in attaining its goals. Both Emery (1959, p.6) and Trist *et al.* (1963, p.6) argued against this view, claiming that the economic dimension could best be understood as a measure of the effectiveness of the other two.

These two systems, the social and the technical, were thought to interact, creating 'forces' that then had psychological effects on individual workers. The sociotechnical system could be designed so that these 'forces' induced task performance, or, on the other hand, task avoidance. The question arose, and was answered in the mining study as to how individual workers could be 'induced' to perform their tasks effectively. Before the introduction of mechanized hewers and cutters on long coal faces, single faces had been worked by groups of two or three men using pneumatic hewers. The most skilled member of the group performed all the tasks required to extract coal—cutting, hewing, filling, etc.—and the co-workers were all self-selected. This single place tradition then had several significant features (Trist and Bamforth, 1951):

> The wholeness of the work task, the multiplicity of the skills of the individual, and the self-selection of the group were congruent attributes of a pattern of responsible autonomy that characterized the pair-based teams of hand-got mining.   (p. 7)

With the introduction of mechanization, the labour process was specialized, and the cycle of operations necessary for coal extraction spread over three shifts. Each shift thus performed only part of the overall cycle, and on a particular shift each man in turn performed only a part of the shift's task. Payment systems were based on at least five different criteria, for different occupational groups, and the net result was a lack of commitment to the 'overall task', the 'primary task' of extracting coal (Rice, 1958; Trist et al., 1963). The mismatch between the social and technical systems on what were called *conventional* long walls, and concentration on the technical at the expense of the social system, failed to generate forces that could induce task performance. The solution to these problems, briefly stated, was to assist the formation of work groups based, not around one skill, such as filling or cutting, but around all of the skills necessary for achievement of the primary task. These 'composite work groups' would enable several features of the single-place tradition to be recovered—workers could be trained in a variety of skills and the group would exercise autonomy in the performance of a whole task. Groups formed on this basis were reported to yield higher output and lower absenteeism, and to perform their duties either on, or ahead of, schedule, when compared to conventional long-wall groups (Trist et al., 1963, Chapters 12 and 26).

The next major theoretical developments were associated with the second Tavistock project—the weaving sheds at Ahmedabad, India. Two studies were conducted there, one with automatic, the other with non-automatic looms, and in both cases the diagnosis of problems, and the solutions offered, were identical. It was suggested the organization of the sheds rested on a contradiction (or mismatch), for although the technology demanded worker interdependence (so as to ensure maximum machine utilization), the workers themselves were organized into independent work roles (Rice, 1958, pp. 57–61, 119–23; also Miller, 1975; Rice, 1953, 1963). The technical and social systems were not being 'jointly optimized'. Rice's solution was therefore to create work groups based on *inter*dependent roles: although each worker might still, in practice, perform one task, he was to be available for all of the activities of the group. Interdependence was to be reinforced by a group payment system (as in the mining study) and by revised responsibilities for individual workers. According to Rice, the workers spontaneously created their own work groups and responded enthusiastically to this arrangement, so much so that the quality of their work fell, although there was a big jump in productivity (Rice, 1958, pp. 69–71, 73–3). After managerial interventions the situation was stabilized, and improved results obtained in both bases in respect of both performance criteria.

At the end of the 1950s Emery (1959) undertook a theoretical synthesis of the findings of the Tavistock work, and it was here for the first time that a major attempt was made to theorize about individual psychology in terms of concepts of motivation and task performance. The latter was said to derive from two sources: firstly from the task structure itself (Emery, 1959, p. 53 ff.), and secondly, from the structure of the individual's work group (Emery, 1959, pp. 30–1). The first point drew on the work of Baldamus (1961), but did not take it much further. Although postulating an optimum task structure that was neither too complex nor too simple, Emery was unable to be more specific. The group was seen as a corrective to two forms of alienation (the first time the concept had appeared in the sociotechnical work): alienation from productive activity, and from one's fellow workers.

Despite his subsequent development of a theory of psychological needs and task attributes, Emery took some pains to point out the limitations of psychological analysis. Workers also belonged to a sociotechnical organization, and this could not be ignored in the explanation of their behaviour. Indeed he believed it was necessary to expand the analysis of sociotechnical systems in order to incorporate relations with their environment: sociotechnical systems were open rather than closed, an insight that was to be crucial in later Tavistock studies.

The next phase of sociotechnical work involved a diversification into two fields. On the one hand Miller and Rice (1967) continued to develop a general theory of organization, and of management, drawing heavily on the earlier work of Emery (1959) and Rice (1958). On the other hand, Emery, Trist and Thorsrud, in Norway, became involved in the Norwegian Industrial Democracy project (Bolweg, 1976; Elden, 1979; Emery and Thorsrud, 1964, 1975; Engelstad, 1972; Gulowsen, 1972; Thorsrud, 1967, 1970; Thorsrud et al., 1976). This was a national programme of research supported by government, employers and trades union bodies, and it forced the sociotechnical researchers to clarify some of their thinking, and to confront new problems. One of the earliest problems they faced was that of job redesign: their work in Durham and India had concentrated on the creation of work groups and roles, and the question of individual job content was either not pursued (Trist) or consciously downgraded in importance (Rice). This problem was solved with the help of work conducted by Davis, in America.

Implicit in the earlier Tavistock work was the idea that individuals should perform various jobs, and that they (or the group) should take responsibility for a meaningful, or whole, task. Work groups were also to provide social forces inducing task performance on the part of the worker, and to satisfy traditional social needs. Four other human requirements of work were added to these two: it should provide conditions for learning, involvement in co-ordination and decision-making, perceptible relations between the job and the outside world and a more desirable future (Thorsrud, 1967, 1972). The second and third of these items had been hinted at by Emery, but the stress on learning, and on a 'desirable future' were innovations. The transformation of these requirements into job specifications owed much to Davis (1957) who had previously delineated 23 criteria for job design. At least nine of these were adopted by the sociotechnical group, and those that were not, such as optimum variety, and length of cycle, were themselves derived from Emery's (1959) paper.

Some of the most well known cases of flexible work groups have been reported in the continuous-process industries, and Section 6.2 examines the economic circumstances of the chemicals and textiles industries in particular, before detailed examination of the cases themselves.

6.2 Continuous-process industries in the post-war period

Chemicals and textiles have featured prominently in popular accounts of flexible work groups, partly because the former, in particular, has embodied for many writers the quintessence of 'post-industrial' organization. Blauner's (1964) account of work in chemicals argued that the skills of monitoring, vigilance and process control that were a hallmark of the industry offered prospects for a dramatic improvement in the quality of work experience and a diminution in alienation. Apart from its higher status, such work was thought to provide challenge, variety and responsibility for workers to a degree that far exceeded opportunities available in more traditional industries, such as vehicles (see Eldridge, 1971; Gallie, 1978, for criticism). Blauner's optimism about the consequences of advanced technologies was taken up by Davis (1971a,b). His argument, stated briefly, is that jobs in advanced technologies require new skills, centred around information processing, and that the incumbents of such new jobs must have more autonomy and responsibility, and show higher levels of commitment to organizational goals. Departures from these requirements will be increasingly dysfunctional, as the costs of poor job performance rise with the capital intensity of such industries. Susman (1970) and Taylor (1971) have taken this argument further by suggesting that there is an actual correlation between 'level' of technology (defined in terms of mechanization, standardization and modes of output control) and actual work organization. Not only does *job content* change with technology: so too does the organization of jobs in the direction of flexible work groups and the decline of individual job assignments and evaluations. What is less clear from these studies is precisely why information processing skills cannot be subdivided, like any other, or why the enormous capital costs in chemicals and related industries result in a *decentralization* of controls to work groups rather than a centralization and tightening up. Davis (1971b), in line with sociotechnical theory, suggests there is in fact organizational choice, but we also need to consider the environment within which such choices (if they are in fact available) are going to be made.

The chemicals industry was one of the fastest-growing industries in the post-war period, and throughout the 1950s world demand continued to outstrip supply (Hay, 1973; Roeber, 1975; Verma, 1969). In these market conditions, rapid growth rates continued well into the 1960s, and as Table 6.1 shows, chemicals production grew approx-

Table 6.1 Growth of industrial and chemicals production
(percent per annum) 1958–1967

	Industrial production	Chemicals production
UK	3.1%	6.6%
West Germany	5.1%	11.0%
France	5.1%	9.9%
Italy	8.9%	13.4%
USA	6.0%	8.3%

From: Chemicals Economic Development Committee (1970).

imately twice as fast as other industrial production in the major chemicals-producing countries.

The buoyant markets for chemical products (which includes fertilizers, plastics, dyes and paints) increased competition on a world scale. The principal effect of this combined competition and demand was to stimulate enormous programmes of capital investment as producers sought to become more competitive by achieving higher productivity and economies of scale (Chemicals EDC, 1973b). Investment programmes were also intended to raise the capacity of the producers to meet world demand, although these new technologies sometimes encountered or created *social* barriers to performance. The fierce competition throughout the 1960s however held down prices below the levels of costs. Between 1963 and 1969, prices rose by only 1½% per annum, but wages and salaries rose 7½% (Chemicals EDC, 1972).

The investment programmes themselves resulted, by the late 1960s in a world over-capacity in chemicals (Chemicals EDC, 1973b; Roeber, 1975). In other capital-intensive and continuous-process industries, such as textiles, world over-capacity was achieved earlier, and import penetration of two of the advanced capitalist countries, the USA and the UK, had reached proportions sufficient to create pressures for import barriers of various kinds in the 1950s, and a multilateral trade agreement in 1962 (Strange, 1979). Increased competition in textiles owed more to the relocation of plant in Third World countries that were able to produce at lower cost, because of the absence or weakness of union organization and the fewer regulations on labour and employment conditions. The British textiles industry has been in decline for many years, although the process seems to have accelerated in the 1950s. In 1953, Commonwealth textiles took 4% of the British market: by 1959 the figure had jumped to 30% (Strange, 1979).

Certain national economies are quite heavily dependent on continuous-process industries, and Bolweg (1976) remarks that in Norway:

> Market conditions for firms within metal manufacturing, textile industries, and pulp and paper looked particularly unfavourable . . . Increasing concern at the national level was voiced regarding the status of Norwegian industry.   (p. 21)

In Norway these economic conditions coincided with a number of political concerns centred on industrial democracy and provided a favourable climate (given the country's size, traditions and industrial-relations system) for a government-led programme of job redesign. Elsewhere, job-redesign initiatives have generally proceeded independently of such explicit State involvement. Indeed responses to changed market conditions varied quite significantly , as we saw with the 'crisis' in domestic appliance manufacturing in a previous chapter. New markets were sought out by some companies; others sold at cost or below-cost prices in existing markets; others again looked for ways of reducing costs still further (Hay, 1973).

Although labour costs constitute a small proportion (relative to other branches of production) of chemicals costs, they were rising rapidly in the 1960s and seemed to be an element that was quite amenable to control (Chemicals EDC, 1973b, 1976; Roeber 1975).

This pattern of circumstances—intensified product-market competition and rising costs—shows some similarity with the factors that led some firms to reorganize their flowlines. But the *form* of job redesign in the continuous-process industries differs significantly from flowline reorganization.

6.3 Origins and mechanisms of flexible work groups

Flowline reorganization invariably retains fixed individual job assignments even where several previously discrete work roles are combined. By contrast in flexible work groups, work is assigned to the group, rather than to particular individuals in particular roles. The reason for this flexibility has less to do with a managerial commitment to group autonomy and decision-making (which is not to rule out its existence), but owes far more to a key characteristic of the industries or sectors using such groups. If we examine the industries in which the major sociotechnical studies have been conducted we find the following: coal mining, textiles, fertilizers, paper making, wire-drawing, light assembly and public transport. With the exception of assembly work, these processes have one feature in common, that of high process variability. Unpredictable short-term variation occurs either in the nature or the supply of the raw material (mining, textiles, wire-drawing, public transport), or in the production process (chemicals, fertilizers, paper making) that require swift intervention by operatives for their correction (see also Davis, 1971b). Such short-run unpredictability is more characteristic of the industries listed above than it is of say, electrical-engineering assembly work, or indeed of much engineering, manufacturing, or clerical work. And it is in the continuous-process industries that both the classical and the later sociotechnical work on job redesign has been concentrated.

The creation of autonomous work groups is intended to allow such 'variances' as they are called, to be controlled as near to their point of occurrence as possible, this being deemed both efficient for the company and satisfying for its employees. But the existence of 'variance' (or variability) in these cases renders the precise allocation of workloads on an individual basis very difficult. Some workers may be compelled to work extremely hard, while others are 'relaxing': precise specification of duties, in the manner prescribed by Taylor may thus be impossible (see Chapter 1). The solution, advocated by the sociotechnical researchers, is to effect a transition from the individual to the group as the crucial unit of analysis and action, for variances in production can then be evenly distributed among its members. This is illustrated in Figure 6.1. With one man – one job allocations any general increase in labour productivity is limited by the effective working time of employee E, who can spend only another tiny proportion of the working day engaged in labour before he has reached its limit. Group working transcends this barrier by creating a situation where workloads can be equitably shared, and where a much greater general

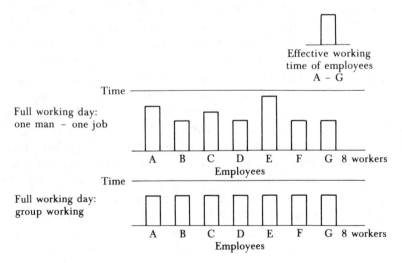

Fig. 6.1 Effective working time with different modes of work organization

increase in productivity is possible. Group working creates the possibility of higher effort levels but this possibility must be transformed into actuality by other mechanisms, and I shall investigate in particular pay rises and labour elimination, in line with the new theory described in Chapter 3.

The discussion hitherto can be summarized diagrammatically, as in Fig. 6.2.

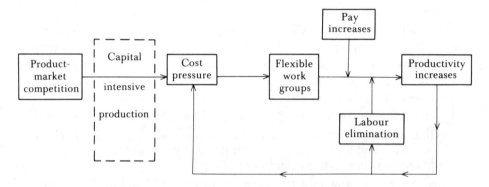

Fig. 6.2 The origins of flexible work groups

In the ensuing sections several major case studies will be described in detail, after which a series of questions will be considered. First, what is the relative significance of flexibility and autonomy for increases in labour productivity? Second what evidence is there for the use of pay and labour elimination in conjunction with flexible work groups? Third, can increases in labour productivity be explained, as sociotechnical theorists suggest, by the joint optimization of social and technical systems and the ensuing improvements in intrinsic motivation?

6.4 Case studies and experiments

I have already described the case studies conducted by Trist *et al.* (1963) and by Rice (1958) within the framework of sociotechnical theory, and will not repeat those descriptions here (see also Kelly, 1978b). The next major group of sociotechnical studies was conducted in Norway as part of a tripartite 'Industrial Democracy Programme'.

Four case studies were carried out at the Hunsfos paper mill, Christiana Spigerverk wire-drawing mill, Norsk Hydro fertilizers and NØBO electric panels.

In the wire-drawing mill, the production system consisted of 20 benches, 10–13 m in length, each manned by one worker. Their task was to weld together bundles of wire, connect them onto one end of the bench, and set the motor running so that the wire was stretched by being drawn along the bench. The researchers proposed that the workers should collectively take responsibility for all of the benches; this would enable the men to allocate labour as and when required (much of their time was spent in inactivity) and would also facilitate increased social interaction. The stress of coping with wire breakages might also be reduced, since it would be shared among the whole group. However, there was a drawback: the researchers insisted there should be fewer men than the number of benches (Emery and Thorsrud, 1975):

> Otherwise it is difficult to see how they would make effective use of the time saved and it was considered that it would be difficult to break the old system of one man, one machine.   (p. 30)

During the first phase of the experiment, reduced manning was rejected, only then to be accepted during the second phase, after workers had begun flexible working to cope with temporary absenteeism (Emery, 1966).

In a more recent study by Trist et al. (1977), two autonomous work groups were established in a US coal mine by voluntary participation and selection, and, after two years' operation by one group and 15 months by the other, the autonomous groups showed higher levels of output per day, and lower absenteeism and accident rates. For the authors, the results vindicated their analysis in terms of sociotechnical theory and through the satisfaction to be derived from working as part of an autonomous group. Several factors, however, complicate these conclusions. Firstly, as the authors admit, the workers on one of the autonomous groups were 'very experienced miners', and thus capable of achieving higher rates of output (Trist et al., 1977, p. 221). But secondly, and more importantly, work in the autonomous groups was paid automatically at the top rates of pay (all the miners were paid time-wages), and of the 29 reasons in favour given by the 24 men who formed the first autonomous group, the most common, mentioned by 7 men, was pay. The attitudes of workers in the non-autonomous groups appeared to show a similar concern with wages and effort: in September

1974, the union local (admittedly on a low turnout) voted to create a second autonomous group, thus extending the experiment. In August 1975, the same local, on a higher poll, voted to curtail it, and an explanation for this change of attitude can be found in the paper itself. In late 1974, the renegotiated union – management contract raised the proportion of workers on top rate to higher levels, and it appears that workers then preferred to stay on their old jobs at top pay, rather than move to the autonomous section for no financial gain. Extrinsic, rather than intrinsic, motivation seems to have played an important role in eliciting higher job performance.

Another well known case is that of the General Pet Foods plant, reported on by Walton (1972, 1974, 1976) and by Schrank (1974). The General Pet Foods company was about to open a new plant, in a greenfield site in Topeka, USA, at the time of the redesign project. Labour for the plant was recruited, and highly selected: of 1200 applicants for the jobs available, only 63 were selected, of whom all were high-school graduates. The new plant was technologically superior to existing plant and was expected to increase output substantially. In addition, however, the company decided to opt for a group-working scheme. The work of processing had traditionally been divided into the roles of: unloading raw materials, storage, removal from storage, mixing preparatory to processing and production. The output end had been divided into the jobs of packaging, warehousing and shipping. It was decided to amalgamate these work roles into two sets, a processing set and a packaging set, and place each under the jurisdiction of a flexible and autonomous team. The team would allocate labour as required, maintain production standards and carry out maintenance, cleaning and quality control duties. According to Walton, the operators much preferred this arrangement, and were less frequently bored, compared with their counterparts in the older plant. Indices of satisfaction, such as turnover and absenteeism, were below the industry average, and production averaged over four tons per man per day, compared with ¾ ton per man per day in the old plant. Much of this improvement was due to the more advanced technology, but not all. According to orthodox industrial engineering, based on precise allocation of function, 110 men were required for the Topeka plant. In fact, it was eventually staffed by 72, a reduction attributed by Walton to 'team work, and the elimination of indirect labour'.

In a study of a textile plant, Janson (1975) reported that the company was experiencing problems of inappropriate incentives, over-specialization, and lack of overall goal commitment. The seven job grades were subsequently collapsed into four, with a utility worker taking over three, formerly separate, functions, and all workers were charged with responsibility for an extra function. All were paid on a group incentive, whereas formerly only the weavers had received any incentive, other workers being in receipt of flat rates. The team also elected its own 'leader', and met once weekly to discuss production problems. As a result of these changes, loom efficiency (actual output as a percentage of theoretically possible output) rose by 5%, and poor-quality material fell from 3% of total production to 0.2%. The results were taken as confirmation of the five principles of job design set out by Janson: variety, task identity, client relationships, feedback and vertical loading.

Another case study, conducted in an aluminium casting plant in the USA, was instigated on a much more articulated theoretical basis—a mixture of Herzbergian and sociotechnical theory (Archer, 1975). Under the old organization of work, there were three groups of jobs: metal casting, furnaceman and metal pouring; saw and shear operating; and truck driving and inspection (Archer, 1975):

> The main change in organization was to form the jobs into a team; it involved the men's rotating and learning each other's jobs. The men would train each other on the jobs during regular working hours and would be paid an increment when they passed a theoretical and practical test for each new occupation. This rotational system would allow the men to change jobs as decided among themselves in order to meet production needs as decided in the team.   (p. 259)

The changes were instigated in order to try and cope with violent fluctuations in workloads which necessitated equally marked changes in manning levels, a procedure made difficult by the insistence of the men on higher payment for any extra duties undertaken. Over the duration of the experiment, a period of 13 months, productivity rose by 12%, most of which (7%) was attributed to the changes described.

Cummings and Srivastva (1977) described two studies, of blue- and white-collar workers, respectively, in an American vehicles company. In the first case, the management negotiated a reorganization of wheel assembly because of recruitment difficulties and because of the inefficiencies in flowline organization. As a result, flexible work groups were established, but the experiment ran into difficulties. Attitudinal measures revealed few changes, but performance was greater in the *control* groups, and the authors attributed the results to inadequate worker training.

White-collar engineers in the company had complained about lack of feedback in their jobs. At the same time, management found it difficult to standardize the work, and decided to introduce flexible project groups. The transition from individualized work roles yielded a less effective form of work organization whether measured in terms of individuals' need satisfaction or of job performance. And indeed after six months, the experiment was terminated by management.

Finally, comes an example from an American paint manufacturer (Poza and Markus, 1980). The site was a greenfield location in Kentucky, and the company was concerned to hold down costs as much as possible because of its competitive and stagnant markets. 160 carefully selected workers (75% of whom came directly from farm work) were recruited to the plant. Work organization was based on flexible groups, and after one year of operation the plant was showing lower levels of absenteeism (2.5% as against 6.7%) and 45% lower costs compared with other similar plants. Productivity and quality were also substantially higher. The results were partly attributed to the lower manning levels made possible by flexibility (160 workers compared with original estimates of 200). The creation of flexible work groups under these conditions will not raise productivity unless the barriers to higher performance can be overcome by mechanisms other than intrinsic motivation. In cases of flowline reorganization, work-methods improvements played an important role vis-a-vis labour intensification in the genesis of higher productivity. By contrast, with flexible work groups the role of intensification appears far more salient than improvements in work methods. The following section expands this point.

(i) The meaning of 'responsible autonomy'

In the Durham mining study, Trist *et al.* (1963) had characterized the hand-got system as one based on 'responsible autonomy'. The workers controlled their own task pace and their internal division of labour, performed a 'whole' task, exercised a multiplicity of skills and selected themselves into work teams. The mechanization of cutting and hewing temporarily eliminated much of this autonomy: tasks were divided and individuals specialized, although movement between work teams and faces was still under the control of the men through their union lodge. The self-selection, known as cavilling, not only allowed men to move between teams, but more importantly it randomized the distribution of coal faces between work teams so that good and bad faces would be more evenly shared out, and hence earnings equitably distributed over the long term (Trist and Bamforth, 1951, pp. 6–7; Trist *et al.*, 1963, pp. 34–5). Not surprisingly, as Trist *et al.* reported, the better workers tended to cluster together in order to maximize their earnings. The cavilling system would not necessarily result in the highest possible output of coal, and nor was it intended to.

The creation of autonomous, or composite, work groups was based on the assignment of responsibility for a complete cycle of mining activity to the group as a whole. What did autonomy mean in practice? It meant that all members of the group were responsible for all of its tasks, a responsibility that was reinforced by the provision of a common paynote, and by training in the requisite skills. These developments went some way to reversing the specialization and isolation of labour that had accompanied mechanization and the creation of separate pay systems, but there was a drawback. According to the researchers, the system of cavilling was out of place, and dysfunctional under mechanization, resulting in sub-optimum deployment of experience. For with the advent of mechanization on a large scale, it becomes extremely costly to allow the machinery to stand idle, or to be under-utilized. The system of cavilling created work teams unequal in ability; some would extract close to the maximum value out of the machines, but others would obtain much less. Given the costs of idle machine time, it became imperative to replace cavilling by 'planning'. Within the plans devised by management and unions, the men would then have their say.

Again, in the mill studied by Rice (1958) it was customary, because of the climate, for workers to deputize for their co-workers while the latter went outside to cool off or relax. This indigenous factory culture with its norms of 'slow' working and long meal breaks, and a tradition of not inconsiderable workers' autonomy, was seen by Rice as incompatible with and inimical to, the requirements of production. By utilizing the norms of sociability inherent in the village cultures of the workforce, Rice was able to undermine the existing factory culture and 'keep the machines running' (1958, p. 241). And in the Norwegian wire-drawing mill, the researchers could only raise the productivity of the then 'autonomous' groups by taking advantage of a fortuitous absence to cut manning levels.

These classical studies would suggest that the prefix 'responsible' before 'autonomy' is indeed apt, because where autonomy clashed with the employer's economic demands (as in Durham and India) or was giving them no advantage (as in Norway), it was curtailed. In these cases, economic imperatives were uppermost, and demanded an end to cavilling, an end to traditional work organization and a reduction in manning.

It was work group flexibility therefore, rather than autonomy that was instrumental in achieving higher levels of productivity in these cases, since there is no evidence that productivity fell after autonomy had been curtailed and flexibility remained. But we need to ask whether flexibility is *sufficient* to raise productivity.

(ii) From flexibility to intensification of labour

It was suggested earlier that the creation of flexible work assignments *per se* might not, under certain conditions, be sufficient to increase labour productivity. The cases just cited serve to identify three reasons, or barriers, to such increases, and point to the necessity for mechanisms of productivity increase over and above those that might issue directly from 'responsible autonomy'. Work-group organization to promote norms of equitable earnings; group norms of effort coupled with the absence of financial incentives; and technical systems whose output is almost entirely machine-paced (the wire-drawing mill); these can all inhibit improvements in labour productivity. Such improvements will arise, on this argument, from an increased intensity of labour. In other words, the effects of 'flexible work groups' may depend on an increased proportion of the working day being spent in productive activity as workloads are raised following the elimination of workload inequalities based on inflexible work arrangements. What evidence then is there for such intensification of labour? And second, what are the mechanisms by which the process is brought about?

In the first of Rice's innovations, we saw that the pace of work did initially increase, although it soon fell, but the volume of work per worker also rose. Theoretically, between 6.2 and 8.3 workers were required for 64 looms (the variations reflect different grades of yarn), but in practice there were seven workers in each group (1958, p. 67).

Consequently when coarse yarn was being employed, and loom stoppage increased in frequency, even management had to admit their figures were too 'tight' and required upward revision (1958, p. 90). In the second case, with manning reduced by 50% (Rice, 1950):

> . . . there were so many complaints of tiredness caused by so much extra walking . . . At all conferences they said that they worked much harder than in the other sheds.   (pp. 146–7)

The same was true of the Durham coalmining study (Herbst, 1962):

> The team delegate later expressed the view that their higher income had been due not so much to the nature of the face or the coal . . . , as to the fact that they had been working hard and, principally, to the greater cooperation they were able to achieve with the composite work method and the advantage it gave in the way of task continuity.   (p. 79)

And what was 'task continuity' (Herbst, 1962)?

> No man was ever out of a job. If he finished his hewing or pulling before others he would join and help them, or go on to some other job which was to follow.   (p. 6)

In the second phase of the wire-drawing mill project, five workers carried out all of the work previously done by six, an extra workload of 20% for each man; output on panel assembly (which was labour intensive) rose by 20%; at Norsk Hydro, a plant that theoretically (according to scientific management theory) required 94 people for its operation, in fact ran with only 56; the additional duties for the operatives included those of the foremen and chargehands (13 eliminated), maintenance workers (4 eliminated), cleaners (all 12 eliminated). In addition, the number of required operatives was cut from 48 to 40 (Emery and Thorsrud, 1975, pp. 41ff., 75–83, 88). In the fourth Norwegian case, the Hunsfos pulp and paper mill, the major economic benefit was in terms of product quality rather than output, whereas in the van Beinum (1966) case no changes in work organization were actually initiated.

It should also be noted that in all of the case studies reported here (with the exception of the Volvo Kalmar plant—see Aguren and Edgren, 1980) the technical system, as conventionally understood, was not altered in any way. Indeed the early Tavistock studies were prompted by technical innovations in terms of mechanization that had failed to deliver their expected benefits. The Tavistock researchers looked for ways in which the social system of work roles could be better adapted to the technology to yield higher productivity. All later sociotechnical work has been of this kind, although the question of new factory design is increasingly (though still to a very limited extent) being pursued by such theorists.

The focus on the social system; the neglect of technical systems; the fact that changes in work methods comparable to those involved in flowline reorganization have not occurred in the course of sociotechnical job design; and direct reports of higher-effort levels; all lead us to the conclusion that, in practice, the sociotechnical imperative of 'joint optimization' is actually best understood as a particular form of intensification of labour. The question that arises is: what are the mechanisms by which this process is brought about?

6.5 Worker motivation, task performance and the question of pay

(i) The Durham mining studies

According to Trist *et al.* (1963) there were four 'bases' for composite, or autonomous, group working: composite work method, workmen, work groups and payment system. Composite workmen were trained in a variety of skills so they were *able* to perform tasks as they arose; their workgroups were self-selected, thus facilitating efficient deployment of labour, and the men were paid on a group basis. Composite work method was the result (Trist *et al.*, 1963):

> ... oncoming men take up the cycle at the point left by the previous shift. When the main task of their own shift is completed they redeploy to carry on with the next ...   (p. 77)

Effective working time was thus increased, as we showed earlier. Of these four features of composite working, the first work method, or task continuity, was thought to be 'essential' (Trist and Murray, 1958). Although pay was clearly important, it was but one part of (Trist *et al.*, 1963):

> A comprehensive agreement which commits a corporate group to an overall task, legitimates motivation to improve performance and releases ability to learn.   (p. 85)

This downgrading of the significance of pay was also evident in Trist and Bamforth (1951), where they discussed the 'displacement' of psychological and sociological problems onto economic struggles, and hence onto worker–manager relations. Questions of pay were thus seen as the expression of more basic, and latent, conflicts, but an alternative interpretation derived from the new theory of job redesign (Chapter 3) is possible.

On conventional long walls, as the authors rightly point out, the existence of different pay criteria meant that for any groups of specialized workers certain tasks went unrewarded (Trist, 1956, p. 13). Minor maintenance, for example, if not the responsibility of Group A, would not be carred out by them since it would only consume time without simultaneously yielding a financial reward. The effect of the 'composite' agreement was to extend the 'cash nexus' to all tasks for all groups. Every task necessary for extracting coal contributed to the final level of pay, and was thus, indirectly assigned a financial reward. But was pay so important that its extension over all tasks for all workers could have such positive effects on performance?

Under the conventional long walls Trist et al. (1963) reported that pay bargaining had been 'rampant':

> . . . , any request to do anything additional is regarded as exploitation unless separately rewarded.   (p. 85)

And what was the nature of the situation before mechanization, with the hand-got systems? Each work group negotiated its own contract with the colliery management, and given the known variability of coal seams, such negotiations would have taken place at quite frequent intervals. And in view of the fairly direct relationship between physical effort and output, the nature of the seam, and the price per unit output would both have been issues of great concern to the work group (Trist et al., pp. 36–7).

In other words, we can say there was a tradition of bargaining in which pay figured as a major element, both in the hand-got and the conventional long wall systems, and it would be surprising if the motivational effects of such a tradition could have been overcome so rapidly with the creation of composite groups. Indeed Trist (1978) notes that the negotiations around the composite groups took almost one year and eventually resulted in a substantial rise in pay.

It was after reaching this conclusion that I came across a follow up study of the coal-mining project by one of the original researchers, and one of its main conclusions speaks for itself (Murray, 1978):

To a degree the original research may have underestimated the salience
of the wages issue, to judge by the emphasis given to it in follow-up
discussions   (p. 14)

(ii) The Indian textile mill studies

The study by Rice (1958) underplayed the signficance of pay for
motivation and performance to an even greater extent than that of
Trist. Although the members of the reorganized weaving groups received increases in basic pay (per month) ranging from nil (for new
entrants) up to 44%, Rice (1958) wrote:

> It was concluded that the first spontaneous acceptance of the new system
> and the subsequent determination to make it work were due primarily to
> the workers' intuitive acceptance of it as one that would provide them
> with the security and protection of small group membership that they
> had lost by leaving their villages and their families to enter indus-
> try.   (p. 110)

More decision-making, over labour allocation for instance, was
assigned to work groups; each worker was to perform a greater variety
of tasks, and he would belong to a group that was itself responsible for a
whole, and 'meaningful' task. However, the behaviour of the weaving
groups showed variations that were quite independent of these features,
but that did correlate with changes in pay levels and supervisory
controls. Before reorganization, only one-third of the workers were on
piece wages (8 weavers and 2 jobbers per group of 30 workers), whereas
the remaining ten occupational groups were paid time wages (Rice,
1958, p. 55). At 85% loom efficiency, a certain sum was paid to the
weavers and jobbers, and variations around this figure resulted in
proportionate gains and losses in pay. After reorganization, all workers
were transferred to an incentive payment system, and on achievement
of the 85% norm, all would recieve 'a small rise in pay' (Rice, 1958, p.
68). The effects of these incentives on performance were predictable
without reference to changed work methods and work organization:
average loom efficiency rose from below 80% to almost 90% as workers
sought to increase their earnings (Rice, 1958, p.76; see also Roy, 1967).

Over the next few months, the high rates of damage to raw materials
were reversed by a tightening of supervision, and by the allocation of
additional labour (one man per half-day) to the groups. Efficiency
remained at 90–93% and damage at 24%, but during November, eight
months after the start of the experiment, efficiency began to fall,

reaching 77%. The workers protested that the quality of the yarn was poor and thus giving rise to more stoppages, too many in fact for them to cope with. They first requested extra help, and when this was turned down, asked for compensation for loss of earnings (Rice, 1958, pp.88–9). According to Rice, the first request signified a 'task-centred' orientation on the part of the workers, but when the request failed, they then 'produced' a cash-centred orientation. Was their acceptance of the reorganization not so thorough-going after all? Or were their attitudes a mixture of 'intrinsic' and 'extrinsic' orientations? Rice bends over backwards to preserve his original hypotheses about the workers' behaviour. After all, he says, they had to contend with absenteeism, machine breakdown, lack of training, etc., from which he concludes it is surprising that efficiency did not fall even sooner and to a much greater extent (Rice, 1958, p.75). A far more parsimonious interpretation is available: the workers' requests for extra help, and extra cash, were not 'separate' requests but two sides of the same coin, that coin being the wage – effort bargain (Baldamus, 1961). Perceiving an upward drift in effort relative to pay, they first tried to realign the two through effort reduction, that is, by asking for higher manning. When this failed they approached the problem from the other end and asked for more pay.

A second experiment involving non-automatic looms, introduced rather similar changes. They consisted of the creation of a group of workers (11 instead of 22) responsible for 40 looms, in which the weavers' duties were now divided up among front, back and smash-tent workers. All workers (instead of just the weavers) went onto piece rates, and bonuses were paid on a composite output and quality index. Efficiency was raised from between 40% and 60% to 85%, 70% being the level beyond which bonus was paid, whereas damage fell from 20% to 5%. However, it appears that many of the results of this case, for example reduced costs, derive quite directly from the 50% reduction of manning levels, and, more significantly, from the furtherance of the division of labour and the introduction of output and quality bonuses for all workers.

(iii) Recent studies

The arguments advanced in connection with these early, classical case studies can also be applied to the flexible-group innovations in Norway and the USA. In the wire-drawing mill and the panel-assembly cases,

output was not increased until management took advantage of fortuitous absenteeism to 'allow' the groups to cope with their workloads
at lower levels of manning. Since both groups were paid under a group
incentive system, the effect of the managerial decision was to allow
higher individual earnings for greater effort, and the wage – effort levels
consequently stabilized at the new levels. In the Hunsfos pulp and
paper mill, the main problem was that of product quality, and the
reorganization of work both allowed workers to take more decisions
affecting quality, and also gave them an incentive in the form of a bonus
tied to quality improvements. The Norsk Hydro fertilizer plant is
difficult to discuss because, although improved productivity (by comparison with other plants) was achieved by setting lower manning
levels, the company tried to attract a highly motivated and able workforce (Emery and Thorsrud, 1975).

Equally, we saw above that in one of the more recent sociotechnical
cases (Trist *et al.*, 1977), pay levels exerted a significant influence on the
motives and willingness of workers to volunteer for membership of
autonomous groups. In a study by Locke *et al.* (1976), of American
female clerical work redesign, early improvements in attitudes and
absenteeism were not sustained, although productivity improved, because:

> ... there was a clear expectation (and strong desire) on the part of the
> employees that practical benefits in the way of extrinsic rewards would
> result from the program even though they were told explicitly at the
> beginning that such benefits could not be promised.   (p.709)

In this case, productivity improvements were attributed largely to
changes in work methods, rather than to increases in motivation.

(iv) Changes in pay levels and systems

If we consider all 35 cases of flexible work groups with known productivity outcomes, in which information is also available on the provision
of pay increases, it is found that in 29 (83%) cases employees received
an increase in pay. If we broaden the base of study, and add 18 cases not
reporting productivity data (to give $N=53$), we find a similar proportion (82%) where employees received pay increases. Information on
payment systems from the larger data base yields the pattern shown in
Table 6.2. There is also a discernible relationship between the provision of pay increases and the elimination of labour, and therefore
increases in labour productivity.

Table 6.2 Pay systems and flexible work groups[1]

Incentives introduced	1
Incentives eliminated	3
Incentives retained	29
Incentives absent	6
Don't know	14
Total	53

Table 6.3 Labour elimination and pay increases in cases of flexible work groups[2]

	Labour eliminated	
	Yes	*No*
Pay increased	25	11
Pay not increased	0	5

Cells show the number of cases to be only 41 because 12 cases have been excluded owing to inadequate data

Fisher's $p = 0.006$

Table 6.3 shows that where labour was eliminated, this was invariably accompanied by an increase in pay for the remaining employees, and indeed in 11 cases employees were able to secure pay increases *without* shedding labour. What do these figures tell us about the role of pay rises in the genesis of productivity increases? I would argue that productivity increases stem from labour elimination, rather than arising from enhanced intrinsic motivation, and that such elimination arises because employees trade-off jobs for wage rises through collective bargaining. In the 25 cases of labour elimination coupled with pay increases, 19 authors reported on the position of trade unions: in 18 of the plants employees were organized in unions, whereas in only one was there no union.[3] Even more telling is the position where pay was increased without loss of labour, for in all 9 cases reporting on unionization, trade unions were in fact present.

It might be argued, in line with sociotechnical theory, that pay rises were the result, not the cause, of productivity rises. Certainly in one case (Peacock, 1979) pay rises followed six months after job redesign, but this is the exception, not the rule. Let us therefore turn to direct evidence on worker motivation. First, we can examine productivity increases as a function of the number of supposedly relevant job dimensions altered, these dimensions being: autonomy, task identity, variety, feedback, responsibility and participation in decision-making.

My coding of case studies of flexible work groups was performed long before any alternative hypotheses were thought of, and it is therefore unlikely that the coding has been retrospectively influenced by a desire to refute conventional hypotheses. The coding of each individual case study proceeded in such a way that the job dimensions were noted *before* the results, thus again helping to eliminate bias. Of course the information in the studies may be incomplete, and in addition it is difficult to assess to what degree any particular dimension has been affected. Bearing these problems in mind, the pattern is as in Table 6.4.

Table 6.4 Median productivity increases in cases of
flexible work groups as a function of number of job dimensions altered[4]

Number of job dimensions altered	Productivity increase	N	
2–3	22.0%	18	$U = 71$
4–5	28.0%	10	ns

On the assumption that improvements in motivation (and therefore productivity) would correlate with the *number* of job dimensions altered, the result shown in Table 6.4 is not consistent with a motivational explanation. A conclusion equally unfavourable to classical job-redesign theory emerges also from more detailed examination of individual studies.

During the first phase of the Christiana Spigerverk wire-drawing study, the attitudes of five group members changed from scepticism to being 'positive', and satisfaction was expressed with the faster passage of time and increased social contact. Productivty, nevertheless, did not increase (Emery and Thorsrud, 1975). In the study at the Aluminium Casting Plant by Archer (1975) the Herzbergian Job Reaction

Survey—an instrument for measuring work motivation—was administered to workers both before and after a series of job changes, but statistical analysis revealed no significant difference between pre- and post- change scores. Again, despite this fact, the majority of workers were in favour of continuing the scheme, and productivity did increase by 7%. In a study by Kuriloff (1963) that involved many changes over a period of time, including changes in pay levels, participation and job content, productivity rose by 35%, whereas 'worker attitudes to the job' remained unchanged. In a study in the Netherlands, a group of clerical workers was formed into an 'autonomous group' and allowed to distribute several clerical functions amongst themselves as they wished. Although productivity rose by 14%, job satisfaction increased only slightly (unfortunately we do not have information on the way satisfaction was measured: Anon, 1975a). Finally, in a study by Rush (1971) no clear relationship was discovered between changes in work motivation scores and changes in production or error rates.

Taken as a whole, the results of these studies contradict the claim of classical job-redesign theory that there exists a correlation between changes in intrinsic motivation, job performance and job attitudes.

There are, of course, studies in which job satisfaction and job perceptions changed in the directions predicted by job-redesign theories, as for example, in the cases of NØBO and Norsk Hydro (where there were also pay rises), reported by Emery and Thorsrud (1975), and the case at Philips, described by van Vliet and Vrenken (n.d.). In all of these cases, employee output per man-hour and/or product quality improved simultaneously. On the other hand, if we consider the cases in which employees received no pay rises, performance improvements were inconsistent (Rush, 1971), attributable to 'technical' factors (Locke *et al.*, 1976), or failed to materialize (Cummings and Srivastva, 1977).

Taken overall, the evidence on mechanisms of motivation and performance would seem, on balance, to be more consistent with the view that performance increases (measured in terms of productivity) arising from flexible work groups owe more to negotiated changes in wage payment levels (and in some cases, in payment systems) and manning levels than to improvements in 'intrinsic motivation' arising directly from redesigned jobs. Since the elimination of labour to reduce manning levels has been covered only briefly, it will be useful to explore its significance in more depth.

(v) The role of labour elimination

In some cases of flexible work groups, the volume of labour operating the technical system in question remained constant, yet in others it was reduced. This variability raises the important question as to the role of elimination of labour and the extent to which (if at all) it is an essential requirement if flexible work groups are to perform at higher levels of productivity. It is clear that if the output of a production system remains at least constant while some labour is eliminated, then labour productivity must increase, other things such as hours of work being equal. I have suggested that the close coincidence of pay rises and labour elimination supports the notion of bargained changes in workloads and manning levels.

However, we may ask what productivity improvements have been obtained in the absence of labour elimination, and to what other factors the increases can be attributed. There are eight cases in which labour was not eliminated, and for which we also have data on productivity. In one of them, the data measured sales performance, an index that could have changed for various reasons, such as different pricing policies, or sales concentration on more expensive items (Paul and Robertson, 1970). In a second case, so many other changes were introduced simultaneously, and the results were taken after such a long interval of time, that the results cannot be taken at face validity. This leaves six cases, reported by Archer (1975), Emery and Thorsrud (1975), Lindholm and Norstedt (1974), Rice (1958) and Trist et al. (1963), whose median productivity increase was 12.0%. In the study at Christiana Spigerverk (Emery and Thorsrud, 1975), the work of wire-drawing was conducted at separate benches by individual workers, each of whom was responsible for loading the drawer, monitoring its progress, and rectifying any defects. It was proposed that a group of workers should take responsibility for a group of machines, and that labour should be eliminated.

The study at Volvo (the Torslanda plant)—Lindholm and Norstedt (1974)—was similar to the wire-drawing case, insofar as the press shop was largely automated, and the operator interventions were relatively few. Their role, in other words, was to monitor the machinery and carry out minor repairs. In both cases, Volvo and Christiana Spigerverk, labour productivity was not increased as a result of job redesign, because the nature of the technical system prevented performance improvements arising solely from increased effort expenditure by workers. The production systems were operating close to their technical limits and machine down-time was low. The analyses by Emery and Thorsrud and Lindholm and Norstedt amounted, in effect, to the assertion that the respective departments were overmanned.

In the Trist and Rice studies, in the Durham coal mines and Indian textile mills, respectively, we find situations different from those described above. Although both production systems were highly mechanized, the role of labour was far more significant than in our two previous cases, for different reasons. In coal mining, only part of the cycle of coal-getting was mechanized, and several aspects, such as filling and stonework, were labour intensive. In textiles, production runs could be as short as 20 min, after which the machinery would have to be emptied and reloaded with yarn. Since each weaver was responsible for between 20 and 48 looms, there were clearly times when looms would be standing idle, awaiting reloading. In both cases uneven distribution of workloads between different jobs restricted the performance of the technical system, as illustrated above in Fig. 6.1.

In both cases, a theoretical averaging of workloads through flexibility was followed by the rasing of this average all round. The increase in workloads was based on the extension of pay incentives to all workers (in the Rice study) and to all jobs (in the Trist study).

In these cases, labour productivity could be raised without labour elimination, because the technical systems were initially operating some way below their capacity.

The study (Emery and Thorsrud 1975) of the NØBO Fabrication Department succeeded in raising productivity without labour elimination becuse it was possible for the workers to increase output by increasing their effort levels. They did eventually increase effort expenditure beyond the group norm to compensate for absenteeism, but once the norm had been exceeded in this way, it fell into disuse, and productivity remained at its new higher level.

Finally, we come to the study by Archer (1975), of the aluminium casting plant, described above. There is a problem in discussing this case, since it is unclear (a) whether labour was eliminated from the casting department, and (b) whether, if it was, this was included in the assessment of the productivity increase. In addition, the description of the production process was inadequate to allow an assessment of the relative contributions of machinery and labour to productivity. Nevertheless, it appears that labour was not eliminated and the productivity increase was small, 7%.

These few studies then, suggest that productivity may be increased in the absence of labour elimination where a production system is working some degree below capacity, and where changes in operator effort levels can raise productivity. On the other hand, where a system is working close to capacity, or where changes in effort levels cannot affect productivity, increased flexibility of labour *per se* cannot be expected to raise productivity without labour elimination.

How far should labour elimination be seen as a consequence of productivity increases, and how far as a cause? For production systems operating close to their theoretical limit and/or technical capacity, the elimination of labour is a major factor in securing higher productivity. Schematically, we could suggest that, from the standpoint of productivity, the intensification of labour necessitates the elimination of labour. On the other hand, in production systems operating below capacity, increased flexibility of labour, in conjunction with other incentives, may raise productivity, and thus *permit* the elimination of labour.

(vi) Quality improvements

In discussing quality improvements in reorganization of flowlines, it was observed that the difference in outcome between cases where workers were assigned responsibility for quality and those where they were not, was less significant than the fact that substantial improvements in quality were found even in the latter type of case. To what extent can theories of job redesign account for variations in results between case studies of flexible work groups? If we divide those cases for which information about work quality is available, into those involving major and minor changes in job content, we can then compare the quality improvements in the two sets of cases. The procedure for making this division is the same as that used above in relation to productivity increases, and results are set out in Table 6.5.

Substantial improvements in work quality were obtained irrespective of the number of job dimensions altered. There are, of course, problems in interpreting data of this sort. For instance, we need to know about the differences, if any, in quality standards between companies, and about the accuracy with which quality levels were assessed. Equally, we need to consider, in any particular case, not only the actual degree of improvement, but also the degree of improvement that was possible. Nevertheless the data are suggestive, and indicate that job-content changes do not appear to have a significant effect on quality improvements. Unlike flowline reorganization, where worker visibility and accountability was increased, it is possible that the opposite process occurs with flexible work groups since allocations of one employee to one job are replaced by a more diffuse assignment of responsibility to the group as a whole.

Table 6.5 Median quality improvements as a function of number of job dimensions altered in studies of flexible work groups[5]

Job dimensions altered	Quality improvements*	N	
2–3	40.0%	8	$U = 19$
4–5	31.3%	5	ns

* Measured in terms of error rates, rejects or scrap

There is again insufficient information on the majority of these cases of flexible work groups to enable any reasonable appreciation of the factors that might be operating, but we know that in four cases wage incentives were extended so as to make them dependent on product quality as well as quantity.[6] Three of these cases involved textile plants, where product quality is a variable subject to many influences. Operator responsibility for quality was thus initiated, or perhaps extended, via the mechanism of financial incentives. The fourth case was at the Hunsfors paper-processing plant in Norway, which was operated on a continuous basis. The effects of operator interventions were thus chiefly concerned with controlling variations in product quality, although interruptions in processing could also be influenced to some degree by the operators. The paid bonus reflected only the latter degree of influence, and with its experimental extension to several indices of product quality these same indices showed dramatic improvements.

6.6 Scientific management and flexible work groups

The principles and practices of scientific management were developed under industrial conditions in which advance planning and allocation of work was possible, and where large and irregular variations in work volume were infrequent. These conditions included labouring, machining, and brick-laying, all of which allowed considerable operator control over production volume. If however we compare the industries which have employed flowline reorganization (analysed as a contemporary application of Taylorism) as opposed to flexible work groups, we can discern a striking difference, as shown in Table 6.6.

Table 6.6 Incidence of job-redesign techniques, by industrial groups[7]

	Flowline reorganization	Flexible work groups
Metals, mining, textiles, chemicals, food, glass, paper	1	31
Electrical engineering, vehicles, clothing, footwear	36	20
Insurance, retail, transport, communications	10	10
Mechanical engineering, instrument engineering, furniture, other manufacturing	11	14
Totals	58	75

$\chi^2 = 31.6$; $p < 0.001$

The use of flowline reorganization has been concentrated in a relatively small number of industrial sectors: electrical engineering alone accounts for 62% of the cases. Within this industry group, flowline reorganization has been further concentrated in assembly or final assembly departments, that is, in situations where work volume is fairly predictable and where, on non-powered conveyor lines, it is subject to operator control. The industrial dispersion of flexible work groups appears at first sight much greater, since no particular industry group dominates the figures. Metal manufacture, mining, textiles, chemicals, food, glass and paper comprise 41% of the total number of cases. These industries are highly capitalized, unlike the more labour-intensive electrical-engineering industry. In many of them production takes place on a continuous, or semi-continuous process basis, in which the role of the operator is rather different from that of his counterpart in product assembly. Work in the process industries more frequently involves machine or plant monitoring, and attempts to reduce machine down-time, with the overall pace of production under a much smaller degree of operator control as compared to product assembly.

The work conditions are therefore rather different in many of these cases of flexible work groups from those conditions that furnished Taylor with the basis of his theory of scientific management. These differences—in machine control, process variability and operator functions—require rather different techniques in order to achieve Taylorian goals. Precise allocation of duties and of workloads is rendered difficult by irregular variations in the product or the production process. Thus, on certain occasions operators may be overworked, on others underworked. As I have argued elsewhere (Kelly, 1978b) the significance of sociotechnical theory, and of flexible work groups to which it gives rise, is that it has, if only implicitly, discerned the limiting conditions beyond which precise allocation of work on an individual basis becomes increasingly difficult. Hence the recommendation that work groups take responsibility for a series of duties. Of course, there will be variations in workload even at the group level, but it can be shown that these will constitute a smaller proportion of total man-hours than would be the case were duties allocated individually. In general then, we may suggest that flexible work groups have abandoned certain features of scientific management (individual allocation of work, accountability and payment) but only to the extent that there have been encountered limiting industrial conditions beyond which scientific management principles become less effective in achieving their stated goals.

There is however, an immediate objection that may be raised against this argument: since it could be pointed out that this brief discussion of industrial variability and flexible work groups refers only to 41% of the cases listed—what about the other 59%? It is true that many of the flexible work groups were created in situations where there may not have been considerable variations in production, and hence inequalities in workloads, such as furniture manufacture, vehicles, insurance and electrical engineering. However, there is often insufficient data to make a judgement on this issue. In other cases, it is possible to suggest that flexibility of labour was not a major factor in raising productivity. For instance, in the study by Bryan (1975) of the Cummins Engine Company, productivity of labour on a new production line was raised 'theoretically' by collapsing several jobs into individual roles, and thereby reducing total labour requirements. In addition, labour was flexible between jobs, but the major increase in output per man-hour had already been achieved. In the study at NØBO, reported by Emery and Thorsrud (1975), it has already been observed that output was only raised when the workforce were induced to cease restriction of output. The productivity rise in this case, again, was not predicated chiefly on labour flexibility. In the Philips study, reported by van Vliet and Vrenken (n.d.), method study was used to reduce unit production time, but over and above this productivity rose only a few per cent.

In conclusion, flexible work groups may be seen as a new 'best way' of organizing work under conditions of product and/or process uncertainty. Nevertheless the emphases on group working, and on flexible work assignments serve to differentiate this form of redesign from classical scientific management.

6.7 Conclusions

In many respects the themes identified in the origins and mechanisms of flowline reorganization—the first category of job redesign (Chapters 4 and 5)—have also been found to have a significant influence with regard to this second category, flexible work groups. The growth of international competition in several capital-intensive industries, such as chemicals and textiles, resulted in various organizational strategies to improve profit margins, hold down costs and/or raise productivity. Labour costs in such industries constitute a small, but potentially variable, element and have constituted the object of attention in many leading companies.

A second key characteristic of such companies, which distinguishes them from product-assembly companies, is the unpredictable variability in the product and/or production, process, which renders individual job specifications either difficult to write and/or costly to operate.

These factors, sometimes acting in combination with managerial interest in behavioural sciences and 'motivation' (as at ICI) or with political interests in 'industrial democracy' (as in Norway) have resulted in the creation of flexible work groups.

The epithet 'flexible' is more accurate than autonomous (however qualified), since autonomy has often been limited and subordinated to managerial objectives, and since flexibility denotes that feature of the groups that is most closely linked to productivity improvements. 'Autonomous' groups without flexibility could not have improved productivity in these cases: flexible groups without autonomy could have done so. I have argued that the key mechanisms that translated flexibility into higher labour intensity were labour elimination (especially where plants operated close to technical capacity) and changes in pay levels and systems. The evidence on changes in intrinsic motivation and job attitudes is conflicting, but there may be cases where the 'instrumental' attitudes required to underpin changes in workloads and pay are only weakly held, as in greenfield sites with specially recruited labour.

Whatever its heuristic advantages, sociotechnical-systems theory has seriously underestimated the importance of traditional mechanisms for raising labour productivity, and has underestimated the salience of the corresponding instrumental attitudes on the part of workers faced with job redesign.

Notes

1. Table 6.2 is based on the following cases: Agersnap *et al.* (1974), Anon (n.d., 1975a), Aquilano (1977), Archer (1975), Armstrong (1977), Birchall and Wild (1974), Bryan (1975), Butteriss and Murdoch (1975), Cummings and Srivastva (1977), Daniel (1970), Davis and Werling (1960), Emery and Thorsrud (1975), Fantoli (1979), Hallam (1976), Hepworth and Osbaldeston (1979), Hill (1971), Incomes Data Services (1979), Janson (1974), Kenton (1973), Kuriloff (1963,1977), Lindestad and Kvist (1975), Lindholm and Norstedt (1975), Locke *et al.* (1976), Mills (1976), Mukherjee (1975), Nichols (1975), Noren and Norstedt (1975), Peacock (1979), Pocock (1973), Poza and Markus (1980), Prestat (1972), Rice (1958), Roeber (1975), Rush (1971), Taylor (1977a), Taylor (1973), Trist *et al.* (1963), van Vliet and Vrenken (n.d.), Waldman (1974), Waldman *et al.* (1976), Walton (1972, 1974).
2. Table 6.3. is based on the same cases as Table 6.2.
3. The 19 cases are reported in: Agersnap *et al.* (1974), Bryan (1975), Daniel (1970), Davis and Werling (1960), Emery and Thorsrud (1975), Hallam

(1976), Hill (1971), Incomes Data Services (1979), Lindestad and Kvist (1975), Mukherjee (1975), Nichols (1975), Rice (1958), Roeber (1975), Torner (1976), Trist *et al.* (1963), Wall and Clegg (1981), Walton (1972, 1974).

4. Table 6.4 is based on the following cases: Anon (n.d., 1975a), Archer (1975), Bryan (1975), Butteriss and Murdoch (1975), Davis and Werling (1960), Emery and Thorsrud (1975), Hallam (1976), Hepworth and Osbaldeston (1979), Hill (1971), Janson (1974), Kuriloff (1963, 1977), Lindestad and Kvist (1975), Lindholm and Norstedt (1975), Locke *et al.* (1976), Prestat (1972), Rice (1958), Rush (1971), Trist *et al.* (1963), van Vliet and Vrenken (n.d.), Waldman *et al.*, (1976), Walton (1972, 1974).

5. Table 6.5 is based on the following cases: Agersnap *et al.* (1974), Armstrong (1977), Engelstad (1972), Janson (1974), Kuriloff (1963, 1977), Prestat (1972), Rice (1958), Rush (1971), Trist *et al.* (1963), van Vliet and Vrenken (n.d.), Walton (1972, 1974).

6. The four cases were reported in Engelstad (1972), Emery and Thorsrud (1975), Janson (1974) and Rice (1958).

7. The cases of flexible work groups are those listed in Note 1 (above) with the addition of: Anon (1972, 1974a,b; 1975b,c,d), De (1980), Frank and Hackman (1975), Jenkins (1974), Lindholm (1973), Moors (1977), Norstedt and Aguren (1974), Terisse (1975), Wall and Clegg (1981), Weir (1976). The cases of flowline reorganization are those listed in Table 4.1.

7 Vertical role integration: Herzberg's job enrichment

7.1 Introduction

For many people, job redesign is synonymous with the concept and programmes of job enrichment pioneered by Frederick Herzberg, and although the identification is less than accurate, it does contain an element of truth. Herzberg is one of the very few academics in this field to have made both an original theoretical contribution (the two-factor theory of job attitudes) as well as a distinctive practical innovation (job enrichment). The significance of his own work has been further enhanced by his unflagging efforts to promote it through books, articles, seminars, films and consultancy, and by his equally firm insistence on the shortcomings of alternative approaches. Furthermore both his name and his ideas have been closely linked with several widely known job-enrichment projects, notably those conducted by Robert Ford at AT&T in America, and by Paul and Robertson at ICI in England.

Herzberg's approach to job enrichment is distinctive and original. Where writers from 1950 onwards had pointed to the advantage of 'broadening' jobs so that they should embrace a wider variety of tasks, Herzberg opposed what he described as a 'Cooks tour' in which workers performed various tasks 'unrelated in any meaningful sense' Herzberg *et al.* (1959, p.133). Instead, he came to argue that responsibilities should be devolved down the organizational hierarchy in a process of what I call *vertical role integration,* a term that avoids the evaluative overtones of 'enrichment', and which was defined in Chapter 3. This is the third type of job redesign in the classification employed in this book.

Herzberg's original study of job attitudes used a white-collar sample, of accountants and engineers, and it is interesting that vertical role integration has been applied to white-collar workers more than the

other forms of job redesign; this point has been documented in Table
3.5. The emphasis on white-collar work in this chapter reflects the
distribution of cases shown in Table 3.5, but it also derives from the fact
that vertical role integration for manual workers has been dispersed
throughout a wide range of industries and its origins are difficult to
discover.

This chapter begins with an outline and appraisal of Herzberg's
theory of job attitudes and his proposals for vertical role integration. It
then considers developments in white-collar work in the post-war
period, focusing on the employment relationship: qualification levels,
pay and status, the rising cost of white-collar workers, and
unionization. The next section then reviews some of the major case
studies of vertical role integration in this context, and seeks to assess the
merits of different explanations for the observed outcomes.

(i) Development of the theory

Herzberg's two-factor theory of job attitudes had its origins in a review
of job satisfaction studies published in 1957 (Herzberg *et al.*, 1957). The
literature appeared to offer contradictory findings on the determination
of job attitudes, but Herzberg and his co-workers suggested a possible
resolution. They argued that the results obtained in the studies varied
according to whether employees were being asked about their job *likes*,
or about their *dislikes*, and they conducted their own research to test this
hypothesis. The original pilot study spanned a considerable range of
occupations, but on finding professional workers to be more fluent and
articulate, the final study used a sample of 203 engineers and accountants from the Pittsburgh area (Herzberg *et al.*, 1959). The basic
interview question asked them to 'think of a time when you felt exceptionally good or exceptionally bad about your job, . . .' and the nature
and meaning of the events mentioned were explored in a series of
further questions. The replies were then subjected to content analysis,
and out of this procedure emerged the most original feature of Herzberg's theory. He suggested that, whereas previously any job factor,
such as recognition, pay or conditions, had been assumed to act on a
continuum, from high satisfaction through to high dissatisfaction, his
own findings suggested that these factors were bipolar. One set of
factors, called hygiene factors, e.g., pay, supervision and work conditions, created dissatisfaction when absent, but when present only re-

moved this dissatisfaction. The generation of satisfaction itself was the product of another, different set of factors called motivators: when present they created satisfaction but when the factors were absent, employees lacked feelings of satisfaction but did not experience feelings of dissatisfaction.

In full, Herzberg *et al.* isolated 16 first-level factors (situations or events) and 12 second-level factors (meanings attached to events), but the motivator – hygiene dichotomy has usually been taken to cover 10 first-level factors. The motivators were defined as: achievement, recognition, work itself, responsibility and advancement. The hygiene situations/events were: company policy and administration, salary, supervision – technical, supervision – social aspects, and working conditions. The labels 'motivator' and 'hygiene' were assigned because the former sets of factors seemed to revolve around an employee's work and its performance—job *content*—whereas the latter appeared to be located in the environment, or the *context* of work. These two sets of factors were associated not only with good and bad feelings, respectively, but also, according to Herzberg, with work performance and absenteeism, respectively.

Since most hygiene factors, were well catered for in most industrial establishments (Herzberg *et al.*, 1959, p.124) and since, according to Herzberg these could not in themselves generate job satisfaction or high performance, it followed that the route to increased productivity lay through the 'motivators'. Only by attending to the content of work, rather than its context, could these goals be achieved.

Several assumptions of two-factor theory, implicit in *Motivation to Work* (Herzberg *et al.*, 1959), were rendered far more explicit in *Work and the Nature of Man* (Herzberg, 1966), ostensibly an attempt to generalize the earlier findings into a more far-reaching theoretical form. This later work has two features of particular interest. First, Herzberg overtly adopted a form of need – hierarchy theory (similar to Maslow's, 1943, ideas) to underpin the hygiene – motivator distinction. People's needs were similarly divided into two broad classes centred on the avoidance of pain and on psychological growth, respectively. The employment of need theory served to undermine the social aspects of the earlier work and in particular the explanation of occupational differences in job attitudes. In 1959, these differences were attributed to corresponding variations in work experiences and work conditions, but in 1966 Herzberg wrote:

A hygiene seeker is not merely a victim of circumstances, but is *motivated* in the direction of temporary satisfaction. It is not that his job offers little opportunity for self-actualization; rather, it is that his needs lie predominantly in another direction, that of satisfying avoidance needs . . . his resultant chronic dissatisfaction is an illness of motivation   (p.81)

Coupled with the emphasis on a more explicitly psychological account of individual differences in job attitudes was the philosophical corollary of an increased attachment to individualism. Herzberg *et al.* (1959) had strongly criticized the 'human relations' emphasis on informal social relations and supervisory styles, and the complement to this view was that of the isolated individual (Herzberg, 1966):

The primal fact is that each human being is separate, distinct, and a unique individual . . . after the umbilical cord is cut; all connections become the inventions and delusions of man.   (p.66)

And not only was individualism a biological fact, it was a psychological and social value (Herzberg, 1966, p.67), and these views help to explain Herzberg's lack of attention to trades unions insofar as unions assert collective as against individual rights. In a recent publication, the logic of this position has been drawn out in relation to sociotechnical systems theory, which was criticized on the grounds that it sought to impose 'the tyranny of the group over the individual' (Herzberg, 1974, 1976a).

Finally, we should notice the assumption, common to all theories of job redesign, and to Taylorism, that the interests of workers and their employers can be harmonized. The basis on which Herzberg proposed to achieve this was also common to all these theories. Changes in job content will lead to higher productivity, and lower turnover and absenteeism for employers, and (Herzberg *et al.*, 1959):

To the individual, an understanding of the forces that lead to improved morale   would   bring   greater   happiness   and   greater   self-realization.   (p.ix)

The view is that the employer gains economically, the employee gains psychologically.

(ii) Vertical role integration

The implications of two-factor theory for job redesign were only barely worked out in *Motivation to Work* (Herzberg, 1959): individual control over work methods was advanced as one tentative conclusion, and this was accompanied by some rather ill-informed criticism of 'job enlargement'. The key principle was that (Herzberg *et al.*, 1959):

> ...jobs themselves have to be set up in such a way that, interest or not,
> the individual who carries them out can find that their operations lead to
> increased motivation.   (p.134).

By 1968, a series of job-redesign principles had been developed, and they have informed Herzberg's major vertical role integration exercises—those at ICI and AT&T. Translated into more conventional terms they prescribed greater autonomy, responsibility, feedback, task identity and increased skill requirements.

As one would expect, the type of job-redesign advocated by Herzberg is individualistic: work groups are studiously avoided (Herzberg, 1976a,b). Equally, it is accepted that certain workers in some types of jobs may not be amenable to job enrichment (hygiene seekers and those in technologically constrained jobs), and there is no notion anywhere in Herzberg's writings of the possibilities of development for such people. Once a hygiene seeker, always a hygiene seeker, or so it seems. The separation of motivators and hygiene factors carries within it the practical possibility of job redesign without pay increases, a possibility to which Hughes and Gregory (1973) have paid particular attention; in practice, as we shall see, many American firms have not granted wage rises in their attempts at vertical role integration.

One of the most distinctive features of Herzberg's approach is the claim that participation in job redesign by those to be affected 'contaminate(s) the process with human-relations hygiene' (Herzberg, 1968, p.123). It produces no worthwhile results, and is therefore to be avoided.

(iii) Criticisms and limitations of the theory

Herzberg's conclusions have given rise to an immense amount of research and a considerable degree of controversy. Three major criticisms have been made, each of which has differing implications, both for the theory and its accompanying strategy. Firstly, it has been claimed by several researchers that Herzberg's conclusions are artefactual since they result from features of the method of content analysis of employee responses that he employed. Studies using different methods have tended not to reproduce the motivation – hygiene dichotomy (King, 1970). Secondly, it has been pointed out by King (1970) and by Wall and Stephenson (1970) that there are in fact five possible formulations of the two-factor theory, for two of which there is no empirical support. A third possibility is supposedly artefactual, whereas the remaining two have yet to be adequately tested. These conclusions have also been reproduced, and accepted, by Miner and Dachler in their contribution to the *Annual Review of Psychology* (1973). Indeed they went as far as to suggest the two-factor theory should be either modified or else '. . . laid to rest'. Thirdly, Vroom (1964) suggested that although the bipolarity discovered by Herzberg was a genuine, rather than an artefactual phenomenon, its basis did not lie in the distinction between job content and job context. Rather, it reflected the fact that people tended to lay the blame for dissatisfaction at the feet of others—company or supervisors—while claiming their own activities as the source of satisfying experiences. Wall and Stephenson (1970) investigated this idea and claimed that there were differences between people in the direction predicted by Vroom.

There are three further points that merit examination since they have implications for the strategy of job enrichment. Herzberg argued that salary was a hygiene factor, and therefore an alleviator of dissatisfaction but not a promoter of satisfaction. Nevertheless 'salary' was mentioned as often in the genesis of 'good' feelings as of 'bad', an awkward finding that Herzberg circumvents by emphasizing that its more frequent occurrence in long-time-span situations associated with 'bad' feelings demonstrates its greater potency as a hygiene factor (Herzberg *et al.*, 1959, pp.82–3). Rather less satisfactory is his attempt to explain productivity improvements following the adoption of the Scanlon wage-incentive plan by the Lincoln Electric Company. First he attributes the improvements to worker participation, rather than to financial incentives and thereby contradicts his description of 'company policy and administration' as a hygiene factor (Herzberg *et al.*, 1959, pp.117–8). Second he admits that where output restriction is practised, incentives can raise performance levels to an unspecified 'norm'. And since he also admits that such restriction is practised on 'an enormous scale' it follows that (contrary to popular misconception) he accepts that pay can motivate performance on a similar scale!

The next major point to be noticed is the conflation of motivation and satisfaction. The thrust of Herzberg *et al.*'s 1959 study was to show there was a systematic relationship between particular job experiences and job *satisfaction*. The argument that these experiences engendered *motivation* as well was based only on indirect and subjective accounts of behaviour by his respondents. Company records or other direct, or behavioural measures or indices of motivation were not used, and the correlation therefore between satisfaction and motivation, and hence between satisfaction and performance, must remain open to question.

Even had such a correlation been shown in the 1959 study, the occupational bias of the study would cast doubt on its generalizability. The work attitudes of the respondents were aptly summarized in the report that (Herzberg *et al.*, 1959):

Workers complained of too little work more than of too much.   (p.74)

From the point of view of vertical role integration, Herzberg's research poses several interesting questions and ambiguities: the role of pay as a motivator; the significance of participation in job redesign; the occupational groups to whom the strategy may be applicable; and the possibility that the strategy may affect job satisfaction (or job attitudes) more than job performance. These issues will be examined in the light of the case studies, but first we must take a wider look at the growth of white-collar work in the post-war period.

7.2 White-collar and office work

The growth of white-collar and office work during the past 60 years is one of the most striking features of the occupational distributions of advanced capitalist (and socialist) economies (Braverman, 1974; Lockwood, 1958). The increase derives both from the expansion of non-industrial employment, such as public services, and from the growth of managerial, administrative, technical and clerical staff within industrial organizations. Brearley (1976) points out that, although the terms 'white-collar' and (to a lesser degree) 'office' worker are not always clearly defined, the terminological debates leave the broad pattern largely unaltered. For example, in 1911 white-collar workers formed 18.7% of the UK working population, but by 1961 this figure had risen to 35.9%, and by 1971 to 41%.

Their growth in numbers has easily outstripped the growth of manual workers. Between 1951 and 1961, the UK working population grew by an average of 0.5% per annum, but the office population (only part of the white-collar population) grew by an average 2.6% per annum

(Brearley, 1976). Across the advanced industrial countries their growth has been uneven, as Table 7.1 shows.[1]

Table 7.1 Increase in non-industrial employment (excluding agriculture) as a percentage of industrial employment 1962–73

Japan	Italy	West Germany	France	USA	UK
7%	7.5%	8%	15%	19%	19%

It is interesting to notice that the two countries in which most extensive use has been made of vertical role integration are also those with the fastest growth rates of white-collar work. To discover the reasons for this association, we must examine some specific features of white-collar work in general, and office work in particular.

Although ways are now being developed of measuring office work using method study (and indeed some date back to the 1950s), the degree of conceptual work in office tasks presented serious obstacles to such endeavours. In addition, the expansion of office work has been tied to status considerations of managerial superiors, and both these features (among others) have resulted in a very much slower rate of productivity growth in this sector, as compared with industrial work. In the USA factory unit labour costs rose by 9% between 1959 and 1969, but the equivalent costs for clerical and service workers rose by 42% (Brearley, 1976, p.140). This is partly because the growth of earnings has outstripped productivity growth. In the finance and insurance industries, white-collar pay increases averaged 6.3% per annum between 1950 and 1970, whereas productivity rose at an annual rate of only 1.9% (Brearley, 1976, p.141).

The expansion of jobs did not correspond to the growth in qualifications of the work force, particularly in the USA which has one of the highest age participation rates in higher education of all the advanced countries. International comparisons are illustrated in Table 7.2. Associated with the growing qualifications of the workforce in the USA was an even faster rise in the qualifications demanded by employers, which were in turn disproportionate to the actual requirements of job performance (Berg, 1970). There were obviously technical advances, especially in manufacturing, which necessitated some upgrading of skill requirements, but with clerical work there is little evidence of such processes. Rather it appears that employers upgraded job entry requirements because of their beliefs in the personal characteristics—such as reliability—associated with higher education (Berg, 1970).

Table 7.2 Age participation rates * in higher education

Country and age range	1965	1975
USA (18)	38.8	42.1
France (18–20)	23.4	28.3
Japan (18–19)	14.5	37.1
Italy (19–21)	12.0	28.3
West Germany (20–22)	11.6	20.2
UK (18–19)	11.5	19.8

* Age participation rate is the number of people of the age group (shown in brackets) attending an institution of higher education, expressed as a percentage of the total national population of the same age(s).

It is also worth noting (a point all too rarely mentioned in the job-redesign literature) that many of the new posts in offices were taken by women, and it is at least possible that the hiring of over-qualified female staff was considered uproblematic because of beliefs about their weak attachment to employment (Mumford and Banks, 1967).

The proliferation and the costs of white-collar work eventually resulted in a concern with the 'control of staff-related overhead' (Brearley, 1976). This led to various actions, and Braverman (1974) documents the growing use of work-measurement techniques in offices and the extension of fragmentation of labour, mechanization and hierarchy into these settings. Other companies have used forms of systems analysis and target-setting to raise white-collar productivity and to control costs (Brearley, 1976). A survey of 260 American companies in all industrial sectors found that 90 were using some form of 'formal, organized approach to improving clerical productivity' (Brearley, 1976, p.141). In banking, insurance and finance, the figure was even higher, and 58 out of 103 companies (56%) had employed such programmes. Systems analysis and work measurement appeared to be the most successful, featuring in 70% and 67%, respectively, of the 30 most successful programmes, defined by productivity improvements, side-effects or duration. In 37% of these programmes, 'job enrichment' had figured, and this often appeared to centre on an employee involvement in job improvements. A more focused survey by Birchall and Hammond (1978) obtained responses from 32 British organizations that had restructured clerical work in line with job-redesign theory. The most frequently cited reason for embarking on such programmes was to improve efficiency (mentioned 14 times), followed by job satisfaction (10 mentions). Labour turnover or absenteeism were cited by only 7 (21%) of respondents.

My own survey of published cases of vertical role integration shows the distribution of reasons for undertaking such initiatives set out in Table 7.3. Particularly interesting is the blue-collar – white-collar difference, which is consistent with the 'problems' of white-collar work outlined above.

Table 7.3 Reasons for undertaking vertical role integration (number of cases citing) for blue and white collar workers[3]

	Personnel (absence, turnover, morale)	Production (productivity, costs)	Other
Blue-collar workers	10	15	3
White-collar workers	10	4	7
Totals	20	19	10

This brief survey of white-collar work is sufficient to indicate that, as with the previous techniques of flowline reorganization and flexible work groups, we need to analyse white-collar job redesign not as an inevitable response to novel sets of problems, but as one possible response to fairly conventional problems. In examining case studies in the next section I will consider factors that dictate the adoption of one response rather than another. The same examination will also throw some light on vertical role integration among blue-collar workers, which because of its industrial dispersion permits no obvious explanation at present, by reference either to product or labour markets.

7.3 Case studies and experiments

(i) Blue-collar workers

I shall begin with a discussion of several cases of vertical role integration involving blue-collar workers, the earliest example of which
was reported by Walker (1950). The division of labour in several
machine shops was reorganized, so that the machine operatives no
longer simply fed the machine, turned it on, and picked up the output.
They were also assigned the tasks of setting up the machine, of carrying
out minor maintenance duties, and of inspecting the products. Before
this redesign, division of labour had been taken to the point where none
of these groups of workers had, or could be guaranteed, a 'full' workload
(in Taylor's sense) and the division was thus counter-productive. Each
group of workers could carry out their tasks only while at least one of the
others was idle, and this inefficiency was transcended by assigning all
duties to the machine operative. At the same time 35 setters and
checkers were eliminated, and because of this higher wages could be
paid at the same time as total labour costs fell.

A similar case was reported by Powers (1972) in which a work
organization comprising one operative and two inspector – packers per
two machines was progressively altered. Firstly, one inspector – packer
was eliminated from each pair of machines, and then the second man
was also eliminated, leaving all the duties to be performed by the
remaining operatives. The output from 18 machines, originally
obtained by the employment of 27 workers (9 operatives and 18 inspector – packers) was finally obtained with only nine workers, each responsible for machine operation, goods packing and inspection. In
terms of output per man-hour, this represents an increase in productivity of 200%.

In both of these cases it might be argued that higher productivity
arose from increased motivation due to the variety and responsibility
involved in the new jobs, and that the elimination of labour was a
consequence, or by-product of this. But why did the employees accept
the new jobs in the first place? And why did this result in increased
output per man, rather than (as some writers have suggested it should)
increased product quality? In the absence of attitude surveys of the
employees, no definitive answers can be given. But it can be suggested
that in both cases employees accepted higher levels of effort expendi-

ture in return for higher wages. The elimination of labour was based on this 'agreement' and was *not* reported as following, some time later, the redesign of jobs.

Indeed in a report of a case in which supervisory duties were transferred to operatives and one layer of supervision eliminated, Ross and Screeton (1979) remark:

> A central problem in the failure to obtain worker commitment was the poor relation between effort, performance and reward. When the workers asked what was in it for them, the answer was — not very much. Pay was not linked to production levels.   (pp.110–111)

There are other cases that have involved labour elimination, where it would seem difficult to defend a theory of motivation and performance based on job content. Rush (1971), for instance, describes a case in which the operatives of twisting frames, in fibre-glass manufacture were 'assigned' the job of frame cleaning. The assignment is unlikely to have been eagerly accepted by the workers since, as Rush states, the job of frame cleaning was 'unskilled, disliked, dirty, boring, low status and low paid'. Yet the fact remains that this work, performed by 28 cleaners, was assigned in full to the 92 frame operatives. Initially the operatives increased in numbers, from 92 to 108, but after another few months, the number fell back again to 92, and the whole process was achieved without a pay rise. The fact that the plant had no recognized trade union may be relevant here in accounting for the absence of any apparent benefits for the frame operatives, and one can only suggest that management simply exercised its uncontested authority to effect this change, or else convinced the workers of the economic necessity for such changes, or both. Certainly, the intrinsic merits of the job would not account for its acceptance, and performance, by the work force. The other alternative explanation is that insofar as the job of frame twisting, as with that of machine operative in Walker's case study, involves a considerable amount of 'machine-minding', operatives may have welcomed any extra duties because they helped pass the time. This appeared to be the case, to some degree, in the study by Cotgrove *et al.* (1971), which suggested that the increased effort necessitated by job redesign was appreciated because it helped speed the passage of time.

In Cotgrove *et al.'s* (1971) study involving over 2000 employees in a British textile plant, loom operatives were assigned several minor maintenance duties, to be carried out either before the machines started up, or when they had broken down. In other words, portions of unoccupied time within the operative's working day were filled up, and (the other side of the coin) the maintenance labour force was reduced by 14–15%. Had this not been done, approximately the same level of output would have been obtained with the same volume of labour: the productivity of labour would not, in other words, have increased. The same point holds true for the previous cases. Again, we must ask why did employees accept these arrangements and agree to perform extra duties? It was not because the duties were more highly motivating, for in this case the extra duties were negotiated between unions and management, and accepted by unions and workforce *in advance*. The inducement to accept these arrangements was an average increase in pay of approximately £3 per week.

It may be more useful to interpret cases of this kind in terms of negotiated changes in the wage – effort bargain. Employees put out higher levels of effort in return for higher earnings, and labour productivity is enhanced by labour elimination. The Rush case is an exception here, but we have already noted that job-redesign theories could not account for these outcomes either.

All these cases have involved blue-collar workers, and two of the mechanisms postulated in the present theory, namely pay rises, and labour elimination and raised individual workloads. There is little evidence to suggest the existence of specific work methods improvements in this category of job redesign (apart from the case reported by Weed, 1971, and by Rush, 1971, in which cleaners were supplied with improved materials and appliances), so it is interesting to enquire what productivity outcomes have been achieved in the *absence* of these mechanisms among blue-collar workers. Without labour elimination or pay rises, or the introduction of pay incentives, we find only small or non-existent increases in productivity in situations where increased effort expenditure could, in principle, have increased output: Agersnap *et al.* (1974), 0%; Paul and Robertson (1970) (toolsetters case), 3.9%; Wyatt and Fraser (1928) 3–4%. The one blue-collar case that deviates from this pattern was written up by Hill (1971), and reported a productivity increase of 20%. But this increase derived both from the delegation of extra duties (in this case, maintenance work) to operatives, as well as from various technical suggestions advanced by the employees. It is impossible therefore to disentangle the effects of these two factors.

(ii) White-collar workers

Let us turn now to studies of white-collar workers. As with the blue-collar cases reported above, many of these suffer from the absence of control groups, and the failure to employ measures of job attitudes. But this is by no means universally true, as shown in the study by Locke *et al.* (1976). This investigation explicitly set out to investigate the mechanisms of job redesign, the role of pay increases and the relation between attitudes and behaviour. As such, it provides one of the closest approximations in the literature to a test of my theory. Three different types of job change were introduced (each with matched control groups) in the clerical section of a local-government agency, involving, respectively, increased control over labour allocation and task variety; increased decision making, liaison and control of work scheduling; and increased variety and reduced external control.

A job-attitude questionnaire was administered both before and six months after the start of the change programme, and the results are summarized in Table 7.4.

Table 7.4 *Behavioural and attitudinal results in a study of vertical role integration (Locke et al., 1976)*

Measure	Experimental groups (N=46)	Control groups (N=49)
Productivity	+23%	+2%
Absenteeism	−5%	+7%
Turnover	−6%	+20%
Complaints and disciplinary actions	0	4
Attitudes	No change	No change

The changes in productivity were attributed by Locke *et al.* to improved utilization of labour (employees moved from job to job as required), elimination of unnecessary procedures, more feedback on performance, and in one group, inter-individual competition. But what of changes in absence and turnover? These are often taken as indices of job satisfaction, yet in this case attitudes remained unchanged. The authors suggested that attitudes *did* improve in the early stages of the study, as reflected in turnover and absence figures, partly in response to job redesign and partly in anticipation of pay rises to accompany new responsibilities. When the latter were not forthcoming, employees were disappointed. Locke *et al.* (1976) comment that their findings:

> ... do not completely support the view that employees at lower job levels dislike or are indifferent to mentally challenging work. They do want it, but predominantly *as a means to an end, not as an end in itself* (p.710).

The study then provided indirect support for the importance of pay increases in job-redesign exercises (although suggesting these are related strongly to attitudes); the significance of improvements in work methods, and better utilization of labour, i.e., labour intensification; and the possibility of attitude – behaviour discrepancies.

The link between job redesign and performance was also questioned in a study by Umstot *et al.* (1976), which also was methodologically rigorous, although it used only part-time employees hired for a few weeks. Nevertheless, it appeared to suggest that the mere assignment of goals raised job performance, regardless of the degree of job enrichment, whereas the latter change had a greater impact on job satisfaction. Direct measurement of job perceptions and intrinsic motivation in these cases (Paul and Robertson, 1970) also called into question the salience of intrinsic motivation for job performance. These studies involved the delegation of higher administrative and managerial duties, including scope of decision-making, to groups such as sales representatives, design engineers, experimental officers, draughtsmen, and foremen. The authors used the Job Reaction Survey (JRS), a measure designed by Herzberg himself to tap employee job perceptions along the 'motivator' dimensions. Scores on this scale can range from 0 to 80, and the results for sales representatives showed an increase in mean JRS score for the experimental group from 50.1 to 55.4, whereas the mean control group score shifted from 51.8 to 52.0. This difference is very small indeed, and assuming a standard deviation of only 2 or 3 points, is unlikely to be statistically significant. Although quantitative performance data are unavailable for the other four groups in the study, ratings by superiors, and other indices, suggest there were definite performance improvements in all cases. With one exception — that of the design engineers — the results, in all probability, show no statistical differences in job perceptions and intrinsic motivation between experimental and control groups after job redesign. In other words, performance effects may appear quite independently of improvements in intrinsic motivation in the cases reported here. One possible explanation is that levels of intrinsic motivation may have been high at the outset. Job redesign may therefore have facilitated the emergence of behaviours which were previously constrained rather than being the cause of those behaviours (see Kynaston-Reeves, 1968).

Pay levels and systems, and volume of labour, remained unchanged throughout all these studies, and there was little systematic evidence of work methods improvements. The explanation of changes in job performance may therefore require resort to one or other of the 'classical' theories of job redesign, with their stress on intrinsic motivation, especially in view of the highly skilled (and probably motivated) nature of the employees in these studies.

The study by Morse and Reimer (1970) also failed to discover any simple correlation between job performance and overall job satisfaction, following an increase in autonomy for clerical workers. In the experimental group productivity rose but job satisfaction was unchanged. In the control group, productivity also rose, to an even greater extent, and job satisfaction fell, though it should be noted that this group experienced a *reduction* in autonomy, rather than a situation of no change. The study also showed however that a *reduction* in employee control over their immediate work could yield a productivity increase. In addition, some (unknown) portion of the 21% productivity increase in the experimental group was due to work methods improvements suggested by the employees.

The classic study by Ford (1969) at AT&T should also be described here. 120 clerical workers (70% of whom were college graduates) were involved. Two groups, (total $N = 36$) were allowed to sign the letters they wrote, to choose the form of the letter, to dispense with external verification, and were to be held responsible for the quality of their work (previously, supervisors had been responsible). Three groups ($N = 59$) acted as controls. Employees were asked to fill out the Herzberg JRS (see above), and performance was measured by a Customer Service Index (CSI), a combined measure of work speed and quality.

Six months later job performance in the experimental groups had risen, but job perception and motivation scores rose in only one of the two groups. Performance improvements were also found in the control groups (though to a lesser extent) and JRS scores were unchanged, as one would expect according to classical job-redesign theory.

No pay rises were given in this study, and labour was not eliminated, but one of our postulated mechanisms *did* change. Formal accountability for job performance was vested in the clerks themselves, rather than their supervisors, and deviations from required performance standards would thus have been brought more directly to the clerks' notice than before. This may well account for improved performance by the experimental groups. Nevertheless the results of this case are quite consistent with Herzberg's theory, as indeed, to an even greater degree are the findings of Janson (1971). In that case, a group of production typists was responsible for typing blocks of information onto computer tapes. After some analysis of their own and various ancillary operations, it was decided to allow them to dispense with supervisory verification of their work, and to correct their own mistakes. They were also allowed to change their own computer tapes (a job previously carried out by supervisors) and were assigned responsibility for a particular group of companies, thus permitting easier identification of the source of errors. Number of blocks typed per hour rose from 70 to 85 in the experimental group, but remained at 68 in the control group, whereas the number of errors per week fell from 15–20 to less than 5, the figure for the control group again remaining constant. Scores on the JRS rose from 50 to 60 for the experimental group, but fell from 53 to 47 in the control group.

Similar results were obtained in another study reported by the same author (Janson, 1975), and in studies by Bryan (1975), Gorman and Molloy (1972), Kraft (1971), Maher and Overbagh (1971) and Randall (1973). Several of these cases did not utilize control groups, although all of them reported improvements either in performance or product quality. In some cases, e.g., Gorman and Molloy and Maher and Overbagh, higher wages were paid for the new jobs, and indeed in the former case employees were so concerned to maintain their level of earnings that they strongly resisted the introduction of a group bonus scheme, fearing that an influx of new employees would lower their earnings. The other cases, however, conform to the predicted job-redesign pattern: changed job content was followed by improved performance and attitudes.

7.4 Mechanisms of productivity improvements

The classical theories of job redesign would have difficulties with some of these cases. For example, as described in Chapter 4, the principal task design theorists (Hackman, Lawler and Oldham) postulated that it is *perceived* rather than *actual* job content that is motivating, and that jobs must be changed on each of the dimensions of autonomy, variety and task significance for improved motivation. Several of the cases above showed instances of performance improvements in the *absence* of changed job perceptions or changes in intrinsic motivation, or showed instances of performance improvements with changes in only two of three key job dimensions.

If one examines the Herzberg postulate of increased satisfaction, motivation and performance as a result of vertical role integration then the occurrence of performance improvements in the absence of changes in satisfaction and job perceptions must indicate a deficiency in the theory. The importance of pay increases *need* not contradict Herzberg's theory, since Herzberg did not deny their efficacy (though he thought it limited), and he could argue that workers responding to pay increases were motivationally 'sick', and hence outside the scope of his theory.

If we examine the incidence of pay rises and labour elimination — two of the principal mechanisms referred to in the theory presented in Chapter 3—and confine our attention to the 26 cases with known productivity outcomes, we find the figures shown in Table 7.5. Only 5 cases involved the elimination of labour *and* pay rises (compare the much higher figure for cases of flexible workgroups, Chapter 6) although at least 12 (almost half) of these 26 cases entailed the provision of pay rises and/or the elimination of labour. But given the large number of 'Don't knows' in Table 7.5, it is difficult to indicate the extensiveness of these two mechanisms. All we can say, so far, is that their occurrence in almost 50% of the cases with reasonably reliable productivity data gives us some confidence in their significance for raising productivity.

However, if we divide the case studies into blue-collar and white-collar studies, two very different patterns emerge. Four of the five cases of vertical role integration which involved the joint operation of pay rises and labour elimination were carried out with blue-collar workers.[4] Further, as noted earlier, productivity improvements were poor in the absence of these two mechanisms in the blue-collar studies. Finally the origins of vertical role integration with blue-collar workers derived mainly from product-market pressures.

With white-collar workers, there were many more cases of vertical role integration that did not involve any of the mechanisms of productivity improvement posited in the new theory. Nevertheless substantial improvements in productivity were still obtained in these cases: e.g., Locke *et al.* (1976), 12.5%; Morse and Reimer (1970), 21%.

Table 7.5 Relationships between pay rises and labour elimination in cases of vertical role integration (N = 26)[5]

	Labour eliminated	No labour eliminated	Don't know	Totals
Pay rises given	5	0	1	6
No pay rises given	1	5	2	8
Don't know	5	3	4	12
Totals	11	8	7	26

The origin of such initiatives owed far more to labour market, or personnel problems of turnover and absenteeism, than to the product-market competition which was more salient in the blue-collar cases (Table 7.3). This is as would be expected on the basis of the account presented above of developments in white-collar work in the post-war period.

In view of the operation of both intrinsic and extrinsic mechanisms of motivation in different segments of the population of cases (*cf.* Centers and Bugenthal, 1966), we would not expect to find a clearcut difference in productivity improvements in favour of extrinsic mechanisms. The figures are shown in Table 7.6. Clearly, labour elimination does appear to be associated with significantly higher degrees of productivity increase, but the same does not seem to hold for pay rises.

Although the evidence for white-collar vertical role integration is broadly consistent with Herzberg's theory, it is worth noting one problem thrown up by the data, and remarked on in the earlier discussion of two-factor theory. Several studies showed non-significant increases in intrinsic motivation, and it may be necessary to rethink the argument that job redesign improves performance by increasing intrinsic motivation. With white-collar workers, motivation may be relatively high before job redesign, but performance effects may be inhibited by job design. Once these barriers to performance are removed, the effects of high motivational levels may then appear.

Table 7.6 Median productivity increases as a function of pay rises and labour elimination in cases of vertical role integration[6]

		N			N
Labour eliminated	49.5%	11	Pay rise	22.0%	6
No labour eliminated	2.0%	8	No pay rise	18.3%	8
Don't know	15.0%	7	Don't know	13.5%	12
Total		26	Total		26

$U = 2, p < 0.001$ (one-tailed) $U = 1$ns

7.5 Quality improvements

Several of the case studies discussed above reported improvements in product quality, or reductions in error rates. The majority of these were not subjected to tests of statistical significance, although if the figures are taken at face value, then some of them certainly appear to have been significant. The data reported by Ford (1969) covered both work quality and quantity and suggested that there was an improvement in the experimental, as compared with the control groups. A case study of inspectors by Maher and Overbagh (1971) in which inspectors were assigned more autonomy and responsibility, showed a reduction in defective products, after 9 months, from 7% to 2.5%, although no control group was used. Paul and Robertson (1970) carried out a study of tool setters, in which the men were given responsibility for product quality from a particular group of machines and for ensuring proper use of machinery. Although there were other factors involved in the rate of rejects, and the control group was inadequate, the figures showed no improvement in the scrap proportion after five months. A study by Janson (1971) yielded a reduction in error rates of over 50%.

Clearly many other factors may have been responsible for these improvements in quality apart from those posited by theories of job redesign. It is interesting to note, for instance, that in Ford's study work quality and quantity improvements were found in the control as well as the experimental groups, underlining the point that these outcomes are subject to many influences. Employees were often given more direct and/or precise feedback on their performance, and it may be the case that this was motivating in, and of, itself. But it is also possible that feedback facilitated the performance of employees who were already motivated to perform well. All but one of the cases involved white-collar, clerical workers, and, certainly in the Ford study, a high proportion (70%) of these were college graduates whom one might expect to hold more intrinsically centred orientations to work.

Theories of job redesign that stress the importance of intrinsic motivation may therefore provide an explanation for some of these quality improvement data.

7.6 Vertical role integration and scientific management

Table 7.7 lists the duties that have been assigned to workers in cases of vertical role integration. These duties can be broadly divided into sets. The first set includes work traditionally carried out by manual or lower-grade clerical workers, and is listed in the left-hand column; the right-hand column lists duties that have more commonly been performed by supervisors and managers, i.e., by those with authority over manual and clerical workers.

The rationale for the combination of various manual or clerical work tasks within a single job is that savings in labour costs can be realized, since each of these tasks, in itself, is insufficient to occupy a worker for the duration of the working day. Taylor himself recognized the existence of such fractional work roles, and ironically, the example he gave us was that of cleaning and maintenance, suggesting that the two could, under certain conditions, be combined. Cleaning work has, in fact, been assigned to machine operatives in two cases of job redesign, although in general the extra duties assigned usually required more rather than less skill than current duties. If we understand that Taylor sought to assign maximum workloads to as cheap a labour force as possible, then the relocation of maintenance, inspection, etc., can be seen as a development that is quite in line with Taylorist principles.

McBeath (1974) was more explicit about the affinity between vertical role integration and scientific management, when reporting a case in which welders lost some of their simpler duties to a new grade of assistant welder, while simultaneously acquiring some of the work previously undertaken by supervision:

> Strictly speaking, this regrouping of work may be considered as 'deskilling' some jobs. However, the deskilled work did not require higher skills anyway ... (p.123).

Indeed it may be considered as deskilling, and the way one considers the process depends very much on the standpoint from which it is viewed, that of the worker losing duties, or of the worker who acquires them in a process of 'enrichment'.

If we examine the second type of labour transferred down the status hierarchy, namely 'managerial' labour, then this does violate the separation of execution and conception argued for by Taylor. In that regard, vertical role integration can be said to have transcended Taylorism. The abandonment of the Taylorist principle here is clearly of some significance, but it should not be over-stated. The overall division of managerial and non-managerial labour persists despite the introduction of job redesign, and it may be that this abiding division can only be transformed by mechanisms of participation and representation, rather than job redesign.

Table 7.7 Additional duties assigned to workers in cases of vertical role integration

Clerical/manual tasks	Managerial tasks
Answer clients' queries	Inspection/testing
Maintenance	Work scheduling
Machine set-up/tool setting	Responsibility/accountability
Paperwork/documentation	Participation in decision-making
Materials supply	Sign letters
	Labour allocation
	Authority for decision-making

7.7 Conclusions

The case studies of white-collar vertical role integration described here provide the strongest support yet for the classical theory of job redesign. The under-utilization of often highly qualified clerical and technical workers has been extensively discussed by many writers, and there are reasonable grounds for assuming that the work attitudes of such employees will be more favourable than most to the ideas and the reality of job redesign. Indeed explanations of productivity improvements in economic and structural terms have much less validity here than for either of the other two forms of job redesign.

Having said that, it should also be observed that the evidence linking vertical role integration to employee job dissatisfaction, absenteeism or turnover is less convincing for blue-collar than for white-collar workers, and cost and efficiency pressures appear to have been more significant in the genesis of such schemes for the former. Furthermore, the cases of blue-collar role integration are explicable almost solely by reference to negotiated changes in pay levels and systems, and in work loads. In the absence of such mechanisms, productivity improvements have been significantly lower.

There are also a few cases where white-collar job redesign has not yielded the anticipated benefits because of dissatisfaction with the absence of pay increases. But the weakness of the new theory of job redesign in the face of white-collar vertical role integration does not mean that Herzberg's theory is vindicated. Several white-collar cases found no change in measures of intrinsic motivation despite improvements in performance, and it was suggested that job redesign may in fact *facilitate* rather than *cause* performance improvements by removing obstacles in their path.

Finally, although blue-collar role integration can be seen as an attempt to reduce labour costs by the reduction of over-specialization of labour, the white-collar cases do represent a genuine, if limited, challenge to Taylorist principles.

Notes

1. Data for Table 7.1 are taken from Brearley (1976).
2. Data for Table 7.2 are taken from House of Commons Select Committee (1980, p.lxvi).
3. Table 7.3 is based on the following cases: Agersnap *et al.* (1974), Alderfer

(1976), Anon (1975a,e), Bryan (1975), Butteriss and Murdoch (1975), Davis and Valfer (1965), Delamotte (1979), Ford (1969, 1973), Gorman and Molloy (1972), Hill (1971), Jacobs (1975), Janson (1971, 1975), Kraft (1971), Lawler *et al.* (1973), Lindholm and Norstedt (1975), Locke *et al.* (1976), McBeath (1974), McDavid (1975), Maher and Overbagh (1971), Morse and Reimer (1970), Novara (1973), Paul and Robertson (1970), Powell and Schlacter (1971), Powers (1972), Randall (1973), Robey (1971), Ross and Screeton (1979), Rush (1971), Taylor (1973), Walker (1950), Weir (1976), Wyatt and Fraser (1928).

4. The four cases are: Bryan (1975), Cotgrove *et al.* (1971), Novara (1973), Rush (1971).

5. Table 7.5 is based on the following cases: Anon (1975a,e), Agersnap *et al.* (1974), Bryan (1975), Butteriss and Murdoch (1975), Cotgrove *et al.* (1971), Davis and Valfer (1965), Gorman and Molloy (1972), Hackman *et al.* (1978), Hill (1971), Janson (1971), Kraft (1971), Lawler *et al.* (1973), Locke *et al.* (1976), Maher and Overbagh (1971), Morse and Reimer (1970), Novara (1973), Paul and Robertson (1970), Powers (1972), Powell and Schlacter (1971), Randall (1973), Robey (1974), Rush (1971), Weed (1971), Wyatt and Fraser (1928).

6. Table 7.6 is based on the same set of cases as Table 7.5.

8 Job redesign as organizational ideology

8.1 Ideological currents within job redesign

The previous chapters will hopefully have made clear why two common conceptions of job redesign are untenable. According to the first view, job redesign is a technique for reconciling the different objectives of workers and employers; according to the second it is a managerial ploy disguised in the language of harmony, fulfilment and other similar objectives. But we have seen that the three forms of job redesign—flowline reorganization, flexible work groups and vertical role integration—emerged in response to different sets of problems; operated via different mechanisms; had different effects on the parties involved; and enjoyed different relationships with Taylorism.

The conventional picture of unity and coherence requires considerable qualification. It is not simply a question of charting different 'generations' of job-redesign theory (e.g., Buchanan, 1979), or of illustrating cultural differences in response to 'job enrichment' as compared with sociotechnical systems theory (e.g., Birchall *et al.*, 1973), though both of these are important. Chronological accounts can oversimplify the growth of knowledge and are prone to an implicit assumption that what comes later is better, whereas cross-cultural work on the diffusion of theories pays insufficient attention to the less-theorized practices of job redesign. In this chapter, I will analyse job-redesign theory and practice in terms of its *ideological assumptions about organizations*, that is assumptions about organizational structure and goals. The purpose of this exercise is threefold: first it will serve as a corrective to oversimplified views of job redesign taken as a whole; second, it will permit some explanation of variations in patterns of costs and benefits with different forms of redesign; and third, it will place us in a better position to consider the future of the different forms of job redesign in different contexts.

Alan Fox (1966, 1973) produced an extremely influential analysis of three major ideological views of work organizations. The first is the *unitarist* view, which regards the work organization as an entity with a single overriding goal (or set of goals) to which all its members are committed, and which is upheld by the prerogatives and authority of management. Conflicts of interest are not acknowledged, and overt conflicts are regarded as the pathological consequences of external factors (outside agitators, union organizers, etc.) or of poor communications and misunderstandings. Independent, collective representation of employee interests is redundant, and any signs of it are regarded as treachery or pathology. Second, the *pluralist* view portrays the organization as a site of several competing interest groups, who are sometimes, though not necessarily, in conflict. Conflict, however, is considered a normal state of affairs, and it may be constructive or destructive. Employees may be committed to organizational goals, or only to their own; they may be loyal primarily to their employer, or to a union, or indeed to both. The supremacy of management prerogative is not accepted by employees and trade-union involvement in decision-making—through bargaining and consultation—is legitimate. Third the *radical* view portrays the organization in social class terms. The ruling class of employers and its agents—managers, supervisors, etc.— is said to dominate the life of the organization, and its objectives, principally the pursuit of profit and the maintenance of power, hold sway. Even where employees are organized in trade unions they can rarely affect the major parameters of organizational decision-making because of the tremendous power imbalance in favour of owners and managers. Harmony of interests may be possible on a limited or temporary basis, but is more likely to reflect only pragmatic adaptations by subordinates.

In examining, job redesign, it is possible to order the many schools, writers and theorists into these three broad groups, and I suggest this can be done on the basis of six dimensions of organizational structure and objectives. Insofar as job redesign is a technique of organizational change, it must, like any other such technique, possess a certain set of properties. First there must be a set of *objectives* associated with the techniques, and knowledge or assumptions about the *focus* of the technique, in this case a *view of the employee*. The *unit of analysis* should be specified, whether it be the individual, group or organizational levels. Next, the context of implementation, namely *the wider organization,* requires examination, as do the *the mode of implementation* (whether employees should participate in the process, and if so, through what channels), and the *mode of diffusion* across intra- or extra-organizational barriers.

In terms of Fox's trichotomy, many job-redesign writers and theories would fall into the pluralist camp, and because this category is so broad and embraces several different perspectives, I will distinguish, *pragmatic* pluralists and *committed* pluralists thus giving us four rather than three ideological positions. Table 8.1 defines the main content of each of the four positions on the six dimensions listed above.

8.2 The unitarist variant of job redesign

Many of the exponents of the unitarist ideology are American, and some, though by no means all, are collaborators or followers of Frederick Herzberg. In terms of *objectives,* although they are committed (as are all job-redesign theorists) to the mutual-interests thesis, unitarists place greater emphasis on motivation than on satisfaction. As Herzberg *et al.* (1959) wrote:

> Our point is that the jobs themselves have to be set up in such a way that, interest or no, the individual who carries them out can find that their operations lead to increased motivation.   (p.134)

The same emphasis on motivation pervades Herzberg's later work, as evidenced in the titles of his papers—*How do you motivate employees?* and *Efficiency and the military?* A similar concern is evident in Ford's *Motivation Through the Work Itself* (1969), and in the UK, in Armstrong's article *How to Motivate* (1977). There are several related themes in unitarist writings: labour utilization (Sirota, 1973a), productivity (Kraft and Williams, 1975), or, more generally, organizational effectiveness. These three are illustrated in contributions by Janson, Weed and Whitsett in Maher (1971a), in Rush (1971), and the case study by Biggane and Stewart (1963), who are advocates of 'job enlargement'. A similar emphasis is apparent in the insistence of the sociotechnical theorist, Rice (1963), that organizations should be viewed as 'organisms' with a 'primary task'. Where job satisfaction *has* been discussed it

Table 8.1 *The four ideologies of job redesign*

Dimension	Unitarism	Pragmatic pluralism	Committed pluralism	Radicalism
Objectives	Primarily motivation; job satisfaction secondary	Both motivation and satisfaction	Quality of working life; worker participation	Democracy in industry; socialism
View of the employee	Intrinsically motivated; power of extrinsic motivation in decline	Complex; needs and preferences vary	Desires wages and security; may in addition desire influence at work	Desires control; self-direction; growth
Unit of analysis	Mainly the individual	Individual or group	Individual group or organization	Up to societal level
View of wider organiz-ation	Largely ignored	Seen as a set of potential constraints, or as obstacles to be out-flanked	Organization seen as interlocking structures (or systems) so job redesign must be part of organization wide change	Aim is to undermine and transform alienating bureau-cracies
Preferred mode of implemen-tation of job redesign	Ignore or avoid participation and trade unions	Participation used as and when necessary	Participation vital to secure commitment, and as an end in itself	Partici-pation is a first step to demo-cratization
Mode of diffusion of job redesign	Based on consultants' appeal to self-interest of managers	Through more research, knowledge and awareness	Must be changes in values in conjunction with resources available through government and informal 'networks'	Changes in values within trade unions and societal distribu-tion of power

is considered to be a result of job performance (Janson, 1971; Paul and Robertson, 1970).

The unitarist perspective *per se* was most clearly articulated by Robert Ford (1969) who wrote:

> With the rapid changes and large scale redesign of accounting opera-
> tions in the next five to ten years the need for employees who work with us
> instead of for us is more than ever apparent.   (p.69)

Such sentiments are echoed in schemes to make workers 'managers' (sic) of their jobs (Rush, 1971; Myers, 1970), or to make them 'feel . . . like the entrepreneur . . .' (Foulkes, 1969, p.67). Unitarist job redesign also takes a moral as well as an economic form. Slee Smith (1973) argues that 'people' should be placed before profits; Ottaway (1977) defends a vaguely defined 'humanization of work' because it can prom-ote 'working together'.

The unitarist *view of the employee* is of someone strongly motivated to perform a challenging job without the additional attraction of higher pay. Herzberg (1966) described the 'hygiene-seeker' as a victim of motivational 'illness'; Paul and Robertson (1970) reported that jobs could be enriched without having to pay more wages, and Foulkes (1969) cited a case where higher pay was of little interest (p.73). More often, the issue of pay is simply not discussed at all. Sociotechnical theorists have also counted unitarists in their ranks, and Rice (1958) reported that workers simply 'had a need to get on with the job', and attached little importance to adjustments in pay systems and levels. Consistent with the unitarist denial of conflicting interests is their explanation of failed or disappointing experiments in terms of inadequ-ate techniques. Trist (1958), for instance, attributes the absence of job redesign in a section of a British mine to 'misunderstanding'.

The individual is invariably the *unit of analysis* in cases of unitarist job redesign, most notably in job enrichment. For Herzberg, as we saw in Chapter 7, individualism is a philosophical principle and not just a tactical or expedient device; and in his more recent work, such indi-vidualism has if anything become stronger, judging by the use of phrases such as 'the tyranny of the group' in a critique of sociotechnical systems theory (Herzberg, 1976a). The classic Herzbergian job-enrichment exercises involved independent, white-collar job roles and were thus amenable to, and supportive of, the individualist orientations of their authors. The early work by Hackman and Lawler (1972) was also concerned with individual job characteristics and with individual needs and perceptions. Although the implicit thrust of their analyses may lean towards unitarism, their later work is more clearly pragmatic pluralist, a fact that underlines the important point that particular writers do not always occupy an unambiguous ideological position, and their work may straddle different positions.

Unitarists have focused their attention on worker task relationships, and the case studies in Ford (1969), Maher (1971a), Paul and Robertson (1970) or Rush (1971) evince almost no awareness or consideration of the reciprocal relationship between job redesign and the *wider organization*. Typically, case studies describe one or more 'problems', outline the changes introduced in job content, and present various results as if the reorganized section, department or office existed in a vacuum. But views change, and the unitarist, Janson, writing in 1979, noted that 'job enrichment' had developed a wider concern with workflow and organizational structure, largely it seems on empirical grounds (see also Foulkes, 1969).

The unitarist view of the *mode of implementation* is one of its most distinctive and revealing features. Scott Myers (1970, 1971, 1975) has argued that one of the benefits of job enrichment is an increased employee resistance or indifference to trade unions, if not their actual elimination, and it goes without saying that trade union involvement in job redesign is a danger to be avoided. Indeed worker influence or participation in job redesign has been strongly opposed by Herzberg and his followers for various reasons, either because it 'contaminates the process with human-relations hygiene' (1968); because, empirically, it has yielded no benefits (Paul and Robertson, 1970); because it 'takes too long' (Ford, 1969); or because it may raise expectations that cannot be met (Ford, 1969). The diversity of justifications and the obvious weakness of some of them, suggest that there is an underlying, unspoken issue of considerable importance, and this, I suggest, is managerial power and authority, or 'the manager's right to manage'. Defence of managerial prerogatives is consistent with unitarism *per se*, and with the unitarist job redesigners' limited economic objectives, and their lack of interest in organizational ramifications of job redesign. It is nicely captured in Herzberg's (1974) unfashionable dismissal of industrial democracy as 'an equality of ignorance'. Equally telling is the classic unitarist (mis)understanding of trade unionism: Anderson (1970) for instance suggests that workers turn to trade unions because frustrating jobs fail to satisfy their quest for identity. And Gooding (1970a,b) offers the opinion that unions deliberately organize and promote conflict in order to justify their existence.

It is fair to say this orientation towards worker participation in general, and trade unions in particular, is more common in the USA than in any other country. Many job-enrichment cases have been conducted in non-unionized plants in America (*cf.* Rush, 1971), and indeed the absence of unions, or the presence of 'friendly' unions has been identified as a precondition for successful job redesign (Walton, 1974). It should be noted however that union density in the early 1970s was comparatively low at 22%, compared to 20–25% in France, 53% in the UK and 80% in Sweden (Barkin, 1975).

But it is ideology, not low union density, that accounts for Cummings and Srivastva (1977) presenting the following tale as a sign of success:

> When members of another union in the plant threw a wild cat strike, the wheel-line workers were the only members from their union, which represented 95 per cent of the workforce, to cross the picketline. This was unheard of in the history of the company.   (p.208)

The *diffusion of job redesign* has received little direct attention from unitarists. Indirectly however, many of the most prominent advocates and practitioners of unitarist job redesign are consultants who make money by assisting industrial and commercial organizations to improve their resource utilization, increase organizational effectiveness or raise employee motivation. Paul, Robertson, Janson, Ford, Foulkes and Rush are consultants and/or managers who diffuse job redesign as part of the process of earning their living. Unitarist job redesign is diffused by self-interest in the service of self-interest.

A recent trend in unitarist work has broken from this tradition by trying to articulate the social and economic conditions in which jobs can be most easily redesigned, and its clearest expression is the emphasis on new plants or greenfield sites. Walton (1972, 1975, 1977) has studied the Topeka pet food plant in Kansas, and noted that the highly selected and committed work force was an important factor in the plant's success. Poza and Markus (1980) described a similar case in the Southern states of the USA where prospective employees were carefully screened and vetted, and Walton (1974) has suggested that new, small, isolated, non-unionized plants in small rural locations offer the best opportunities for job redesign.

It is these conditions that offer the best prospect of the unitarists' ideal organization—a unified entity with a single purpose—and Lawler (1978) has in fact reported that 'most new-design plants are relatively small and are located in the South, . . . most . . . have remained non-union' (p.12). A different prospect is portrayed by Davis and Taylor (1976) who see the growth of automated, capital-intensive technologies with their labour requirements oriented more towards monitoring and control skills, as providing the pre-conditions for 'community of purpose' (see also Davis, 1971a,b,c).

Taken as a whole, the unitarist perspective is remarkably coherent. Its goals are primarily those of the organizational management, whose authority is upheld by a firm opposition to worker participation and trade unionism, and by an insistence on studying and changing workers and their jobs individually rather than collectively. Any ramifications of job redesign are avoided, since job redesign is largely a technical exercise, not a process of organizational change or reconstruction, and diffusion of job redesign operates on the same principle that governs organizations and the economy as a whole, namely self-interest.

8.3 The pragmatic pluralists

At one level, pragmatic pluralists share the *objectives* of their unitarist colleagues, insofar as both seek to promote motivation and job satisfaction. Within the pluralist camp, however, there is a much stronger emphasis on the inter-relatedness of these objectives, and a relative up-grading of the importance of job satisfaction. For instance, Birchall and Wild (1973), Hackman and Lawler (1972) and others consider both performance and satisfaction as possible outcomes of job redesign. Some writers use the term efficiency (e.g., Wilson, 1973), or effectiveness (Lawler, 1973), or the more general term 'economic results' (*Work in America*, 1972). Psychological outcomes have also been conceptualized as 'growth' (Lawler, 1973), or satisfaction of 'ambitions' (Philips, 1969), or simply as 'human results' (*Work in America*, 1972). The principle however remains the same: the improvement of job satisfaction is an integral part of economic improvement (Lawler and Hackman, 1971), or, in sociotechnical terms, social systems and technical systems must be 'jointly optimized' (Trist and Bamforth, 1951; Trist *et al.*, 1963).

The defining feature of the pragmatic pluralist view of the employee is its anti-universalism, or more positively, an insistence on variation and contingency. Lacking the conviction of the unitarists, or the value commitment of radicals (or committed pluralists), the pragmatic pluralists place a strong emphasis on research findings (e.g., Wild, 1975). Hulin and Blood (1968) followed the work on individual differences of Turner and Lawrence (1965) and applied this argument specifically to job redesign. Hackman and Lawler (1971) hypothesized that reactions to job redesign would vary according to employee's 'growth needs', and later writers have suggested other contingencies (see Morse, 1973; Philips, 1969). The implication of this view for changes in payment systems is unclear: some writers suggest that evidence shows the value of pay rises and incentives (e.g., Lawler, 1971, 1973), but others simply point to payment systems as an issue that needs to be considered in the introduction of job redesign (e.g., Oldham and Hackman, 1980).

The *unit of analysis* also varies among adherents of this ideology. Hackman (1978b) argued that individual job redesign is appropriate with small tasks, but that group redesign may be required for larger tasks. Wild and Birchall (1973) and Wild (1974) have reviewed and installed both individual and group redesign in different conditions but, in line with a noticeable swing towards sociotechnical systems theory and 'autonomous' groups (see for instance, Hackman, 1977), have on occasion expressed a general preference for the creation of work groups.

The pragmatic pluralist *view of the organization* again shows some variation. Hackman (1975a,b) expressed the most common view in describing the constraints imposed by various aspects of organizational structure and tradition, and the same rather negative view appeared in the analysis of a 'failed' case of job redesign (Frank and Hackman, 1975). Blake and Ross (1976) articulated a more refined notion of change as a process. Finally, writers such as Buckingham *et al.* (1975) and Wilson (1973) see the necessity to change other aspects of organizational structure in order to support job-redesign ventures once they are under way. In short, there is little evidence in any of this work of any thorough appreciation of organization theory, but a strong emphasis on pragmatism and clear signs of incremental, empirical learning.

Worker participation in the *implementation* of job redesign is judged largely on its merits and on prevailing circumstances (see Cummings and Molloy, 1976). Taylor (1973) describes a series of cases of vertical role integration with wide variations in the extent of worker participation in the process of redesign, and the message that comes over is once more the importance of pragmatism (and its corollary, flexibility). Hackman (1975b) notes that some cases of job redesign have been unsuccessful because of inadequate participatory mechanisms, but again the suggestion is that in other circumstances, absence of participation need not be problematic (see also Seeborg, 1978). It was this calculative attitude that dictated the avoidance of participation at one of British United Biscuits plants because of a fear of raising expectations. However, the presence of strong trade unions in certain American manufacturing plants has been partly responsible for the new vogue of 'labour – management committees' in the introduction of job redesign (cf. Davis and Sullivan, 1980; Drexler and Lawler, 1977; Greenberg and Glaser, 1980; Nadler et al., 1980). There is some difficulty in locating these committees ideologically, because of variations between them and because of the different meanings attached to them. The emphasis on 'quality of working life' is more redolent of committed pluralists, yet it is clear from reading reports of these initiatives that on the key question of conflict which distinguishes unitarism and pluralism the 'adversary relationship' is often considered to be an unfortunate and rather lamentable feature of organizations. Again, Wild's (1974) suggestion that job redesign is greatly facilitated by a lack of 'instrumentalism' and a surfeit of 'positive and cooperative attitudes to change' on the part of the workers is also more reminiscent of unitarists than of pluralists.

Insofar as pragmatic pluralists have addressed themselves to *diffusion* of job design, their suggestions seem to owe more to the unitarist emphasis on communication as a panacea for many organizational problems. Hackman (1975a,b) suggests that it is a lack of knowledge and insufficient research which is holding up the process, a theme reiterated by Wilson (1973) in the UK. The authors of *Work in America* (1972) also drew attention to the fact that the potential recipients of this knowledge were not necessarily well disposed towards it, and in a later article Hackman (1978a) took up the theme of managerial conservatism, implying that more research and education would not necessarily be sufficient to guarantee adoption. The pessimism of some American researchers contrasts with the guarded optimism of Brekelmans and Jonsson (1976), who have the advantage, it should be said, of working for Volvo, a company committed to innovation in division of labour

(Gyllenhammar, 1977). They argue that job redesign may have to be introduced in conjunction with, or on the back of, other more acceptable changes, such as the introduction of new machinery or new products (*cf.* also Lupton *et al.*, 1979).

The pragmatic pluralist position has the superficial appearance of incoherence. It is often difficult to discern firm views on any issue, and to identify the ways in which views on different issues hang together. The unity of this position is not predicated on a given set of detailed, or substantive themes, but on a procedural principle. Given the objectives of jointly improving organizational performance and individual satisfaction, the means required are based solely on research evidence and practical experience. If evidence suggests participation is necessary in unionized plants, but not in others, this will inform practices in the respective plants. The pragmatic pluralists, in short, are technocrats whose goals are taken as given, and who concern themselves with the most effective means of achieving and evaluating them. It is therefore no accident that it is pragmatic pluralists who have produced more precise and detailed measuring instruments than anyone else, although it should also be said that several of them might better be called reluctant pluralists as their awareness of conflicts of interest was, until recently, quite limited.

8.4 The committed pluralists

For the committed pluralists, the *objectives* of job redesign are not defined by the range of costs and benefits conventionally tied to changes in job content. Job redesign is seen as a managerial technique whose outcomes must be bargained over to ensure that workers' separate (and sometimes conflicting) interests are adequately met (BBC, 1977; Hughes and Gregory, 1973). The International Labour Organisation and the International Institute for Labour Studies both talk of the 'humanization of work' and 'the quality of working life', and the terms are used to denote changes in working conditions, participation, reward systems, health and safety as well as job content and work roles (Burbidge, 1976; Carpentier, 1974; Clerc, 1973; IILS, 1974; ILO, 1977, 1979a, b; Tchobanian, 1975); their committed pluralism is aptly summarized by Delamotte and Walker (1973):

. . . it is abundantly clear that the humanization of work is far from being a consensus issue. (p.13)

Similar sentiments have been echoed more forcefully in America by Fein (1974, 1976):

> The true problem is that *management and workers* are not motivated in the same direction; they have different goals, aspirations, needs and expectations. (1976, p.488, Italics in original)

Equally interesting is the link between job redesign and worker participation in management. Butteriss (1971), Clarke *et al.* (1972), Guest and Fatchett (1974) and the British TUC (1973) view job redesign as one of several modes of participation in managerial decision-making, and therefore as a means for extending workers' influence within the organization. This is not to say that participation serves only workers' interests, and Emery and Thorsrud (1964) make it clear they believe industrial democracy can assist firms to become 'stronger and more competitive' (p.14).

Many of the committed pluralists hold a strongly economistic *view of employees' needs* and interests, and they frequently castigate job-redesign theorists for their utopianism and naivete. Winpisinger's (1973) classic phrase epitomizes this view:

> 'If you want to enrich the job, enrich the paycheck'.

Fein (1976) asserts with equal bluntness that:

> 'Participation failures in all countries, including the UK, stem primarily from *lack of worker interest*. (p.476, Italics in original)

Theoretically Parke and Tausky (1975) have defended a reinforcement interpretation of financial incentives and organizational controls against Maslovian need theory, and an emphasis on pay and control systems as crucial mechanisms in job redesign can be found in some case studies (e.g., Champagne and Tausky, 1978; Cotgrove *et al.*, 1971; Daniel, 1970) as well as in several reviews of job redesign (e.g., Daniel and McIntosh, 1972). The different goals of management and workers, crystallized on the workers' side in trade union organization and class consciousness, were reported as a major stumbling block in a Danish case study (Agersnap *et al.*, 1974) and reports of worker suspicion of management are not uncommon (e.g., Emery and Thorsrud, 1975).

Yet there are also committed pluralists who recognize the predominance of economic motives and interests, but insist nevertheless that many workers do desire greater influence over their immediate work environment, and that job redesign is one vehicle for achieving these goals (e.g., Delamotte and Walker, 1973). Broadly speaking the 'economistic' pluralists emphasize the importance of defending workers' economic interests, and tend to dismiss the concern with 'alienation' and 'dissatisfaction' as 'middle-class myopia' (Fein, 1976; see Brooks, 1972). However, there are those who take seriously the 'problem' of alienation (e.g., Bluestone, 1974; Gomberg, 1973), and/or who are committed to some form of increased worker influence over managerial decision-making.

The *unit of analysis* has been taken a little further by committed pluralists compared to their unitarist and pragmatic counterparts who have moved to the organization and beyond. The national monographs compiled by the ILO all locate job-redesign initiatives in their social, economic and political setting and many of the case studies provide information on organizational structure, reward and control systems, technology, and product markets (ILO, 1979a, b; see also Lupton, 1975). Equally, the economistic writers stress the importance of taking a 'holistic' view of job redesign and of analysing the phenomenon as one of organizational change (e.g., Hughes and Gregory, 1973). The British Work Research Unit also emphasize the benefits of an organization-wide approach to change that includes, but is not confined to, analysis at the level of the individual and the group (1980). This wider focus is not the sole preserve of committed pluralists, since writers such as Walton (1972, 1974) whose commitment to pluralism is weak, if not questionable, also stress the utility of viewing the organization in its entirety.

Coupled with this more comprehensive perspective is a correspondingly more positive appraisal of the connection between job redesign and changes in other parts of the *wider organization*. The British Work Research Unit (1980), for instance, points out that job redesign cannot proceed in isolation but needs supporting changes elsewhere if it is to survive. Clegg (1981) and Fitter (1981) have both analysed the impact of job redesign on other organizational departments and systems in the context of conflicting objectives and interests, and both stress that such conflicts may be managed but cannot be eliminated (see also Malmberg, 1980). Theoretically they both work within the post-Weberian tradition of bureaucracy epitomized by the empirical studies of interdepartmental conflict and collusion, e.g., Blau (1963), Crozier (1964).

Klein (1976) has suggested that top management support is essential for successful job redesign, a theme supported by Wilkinson (1971). De (1980) has pointed out that effective job redesign in India also requires organizational change in a multiplicity of areas and levels. For the 'economistic' pluralists, essential organizational changes are defined more narrowly within the sphere of reward and control systems, but these changes are insisted on very firmly indeed for reasons of efficacy and of rights.

Committed pluralists stress that these changes ought to be *implemented* through collective bargaining, and they share the view that trade union involvement is vital for successful job redesign. Emery and Thorsrud (1964) began their Norwegian studies of job redesign with a preliminary investigation of worker directors as one strategy of industrial democracy, and devoted a whole chapter of their final report (1975) to the role of trade unions. Nash (1976) has argued that trade unions have long been used by workers to reduce the dehumanizing effects of work, a theme pursued by Gregory (1981) in the UK and Gomberg (1973) in the USA. The British Work Research Unit (1980) considers participation by those whose jobs are to be redesigned as an end in itself. A more instrumental view was argued by Weinberg (1974) who claimed that it was only unionized companies with extensive worker participation that had experimented successfully with job redesign in the USA. Indeed, in the Olivetti company in Italy it was union demands for higher pay and promotion that were partly responsible for the management decision to upgrade work through job redesign, culminating in 1971 in a formal written agreement (Butera, 1975; Novara, 1973).

Diffusion of job redesign is an issue that has generated a range of responses, and for good reason. Once it is acknowledged the effects of a particular innovation are contingent on changes in other areas of organizational life, and on the mode of implementation, it follows that the *diffusion* of job redesign will be an equally complex and multiply-determined process. Thus where job redesign has been linked, empirically and/or theoretically to industrial democracy, as in Scandinavia, there is more optimism on the part of writers and practitioners about its future than in countries where the technique remains the preserve of unitarists or pragmatic pluralists. Compare for instance the views of Dundelach and Mortensen (1979) on Scandinavia or the Swedish Employers' Confederation (1975) on Sweden, with Delamotte (1979) on France, Emery (1980) on Australia, or Hackman (1978a,b) on the USA.

An 'institutional' approach to diffusion underlies the committed pluralist emphasis on tripartite initiatives and industrial democracy. In 1975, the Davis and Cherns' volumes on *The Quality of Working Life* carried a report that resulted in the creation of the International Council for the Quality of Working Life, a network of academic proponents of job redesign. The argument ran that knowledge and research in themselves were insufficient to promote change, and that active agents were required to influence the seats of power. In the USA, the promotion of labour – management committees represents a definite commitment (however tenuous) to pluralism, and signifies recognition of the need for institutional support if job redesign is to extend beyond the often successful, but also unique and isolated, experiments (see Greenberg and Glaser, 1980).

Whereas the unitarists are managerial technicians firmly wedded to the 'status quo', and the pragmatic pluralists are technocrats, clear about their objectives, but flexible on means, the committed pluralists have a wider set of objectives and value the process of their attainment in its own right. But more than this they have some grasp, however variable and unarticulated, of organizations as sites of *interest groups* and therefore as *political* entities. That the terms power and authority rarely appear in the literature is less significant than the fact that the realities which they denote are clearly present in many pluralist writings. Job redesign is not seen therefore simply as a technique: such a view would indeed be untenable. Rather it is an integral part of organizational process and change, and it is this emphasis that lends coherence to the committed pluralist views of the wider organization, the unit of analysis, the implementation and the diffusion of job redesign, despite differences between the 'economistic' and the 'political' views of worker interests.

8.5 Radical approaches to job redesign

For radical proponents of job redesign, changes in job content and work roles are invariably located as one component of a comprehensive strategy whose *objective* is often (though not always) one or other form of socialism. This can be seen most clearly in statements made by the

French Communist trade union confederation, the CGT, and by the French Communist Party (PCF). The CGT expressed intense hostility towards 'job enrichment' in a major statement in 1972, but by 1976 it was prepared to consider reorganization of work provided a series of guarantees—on job security, workloads, etc.—were met (Delamotte, 1975, 1976; Tchobanian, 1975). The PCF has gone even further and talks of 'a new labour process' in which work would be more rewarding as well as more efficient (di Ruzza, 1980). Although the French groups remain committed to revolution through class struggle, the Swedish trade union confederation (LO) has pioneered 'a third way' between market capitalism and state socialism, which it calls democratic socialism (LO, 1977; Meidner, 1980). The extension of industrial democracy that is an integral step towards democratic socialism entails the improvement of working conditions, and increased worker influence at all levels of organizations from the immediate job, up to investment and other long-term plans. Other writers continue to use terms such as 'humanization of work' (e.g., Cooley, 1977; Rice, 1977), but they are defined in terms of democratic socialism, and not confined to improvements in working conditions within capitalism. Finally, there are writers who locate their objectives primarily in subjective and/or individual terms, e.g., 'human growth' and 'self-actualization' (Blackler and Brown, 1978), or freedom and competence (Gustavsen, 1980). Again, the meaning of such terms is sharply distinguished from more conservative usage, a point explicitly and interestingly discussed by Blackler and Brown (1978).

Radical *views of the employee* are surprisingly often not made explicit. Blackler and Brown (1978) emphasize the capacity for personal growth rather than any particular set of pre-determined needs, but they are also very critical of instrumental and materialist attitudes to work, a view definitely not shared by the Swedish LO (1977). LO's view of 'humanity' is founded on the socialist values of the equal worth of all people, the importance of freedom, and the intrinsic value of work, but financial rewards for work continue to receive considerable attention. Cooley (1977) also emphasizes the vast reserves of unutilized talent and ability possessed by 'ordinary people' and their desire to engage in useful and creative work. A similar emphasis on activity, based on a dynamic view of people, permeates Gustavsen's (1980) account of work research in Scandinavia, and he shares the scepticism of Blackler and

Brown of concepts of 'needs' and 'states'. Indeed, all of these conceptions approximate to the views of human behaviour adumbrated by the
early Marx (1844; see, also Ollman, 1971), and it is interesting that
Emery (1978b) referred to the radical project of the Norwegian Industrial Democracy Programme in neo-Marxist terms.

It goes without say that the *unit of analysis* in radical works is usually
the whole society, or at the very least 'the organization' (LO, 1972).
The connections between work and non-work experiences gradually
impressed themselves on Norwegian work researchers, especially when
they began to study health and safety at work (Gustavsen, 1980). The
limits of organizational analysis were also illustrated in a case study of
worker participation in a Swedish tobacco plant, when the workers
met a serious lack of information on the company because it was a
subsidiary of a foreign multinational (Gonas and Levinson, 1980).

Indeed the limited nature of democracy within organizations has
come to dominate the radical *view of organizations*. Emery (1978a) uses
the term 'bureaucratic–Taylorist paradigm' to characterize the principles on which contemporary work organizations are designed. Not only
do such organizations combine the principles of bureaucracy (a hierarchy of clearly defined roles, regulation by rules, 'rationality', and the
principles of Taylorism — measurement and fragmentation of work,
etc.) but these two sets of principles are in fact highly compatible
(Emery, 1974). The Swedish LO refers to contemporary organizations
as 'authoritarian' (1972), and the references to 'tyranny' (Gorz, 1976b)
and 'the prison factory' (Bosquet, 1972) by contemporary French
writers preserve the same meaning even if the form of expression is
stronger. The authority structure of organizations is seen as its key
dimension, and criticisms of hierarchy can be found even by writers
who are 'radical' only in the sense of being hopelessly utopian (e.g.,
Thorsrud, 1980).

In terms of *implementation*, it equally goes without saying that radical
writers assign trade unions a key role in the processes of democratiza-
tion and humanization. For some unions, this is a basic question of
principle only, e.g., the CGT, but for others the process of changing
organizations provides an occasion for mobilization of the members
and an experience of effective influence over their conditions of work
that is a vital prerequisite for continued change. The Italian Communist trade union federation (CGIL) and the Swedish LO provide good
examples of this latter position (Bronda, 1980; Tchobanian, 1975).

Trade union involvement in work reorganization is also sometimes premissed on the right of unions to continue the pursuit of issues they have always taken seriously. The pluralist writer Gomberg (1973) articulated this view, and more recently Gregory (1981) has argued that trade union concern with work experience and organizational structure both pre-dates, and is more comprehensive than, that of management.

One consequence of the radicals' emphasis on societal transformation is that the 'problem of *diffusion*' in its conventional sense disappears entirely. This is because the 'problem' is predicated on a strategy that seeks change only within organizations, and that thus confronts the question as to how changes can spread from one organization to another. By working through national organizations (trade unions, and sometimes governments and political parties) and by operating partly through changes in legislation (e.g., the Work Environment Acts of Denmark, 1976, Norway, 1977, and Sweden, 1978) the barriers to change become located within the legal system and at the interface between government, judiciary and corporate leaderships (Blackler, 1981). There is, of course, a problem of diffusion for radicals working through grass-roots initiatives such as the 'workers' plans' movement in the UK. The objective of the movement is to encourage workers to become actively involved in the preparation of alternative plans of production, emphasizing full employment, work reorganization, and the creation of socially useful products (Cooley, 1980; George, 1980).

At enterprise level, the Swedish unions have proposed that a fixed proportion of company profits should be paid into a 'workers' investment fund', and used to purchase company shares, thus transferring the ownership of most major industries into workers' hands within 20 years (Meidner, 1980; Ohman, 1980). Nevertheless, it has to be said that with the exception of the Swedish unions, few radicals have devoted serious attention to the strategies that might be used to democratize or humanize organizations, though some have studied the failure of job redesign to diffuse within organizations (Blackler and Brown, 1980). Others have expressed considerable pessimism in the face of the difficulties of transforming existing organizations, and have placed their hopes in greenfield sites (e.g., Emery, 1980). Radicals more generally have simply been sceptical of the purposes and significance of job redesign *tout court*, and it is to this tradition that I now turn.

8.6 Radical criticisms of job redesign

Ideologically radical criticism of job redesign falls into two main classes, concerned, respectively, with the nature and significance of job redesign. Within these categories, criticism has appeared under three broad headings: social, economic and political. The resulting 3 by 2 matrix of views is shown in Table 8.2.

Table 8.2 Radical criticisms of job redesign

	Nature of job redesign	*Significance of job redesign*
Social criticism	Job redesign contains nothing new and is really a form of scientific management, a neo-Taylorism	Job redesign has little impact on jobs, and is constrained in its application by economic, social and technological factors
Economic criticism	Job redesign claims to be concerned with job satisfaction and alienation, but in reality is concerned solely with profits, costs and speed-up	Job redesign in practice generates a wide range of social and economic costs for workers; such as speed-up, reduced manning and reduced promotion prospects
Political criticism	In reality job redesign is a more subtle and insidious instance of employer and management control over the labour process	Job redesign concedes 'autonomy' to workers in order to allay their demands, but the experience of autonomy and control will generate demands for more and the whole process will threaten to explode in the faces of its capitalist initiators

(i) Nature of job redesign

On the nature of job redesign, the three main arguments contrast the appearance of the phenomenon with its social, political or economic reality. The characterization of job redesign as a form of Taylorism is a French argument produced by Montmollin (1974) on the basis of a highly abstract characterization of the two schools of thought. He observed that both were concerned with the objectives of productivity and harmony, used similar conceptions of individualism and rationality; and accepted the mental/manual division of labour. Equally Aglietta (1979) and Palloix (1976) have noted that job redesign maintains the division of labour and hierarchy of authority within the enterprise, and that the experience of exploitation remains unchanged (see Bernoux and Duffier, 1974). Both Montmollin (1974) and later Chave (1976) acknowledged that some forms of job redesign could not be clearly seen as 'neo-Taylorism', and Coriat (1980) argued more specifically that flowline reorganization was precisely Taylorism applied under new conditions (see Chapters 4 and 5). Coriat's (1980) conclusion is in agreement with my own, and one only needs to add that the level of abstraction used by Montmollin is inappropriate, as it allows so few distinctions between different management practices.

The economic criticism says that despite the rhetoric about job satisfaction, human growth, alienation, work humanization and so on, in reality job redesign is concerned with such mundane and hardheaded matters as productivity and cost reduction (Banks, 1974; Baumgartner et al., 1979; Hales, 1974a; Hughes and Gregory, 1978; Rasmus, 1974; Rinehart, 1975; Rosenhead et al., n.d.; Winpisinger, 1973). Job redesign, in short, is a 'confidence trick' and seeks to secure managerial interests while ignoring those of workers. This line of attack (labelled liberal – radical by Nichols, 1980) might validly apply to the unitarist school of job redesign, though even then one can usually find some expression of the 'mutual-interests thesis' in their writings, but its validity in relation to the pluralist and radical schools is extremely problematic. For within these schools, it is virtually impossible to find any statements advocating job redesign solely or largely as a means to promote job satisfaction, or similar goals. On the contrary, one of the main strengths of job redesign has always been its claim to satisfy the mutual interests, economic and psychological, of employers and workers, respectively. And the argument adducing weaker and less frequently reported data on job satisfaction, alienation, etc., as evidence for the neglect of workers' interests in comparison with their employers, actually succeeds in reproducing the extremely dubious view of job-redesign theory that employers' interests belong to the economic sphere, whereas workers' interests are located mainly in the psychological sphere (Blackler and Brown, 1978; Morrow and Thayer, 1977). Absent from this argument is any sustained analysis of workers' economic or material interests.

The *political* variant of the criticism asserts that job redesign is in fact an instance of a wider and more continuous system of managerial control over labour, and this feature overrides any microlevel changes in 'autonomy' (Brighton Labour Process Group, 1977; Friedman, 1977a,b; Gorz, 1976b; Hunnius, 1979; Nord, 1978; Rasmus, 1974). One of the difficulties with this argument is that it comes dangerously close to elevating control over labour to a position of pre-eminence, as an end in its own right, rather than analysing it in relation to other objectives, such as profit production. And the argument has an abstract character from which it is difficult to see how one could produce more concrete analyses of specific job-redesign practices.

(ii) Significance of job redesign

On the significance of job redesign (the right-hand column in Table 8.2) there are first those radical critics who declare the significance of the phenomenon has been overestimated because it is either inherently trivial, or limited in its sphere of application. The triviality argument asserts that the alterations in division of labour arising from job redesign are insignificant compared with some (usually unspecified) concept of significant change (Barbash 1977; Braverman, 1974; Cooley, 1977; Dickson, 1974; Elliott, 1976, 1977; Hughes and Gregory, 1973; Nichols, 1975, 1980; Nichols and Beynon, 1977). Alternatively, or in addition, it is alleged that the circumstances under which job redesign can be initiated are socially, economically and/or technologically limited (Goldman and Van Houten, 1980; Gomberg, 1973; Levitan and Johnston, 1973; Noble, 1979). The first argument begs the question as to what would constitute 'significant' change and whether this is an appropriate standard by which to evaluate job redesign, whereas the second variant appears to lead in the direction of dismissing job redesign as unworthy of analysis.

Economic assessments of job redesign have drawn attention to the often neglected consequences, such as threats to promotion prospects, manning levels, workloads, labour markets, pay levels, skills, job security and union organization (Delamotte and Walker, 1973; Hull, 1978;

Schlesinger and Walton, 1977; Tchobanian, 1975). Some of these consequences can be shown empirically to have occurred, but others, such as weakening or inhibition of union organization, are found much less frequently in the UK than the USA, and are more characteristic of the unitarist approach to job redesign. Economic reassessment of job redesign is potentially very promising, but its proponents have not located their observations within a coherent theoretical framework that would permit an understanding and explanation of those issues, and that would allow us to discover the degree to which they were necessary or contingent features of job redesign.

The political variant of radical criticism has been advanced by writers such as Bosquet (1972), Edwards (1978), Gorz (1976a,b,c), Skillen (1977) and Zimbalist (1975) and posits an inherent radical dynamic within the concession of elements of autonomy or control to shop-floor workers. By a cumulative process, shop-floor control would escalate to the point where it would threaten or undermine capitalist imperatives and structures. No evidence has actually been adduced in favour of this view (although Emery, 1978c, and Larsen, 1979, provide some), a fact that is not altogether surprising because of its conflation of the concepts of autonomy and control (cf. Nichols, 1975, 1980), and its unilinear, zero-sum view of control (see below).

Finally, we should note the existence of radical 'contingency theorists' (Durand, 1975; Fleet, 1974; Friedman, 1977a,b; Zimbalist, 1979) who have all suggested that job redesign must be examined in the context of class struggle. Its outcomes and effects will vary according to the circumstances of and motives for its implementation, and the degree to which workers can influence its introduction. This type of criticism at least recognizes the potential variability and complexity of job redesign, but hitherto has gone little further than a general statement to that effect without specifying in more detail how one might analyse such variation.

If the failure to appreciate the variability of job redesign is one of the most serious flaws in much radical criticism, the implicit equation of job redesign as a whole with the unitarist approach is almost as striking. Methodologically, it is common to find radical critics declaring their argument and then proving it by citing a few supportive instances from unitarist writers, not stopping to consider the representativeness of their chosen cases. Having said this, several of the arguments do raise important issues, namely the extent of job losses and non-provision of pay rises; the extent to which labour intensification is a feature of job redesign; and the distribution of costs and benefits in particular cases. Section 8.7 therefore attempts to provide systematic information on these topics.

8.7 Costs and benefits of job redesign

The 'mutual-interests thesis' of job-redesign theory, described in Chapter 3, turns on the claim that despecialization of labour will simultaneously provide more job satisfaction for the job incumbent and higher performance (via increased motivation) for the employer. But we cannot properly assess the net gains accruing to all the parties until we have also assessed the costs of job redesign. In addition we would ideally need to measure the duration of costs (and benefits), a task that is impossible if only because of lack of data. Methodologically, cost – benefit analysis of job redesign is still in an extremely crude state, although the important work by Hopwood (1979a,b) is endeavouring to introduce some order into the field, and to appraise the significance of a series of problems, such as under-reporting of 'failures', and the tendency to use results for legitimation rather than evaluation. We can nevertheless make a preliminary, if crude, assessment of the possible major costs of job redesign for different groups of workers and employers.

In terms of my theory of the origins and mechanisms of job redesign (Chapter 3), four issues stand out for immediate investigation, *viz* labour elimination, wage or earnings levels, workloads or intensity of labour, and control and accountability.

(i) Job losses and employee displacement

When discussing the outcomes of job redesign, many authors of case studies have written from the standpoint of the workers whose jobs have been redesigned. They have frequently ignored, however, the consequences for other groups of workers both in the same plant and elsewhere, yet these consequences are both real and significant. Of all the known cases in the literature, where data were available on the displacement or elimination of jobs and/or workers, such displacement occurred in 68% of cases (Table 3.2). And it was shown (Chapter 6) that the creation of flexible work groups often required labour elimination if productivity was to be raised, as also to a lesser extent did vertical role integration. The process may take the form either of a reduction in the number of workers occupying a particular role, or roles, or the complete elimination both of a group of workers and of the roles they occupy. For example, in the study by McDavid (1975), two clerical officers were eliminated, although the position of clerical officer remained, whereas in the study by Walker (1950), 35 setters and checkers were displaced, and their roles amalgamated with that of machine operative.

In all, 60 cases of job redesign were found that contained data on the number of jobs redesigned and the number eliminated (if any).

Many case studies state that labour was eliminated without giving figures, and have been excluded from this analysis. It was found that elimination had occurred in 33 (55%) of these cases. Excluded from the 60 cases were those where job/labour elimination was clearly attributable to other factors, such as mechanization, or where numbers of jobs were only given approximately. Table 8.3 shows the numbers of jobs redesigned and the numbers eliminated for each category of job redesign. Before discussing these figures, one general point must be made: the data have been combined from a series of studies carried out at different times, in different countries, and under different circumstances, such that the final figures take no account of variations in these and other factors. What the figures show, roughly speaking is that for every 100 jobs redesigned, almost 25 have been lost. *If* the figures are correct, this is certainly a 'cost' of some magnitude for workers. And, viewed from the standpoint of the employed population as a whole, such an apparently effective eliminator of jobs, can hardly be considered a 'social benefit', unless countervailing mechanisms exist for

Table 8.3 Job losses in cases of job redesign[1]

	Vertical role integration	Flowline reorganiz- ation	Flexible work groups	Mixed categories	Totals
Jobs redesigned (A)	407	250	1277	383	2317
Jobs eliminated (B)	103	39	342	88	572
B/A %	25.3%	15.6%	26.8%	23.0%	24.7%
N (= Number of cases)	14	18	21	7	60

the creation of an equivalent number and type of jobs in accessible labour markets.

There are of course several possible objections to this evidence, as well as problems of interpretation. Firstly, it could be argued that these job losses might have occurred in companies that were expanding, or in local labour markets where there was no shortage of alternative employment, so that the 'real' costs of job redesign may have been minimal. In some studies this was certainly the case (e.g., Walker, 1950) but in others the numbers involved and the scope of the programme make it unlikely that redundancies could have been avoided, (e.g., Hepworth and Osbaldeston, 1979).

However the fate of displaced workers almost invariably goes unreported. It is also worth noting that the number of workers displaced is lower than the numbers of jobs eliminated, because the latter figure includes four cases where theoretical manning levels were reduced in new plants, but no workers were displaced as none were then employed.

The figures also show, in line with the analyses of labour elimination (in Chapters 4–7) that the process is much less characteristic of flowline reorganization than of the other forms of job redesign, a fact that was explained previously in terms of the availability of other mechanisms of productivity increase arising directly out of flowline changes that are absent in other forms of redesign. But the incidence of job/labour elimination also varies with the national location of the initiative, being very much higher in the USA than elsewhere, as Table 8.4 shows. The reasons for these international differences are unclear, although one could suggest plausible hypotheses, such as differential union densities and union-bargaining strategies, which it would be fruitful to examine more carefully. Union densities in the USA, UK and Scandinavia in the early 1970s were 22% 53% and 80%, respectively (and approximately), and it may be that in the UK trade unions have insisted more firmly on no-redundancy clauses in job-redesign exercises. The international variations cannot be accounted for in terms of unequal distributions of the different *forms* of job redesign, with the most effective job-eliminating form (flexible work groups) predominating in the USA, and the least effective eliminator (flowline reorganization) predominant in the UK. Indeed we find almost the reverse: of the 20 US cases in Table 8.4, 9 are cases of flowline reorganization and only 5 involve flexible work groups. For the UK, there are only 5 cases of flowline reorganization, but 7 of vertical role integration. Equally, there appears to be no significant trend over time. Labour was eliminated in 10 out of 18 cases (55.6%) before 1970, and in 24 out of 42 (57.1%) initiated after 1970.

It should also be said that the existence and scale of job loss may be peculiar to an economy, or an industry, in which labour is regarded as an economic cost that ought, where possible, to be minimized. Under different economic and political arrangements, it is therefore conceivable that job redesign (if it were practised) would not be accompanied by the job losses reported here.

Table 8.4 Job redesign and job losses: international comparisons[2]

	USA	UK	Scandinavia[a]	Europe[b]	Elsewhere[c]
Jobs redesigned (A)	757	441	389	188	562
Jobs eliminated (B)	260	15	108	16	173
B/A %	34.3%	3.4%	27.8%	8.5%	30.8%
N_1 (cases involving some job loss)	17	5	6	3	2
N_2 (cases involving no job loss)	3	12	6	3	2

$\chi^2 = 102.1$, $p < 0.001$. χ^2 performed for data on USA, UK and Scandinavia only, because of the small Ns in the remaining countries

a Includes Sweden, Norway and Denmark
b Includes Holland, Belgium, France and West Germany
c Includes India and South Africa

(ii) Wage or salary increases

The incidence of job-redesign cases *without* accompanying wage or salary increases was found to be only 33% of cases with known productivity outcomes, and 36% of all known cases of job redesign containing the relevant information (see Table 3.2). Both these figures were calculated using only cases in which the provision or absence of a pay rise had definitely occurred. Some of the cases without pay rises are well known and include some of the Philips studies, cases reported in Rush (1971), the ICI studies, and the case of AT&T, described by Ford (1969). In these cases the wage – effort ratio has been tipped in favour of management, as wage costs per unit of output have been reduced, and the incidence of non-provision is highest in the USA (Alber, 1979a,b) where union density is relatively low. Nevertheless such cases are in the minority, and there is a statistically significant suggestion that the incidence of witholding of pay increases may be declining. Pay was increased in 9 out of 19 cases (47.4%) before 1970, but in 29 out of 48 cases (60.4%) started after 1970 ($\chi^2 = 4.61, p < 0.05$).

A final source of evidence on pay can be derived from the nature of the pay systems used in cases of job redesign. The same literature review as reported above yielded information on the type of payment system in 45 cases, and revealed that incentives were paid in 28 (63%) of them (see Table 3.2). In such cases employees would thus automatically receive a pay increase as productivity rose, unless other countervailing changes were introduced, for example, higher work standards.

We can also consider the question of wages from the standpoint of the relation between labour and capital in a particular plant as a whole, for although wages might rise with job redesign, so too (very often) does productivity. It is therefore possible, as happened in one of the earliest job-redesign exercises at IBM, for wages to rise and labour costs to fall (Walker, 1950). In other words the total share of the wealth produced in the plant which went to labour showed a decline, whereas that accruing to other parties (employers, shareholders, etc.) showed an increase. Even if employees do receive wage increases, these may not be commensurate with the increased profits accruing to the employers and others, as a result of improved productivity. Wage rises however have been described as an important mechanism for raising productivity in cases of job redesign, a fact that accounts for their relatively high incidence.

(iii) Labour intensification

Labour intensification has been defined as an increase in the proportion of the working day consumed in actually working (effort level) or an increase in the rate of working (rate of effort expenditure) (see Chapter 3). Theoretically, the salience of effort expenditure in employment relations has been thoroughly described by Baldamus (1961), Behrend (1957) and Ryan (1947), who conceptualized it as a cost to be set against the mainly extrinsic rewards issued by organizations. There are virtually no case studies in the job-redesign literature that have measured intensity of labour, i.e., effort levels, and this theme can only be discussed here in terms of principles and illustrations.

In the first category of job redesign (vertical role integration) disparate work roles with their attendant duties are combined into a new role. In the study by Walker (1950), for instance, the jobs of setter and checker were eliminated and their work performed by machine operatives. Since production could not be executed during machine set-up, and products could not be made and checked simultaneously, then we can say that intensification of labour did occur there. And a similar process has occurred in other cases of blue-collar job redesign where ancillary duties, such as maintenance, set-up and cleaning have been added to operatives' existing work roles and workloads (e.g., Cotgrove *et al.*, 1971; Powers, 1972; Rush, 1971). In several white-collar studies, simple role amalgamation of this type has also taken place, although production volume (measured in such terms as volume of material processed) has remained constant or even increased (e.g., Champagne and Tausky 1978; Janson, 1971). But white-collar reorganization of this type has more commonly involved the addition of conceptual duties to existing roles, such as limited areas of decision-making, or responsibility for error rates in document processing, and in such cases the element of intensification of labour may be minimal (e.g., Ford, 1969; Locke *et al.*, 1976).

In the second category of job redesign (flowline reorganization), much of the increase in productivity in the better documented cases can be attributed to improved work methods, such as the elimination of handling time. However, complete abolition of flowlines, and their replacement by individual work stations, removes balance – delay time ('idle' time arising from unequal workloads and/or work rates between employees on a flowline), and under the influence of mechanisms such as pay incentives, some or all of this time may be transformed into actual working time (see Chapters 4 and 5). Labour is thus intensified, although the incidence and magnitude of the phenomenon may be less than compared with the other categories of redesign.

It was argued in Chapter 6 that the creation of flexible work groups necessarily entails intensification of labour in the first sense defined above, if labour productivity is to be increased. In a number of the most renowned sociotechnical case studies (the Durham mining study, the Indian textile mills, the Norwegian Industrial Democracy studies, and the more recent work of Walton) manning levels were significantly reduced (in two cases these were theoretical levels, before plant open-ing). The corollary, for those remaining workers, was an increase in workloads induced in many cases by the provision of pay rises, directly on basic rates or via incentive systems. The precondition for labour intensification in this type of job redesign is the breakdown of job demarcations, and the assignment of responsibility in principle, to all workgroup members, for all of the group's tasks. Labour is thus de-ployed between jobs as and when required, thereby raising the overall intensity of labour.

Objectively, therefore, we can say that labour intensification is associated with job redesign, and this has been confirmed by attitudinal data collected in a number of studies. According to Rice (1958):

> At the first conference there were many complaints of tiredness caused by so much extra walking. By the second, there were reluctant admis-sions by some workers that they were getting used to it. By the third, they showed a preference for the new methods of work. At all conferences they said that they worked much harder than in the other sheds. (pp.148–9).

And a similar theme was reiterated in the Trist *et al.* (1963) coalmining studies, but without the idea of habituation that emerges in the quota-tion above. In a study of assembly-line reorganization, 23% of the workers remaining on the lines reported being 'bothered by too much pressure', but the figure was even higher, 40%, for workers at indi-vidual work stations (Donaldson, 1975; Thornely and Valentine, 1968), though the difference was not significant. And in a similar study by Conant and Kilbridge (1965) there were complaints about the tightness of work standards on individual assembly, and hence, by implication, of the effort levels required to attain them (see also Smith, 1976).

Labour intensification thus appears to be associated with job rede-sign, though less so in flowline reorganization where methods improve-ments raise productivity, but its effects may be mitigated by counter-vailing forces. Firstly, as indicated in the quotation above from Rice (1958) employees may habituate to higher levels of effort expenditure (see also Guest, 1957). Secondly, a shift in the perceived locus of control may alter perceptions of effort expenditure. Work at an individual work station may be felt to require less effort, despite increased physical output, because the worker can pace himself and no longer has to suffer the strain of assembly-line pacing. Although this issue is by no means as simple as might at first appear, since it is far from self-evident that paced assembly-line work is *ipso facto* stressful, but more likely that this depends on the pace of the line and the operator's ability to adhere to the pace. Thirdly, self-pacing at individual work stations may create a smoother and more continuous flow of work, and thus augment the satisfying elements of 'traction' in the job (Baldamus, 1961; Turner and Miclette, 1962).

(iv) Managerial control and worker accountability

In many cases of vertical role integration and flowline reorganization the authors reported improvements in product quality, which they attributed to the concession of responsibility for quality, and sometimes for quality testing to directly productive workers. Yet most cases of flowline reorganization have in fact involved the abolition of such lines and their replacement by individual work stations. This not only renders individuals more visible to management, it also enables a more direct and accurate assignment of accountability for particular batches of work. This has implications for quality control, as Guest (1957) appreciated many years ago:

> When quality errors were made it became much easier to identify who made the error. (p.13)

Similar observations were made by Ford (1973), Peacock (1979) and Pignon and Querzola (1976). More generally, Sirota (1973a) has argued that such individualization of work roles with consequent augmentation of accountability, is both an objective and a feature of traditional, 'hard' management practice. In several cases the heightened accountability of workers was both formalized and intensified by means of the device of personal worker signatures on products (Biggane and Stewart, 1963; Mumford and Henshall, 1979). In the two other types of redesign, increased accountability may not have occurred, and indeed the creation of flexible work groups could place more obstacles in the path of accountability than had hitherto existed, by blurring individual job assignments.

The relative lack of attention devoted to this process may have stemmed from an implicit zero-sum concept of control, according to which if workers were to exercise increased autonomy or control over immediate aspects of production, as all job-redesign theories prescribe, it would follow that management had simultaneously lost some of its control. But if we explicitly adopt a non-zero-sum concept of control, we can recognize the possibility of workers and managers both increasing their control simultaneously. Workers may experience enhanced control over more immediate aspects of production, such as work pace and work methods, but this is not incompatible with a simultaneous increase in managerial control over performance as a result of the individualization of work organization and work roles. Greater managerial control of this kind has in fact been exercised in several cases as noted above (see especially Chapter 4).

Since it is difficult to measure accountability and worker control over pace and quality, in any meaningful way, it is difficult to compare these two aspects of control in cases of flowline reorganization and vertical role integration and arrive at an overall assessment of the net degree of control (or autonomy) acquired or lost by workers. All one can say therefore is that workers may pay a price for their 'autonomy' in the form of increased control over and accountability of their performance by management (*cf.* also Tausky and Parke, 1976).

(v) Costs to management

Costs to management of job redesign are much harder to specify, because management's role and presence in job redesign has received very much less attention than that of the workers directly affected. Any overall assessment of these costs must therefore be only tentative and provisional. Economically, the costs would seem to be minimal, since no major investment is typically required. Nevertheless there may be higher training costs, particularly for workers in flexible, multi-skilled groups (Hopwood, 1979b); and flexibility between, as opposed to within, work groups may decline if group cohesion rises. But even if these and other costs, such as consultants' fees and management time, are combined (and some writers have opposed costing the latter; *cf.* Mumford and Henshall, 1979), these will generally be weighed against, and paid out of, the long-run increase in labour productivity that the consultants and management have jointly engineered. Thus the authors of case studies at Philips (den Hertog, 1974), Toysite (see Chapter 5), British Steel Corporation (1975) and ICI (Roeber, 1975) estimated that these costs would be recouped within a few years of the project's initiation whereas a similar estimate was produced for two American cases by Bowers (1977). Increases in wages have often

(though not always) accompanied job redesign, but with corresponding increases in labour productivity, the net financial effect has by no
means invariably been negative. Indeed there is evidence that in some
cases total labour costs per annum, or unit costs of production, or both,
have in fact been reduced (Hopwood, 1979b).

However, there may be significant costs associated with reorganization of flowlines. This entails the construction of individual work
stations, and may result in higher levels of stock to cope with improved
materials supplies. Figures for these and other costs were provided by
Persson (1978) in an assessment of job redesign at Saab Scania, but he
concluded that they were balanced by the estimated savings due to
reductions in absenteeism, labour turnover and other costs.

If there are any significant costs of job redesign for management, they
are more likely to be found in the social or political spheres. In flowline
reorganization, a typical innovation is the transition from a progressive
flowline to individual assembly. On the flowline, the pace of work may
be at the discretion of management and mediated via the speed of the
mechanized line. Alternatively, on non-mechanized lines, faster workers may be placed at the head, and slower workers at the rear of the line,
to facilitate maximum production. These mechanisms of control dis-
appear under individual assembly, and although alternative systems
may be brought into play, such as the use of individual cash incentives
or greater responsibilities being assigned to supervisors, they may not
be as effective. Again, in cases of flexible work groups, workers are often
assigned control over labour allocation within a delimited area.
Although there is no evidence that this concession of control has ever
seriously backfired against management, such an eventuality is possible.

Data included here were derived from cases defined as successful, but
in those instances where expected results did not materialize, then the
costs of management and consultants' time, etc., are unlikely to be
recouped. The bias of the literature towards successful studies prevents
any serious evaluation of failures, and hence, of the net costs to management of such schemes. What is also not clear from the foregoing is why
job redesign has not been conducted more extensively, if the benefits
are so substantial and the costs so low. Although one can point to
several factors here—lack of opportunity, lack of knowledge of methods
of implementation, fear of uncertainty or risk, workers' disinterest,
union opposition—there is no satisfactory explanation of the assumed

indifference to job redesign on the part of British, and perhaps to a lesser degree, US managers.

8.8 Summary

The most important point to emerge from this chapter is the significance of separate analyses of the three types of job redesign. Once these have been systematically differentiated using the classification of unitarist, pluralist and radical ideologies of organization, a considerable degree of order can be introduced into what can otherwise seem to be a confusing melee of techniques, theories, hypotheses and assumptions. Not only can differences be more systematically ordered, they can also be related to more or less coherent ideological assumptions about organizations. In this way, it becomes possible to make sense of different patterns of objectives; views of the worker and of the wider organization; different units of analysis; and different views of implementation and diffusion; and to realize that these possess a hitherto unrecognized degree of coherence. A failure to appreciate the extent, the significance and the bases of this differentiation vitiates much radical criticism of job redesign *per se*.

Differentiation is partly a matter of location, or of culture, with the unitarist approach to job redesign being very strong in the USA, whereas pluralist and radical approaches are more common in Europe. It would be misleading however to speak of a European, or an American approach *per se*, because ideological approaches transcend national boundaries, and America has no monopoly of unitarist thought, just as Europe is not the only site of pluralist or radical orientations. The form of job redesign is also important, since some of the major costs of job redesign for workers vary significantly with its form. Job displacement for instance is more commonly found with vertical role integration or flexible work groups than with flowline reorganization, although there is also evidence that national differences can reverse this relationship.

The evidence presented on this and other costs of job redesign is highly pertinent to analysis in terms of ideology, and in particular to the 'mutual-interests thesis' that lies at the heart of job redesign. It does appear there are several major economic and political costs of job redesign both for workers directly affected, as well as for those in ancillary or adjacent work roles (whose interests have frequently been overlooked). Indeed, when it is borne in mind that the costs to management would appear to be much less than for workers, the evidence casts considerable doubt on the mutuality of interest satisfaction arising from the redesign of jobs. Clearly the effects of redesign will vary with the form and the location of the initiative, but this point notwithstanding there are grounds for thinking that the scepticism of radicals and committed pluralists has some basis in fact.

Notes

1. Table 8.3 is based on the following cases: Agersnap et al. (1974), Biggane and Stewart (1963), Bjork (1978), Blair (1974), Bryan (1975), Conant and Kilbridge (1965), Coriat (1980), Cummings and Srivastva (1977), den Hertog (1974), Emery and Thorsrud (1975), Engelstad (1972), Ford (1969), Foulkes (1969), Glaser (1976), Hallam (1976), Hepworth and Osbaldeston (1979), Janson (1975), Kraft and Williams (1975), Lindholm and Norstedt (1975), McDavid (1975), Maher and Overbagh (1971), Mills (1976), Moors (1977), Mukherjee (1975), Orpen (1979), Paul and Robertson (1970), Pocock (1973), Poza and Markus (1980), Rice (1958), Ross and Screeton (1979), Rush (1971), Staehle (1979), Taylor (1973), Torner (1976), Trist et al. (1963), Tuggle (1969, 1977), van Vliet and Vrenken (n.d.), Wall and Clegg (1981), Walton (1972, 1974), Weed (1971), Wild (1975), Wyatt and Fraser (1928).
2. Table 8.4 is based on the same cases as Table 8.3.
3. The cases are as follows: Agersnap et al. (1974), Andreatta (1974), Anon (1975c, e), Archer (1975), Armstrong (1977), Bryan (1975), Conant and Kilbridge (1965), Cotgrove et al. (1971), Davis and Werling (1960), den Hertog (1974), Dunn (1974), Dyson (1973), Emery and Thorsrud (1975), Ford (1969), Gooding (1970b), Gorman and Molloy (1972), Guest (1957), Hallam (1976), Harvey (1973), Hill (1971), Kuriloff (1963, 1977), Lawler et al. (1973), Lindestad and Kvist (1975), Locke et al. (1976), McDavid (1975), Maher (1971b), Moors (1977), Morse and Reimer (1970), Mukherjee (1975), Noren and Norstedt (1975), Novara (1973), Paul and Robertson (1970), Pocock (1973), Powell and Schlacter (1971), Rice (1958), Rush (1971), Taylor (1973), Trist et al. (1963), Tuggle (1969, 1977), van Vliet and Vrenken (n.d.), Waldman et al. (1976), Walker (1950), Wall and Clegg (1981), Walton (1972, 1974).

9 Theory and conclusions

9.1 Summary of findings and conclusions

The tripartite differentiation of job redesign has several implications for theory. Whether the subject matter is worker motivation, job performance, organizational change or managerial decision-making, it becomes important to clarify at the outset which forms of job redesign are under consideration, or indeed whether an attempt is to be made to produce general theory. It is this complex of issues that forms the subject matter of the present chapter. Before proceeding to these it will be useful to recapitulate the main findings and conclusions of the book, starting with Taylorism, and proceeding through the new theory of job redesign and its application to the three forms: flowline reorganization, flexible work groups and vertical role integration.

(i) Taylorism

I began my investigation of job redesign by examining its historical antecedent and supposed theoretical protagonist, Taylor's scientific management. According to job-redesign theorists, Taylor's focus on financial incentives as the key determinant of worker motivation, and his advocacy of rigorous and progressive division of labour resulted in undesired (and undesirable) consequences: job dissatisfaction, absenteeism, turnover, poor motivation and poor job performance. I established, however, that the origins of division of labour predated Taylorism (a point made by other writers) and that output regulation by workers owed less to job dissatisfaction than to rational fears of the negative economic consequences of higher performance, such as rate-cutting.

More important, Taylor's work underwent significant developments throughout his career, in response to external criticism and the requirements of implementation. From an early emphasis on the employment relationship as an individual economic exchange, Taylor shifted to an organizational view of work performance, embracing authority, workflow, machinery and payment systems as means for controlling labour. Towards the end of his career, he developed the concept of the 'mental revolution' to express his view that the implementation of such organizational changes required a radical transformation in attitudes on the part of employers and workers, and he therefore moderated his earlier emphasis on organizational control as the key to the implementation of change. What follows from the delineation of these developments is a recognition of a considerable element of continuity between 'late Taylorism' and early industrial psychology. Both in the USA and the UK, industrial psychologists at the end of the First World War were beginning to investigate the conditions for cooperation in industry. More striking were the actual developments in industrial relations, with Whitley Councils and mechanisms of joint consultation being established in Britain from 1919, and extensive union – management cooperation continuing in the USA from 1917–8. Taylorism was an integral part of this trend, despite its equally apparent differences from early industrial psychology.

The specificity of Taylorism was constituted through its strategy, techniques and objectives. Strategically, it was defined in terms of a tactical and philosophical individualism that assigned key importance to individual motivation and individual rewards and controls in order to fragment the collective power of organized work-groups. The techniques of time-and-motion study and financial incentives were crucial in the substitution of management's definition of appropriate workloads and work methods, although Taylor also assigned some importance to other mechanisms of motivation, such as promotion prospects, friendly supervision, work rhythm and the provision of clear work goals. Taylor's objective was to re-establish control over labour in order to raise its productivity, and thereby increase the earnings of both labour and capital.

(ii) A new theory of job redesign

According to the classical theories of job redesign, it is personnel problems, such as absenteeism, turnover and job dissatisfaction that have prompted managements to redesign jobs in order to make them more satisfying. Employees are said to respond to redesigned jobs with higher levels of performance and the whole process caters for the interests of both employers and workers.

My own theory of job redesign suggested that changes in product markets were more significant than labour-market changes in explaining the genesis of job redesign. Second, it suggested that Taylorist methods of performance improvement (financial incentives, work-method improvements, labour elimination, and increased control and accountability) were likely to provide the best explanation of productivity increases arising from job redesign. Third, it suggested that in the context of an employment relationship based on antagonism and exploitation, the operation of these methods was likely to generate considerable costs for employees. In Chapters 4–7 the new and the classical theories of job redesign were tested against original and secondary case material. One of the key points to emerge from this process was the complexity and variability of job-redesign initiatives and the difficulty in validating propositions for all forms of redesign irrespective of circumstances.

The three types of job redesign identified were: *flowline reorganization*, where a production flowline is reduced in length or abolished and replaced with discrete individual work stations; *flexible work groups*, where a group of workers is allocated collective responsibility for a set of tasks and workers are flexible and move between tasks as necessary; and *vertical role integration*, where a series of discrete work roles in a vertical chain of roles are amalgamated into a single, new role.

(a) Flowline reorganization

Chapters 4 and 5 focused on the reorganization of flowlines, which typically involves a reduction in the number of work stations. Job redesign of this type predominates in consumer-goods industries, especially electrical appliances, using flowline assembly, and the problems leading to redesign of jobs were traced to changes in product markets. The expansion of product ranges in increasingly competitive markets led many companies to a situation where they were actually engaging in batch production but using a system of flowlines designed for mass production. Increased frequency of product changeovers on flowlines reduced total working time and raised unit costs, and companies responded in various ways to those problems, of which job redesign was but one.

By individualizing work organization through the abolition or reduction of flowlines, companies increased the flexibility of their production system and reduced the frequency of product changeovers. Various products could be produced continuously by workers at individual stations (or shortlines), whereas under the previous flowline system, a variety of products could only be assembled by periodically stopping the line, changing over parts, and starting up again on new products. The elimination of idle time and associated improvements in work methods following flowline reorganization made a substantial contribution to productivity improvements. The operation of individual financial incentives and increased control over labour offered an explanation for much of the remaining increases in productivity otherwise unaccounted for. Improvements in job content in the directions specified by job-redesign theory (variety, autonomy, task wholeness and responsibility) seemed to have some effects on job satisfaction but made only a small impact on performance and productivity changes. The validity of these conclusions was confirmed in a case study that allowed a comparison of the effects of changes in pay and work methods, and of job content. It was concluded that flowline reorganization could more fruitfully be analysed as a consistent application of Taylorism.

(b) Flexible work groups
By contrast the second form of job redesign, the flexible work group, entails the loosening of individual job specifications and rewards, and the creation of collective responsibility for a set of tasks. To that extent they are based upon principles of work organization that differ from Taylorism. In other respects, however, flexible work groups show some similarities to flowline reorganization, especially in their origins. Industrially, their use has been concentrated in continuous-process industries, such as chemicals and textiles, and it was shown that over-capacity in these industries had generated considerable competition and cost pressure in the late 1950s and 1960s. Again, managerial responses to these pressures varied, but their attention was focused on labour costs as one of their fastest rising and most easily manipulable elements.

The reason for introducing flexible work groups owes less to enlightened management than to the nature of their technology. Many continuous-process industries are characterized by frequent, but unpredictable, variations in the product and/or the production process, i.e., by high uncertainty, which necessitates corresponding shifts in labour allocation. Individual job descriptions and allocations have the disadvantage of 'locking' employees into 'their' jobs and inhibiting the required degree of flexibility. By effecting a transition from the individual to the group as the unit of work allocation, and by insisting on intra-group flexibility of labour, managements have been able to cope more effectively with production variations. Other things being equal, however, this process constitutes only a redistribution, not an increase, in workloads, and raises the question of how labour productivity is increased. Two mechanisms of productivity increase were seen to operate in firms with different types of production system. Where the firm's production system was operating some way below capacity and where changes in worker behaviour through increased effort expenditure could raise output, we found increased productivity associated with increases in pay. By contrast, where production systems were close to their operating capacity or where workers could not, by changes in effort levels, alter the system's output, we found changes in productivity were correlated with the volume of labour eliminated from the production process. De-manning was associated with increases in pay for those remaining workers, and the frequency of unionization in such plants suggested that these manning, pay and workload changes were bargained over and settled in advance by the parties.

Evidence on changes in intrinsic motivation and job satisfaction was often not reported in cases of flowline reorganization and flexible work groups, but taken as a whole it was inconsistent and failed to provide substantial support for any variant of job-redesign theory.

(c) Vertical role integration
The significance of intrinsic motivation was much greater in vertical role integration, the third category of job redesign. This has been used frequently with clerical and other white-collar workers, particularly in the USA. Studies of the evolution of office work, particularly in banking, insurance and finance, showing two conflicting trends: on the one hand a progressive fragmentation and subdivision of work coupled with increased regulation through method study and other work rules; on the other hand, a growing tendency for employers to recruit more qualified employees. This growing divergence between employee qualifications and job requirements was well described by classical job-redesign theory, but various responses to this potential (and sometimes

actual) problem were noted. Job enrichment, or vertical role integration, was used by many employers to stem turnover, curb absenteeism or ease recruitment, and there is evidence to suggest that the enhanced challenge and responsibility built into jobs was appreciated, and responded to as the classical theory predicts. Improvements in performance and productivity were often reported and simultaneously or subsequently several companies were able to increase productivity still further by eliminating supervisory or inspection jobs.

Vertical role integration among blue-collar workers has been seen to take a rather different form, often involving attempts to transfer maintenance or other ancillary duties to production workers. There is evidence from some of the better documented cases that these changes in work roles were bargained over in advance and accepted by employees in exchange for improvements in wages and fringe benefits. Attitudinal changes occurred in some cases, but seemed to lag sometime behind changes in both job content and job performance.

The overall conclusions from these chapters were firstly that classical job-redesign theory offered inadequate explanations of the origins of job redesign in general. Although the determinants of their origins, and the mechanisms by which redesign of jobs raises labour productivity, are logically separate questions, the fact that personnel problems did not predominate in the genesis of redesign does weaken (though not irreparably) the case for improved job content as a major route to improved job performance. The weakness of the job-redesign case was confirmed in my analyses of the mechanisms of productivity improvement in the three forms of job redesign, where changes in intrinsic motivation were seen to be of relatively little overall significance. Nevertheless, in cases of vertical role integration involving white-collar workers, intrinsic motivation did appear to be a crucial variable in the explanation of changes in job performance.

The general theory of job redesign outlined in Chapter 3 owes a considerable debt to contingency theory, and the investigations in subsequent chapters revealed the importance of (a) product- and labour-market characteristics as influences on the use of job redesign; (b) technological variations in explaining the form of job redesign; and (c) variations in the mechanisms of productivity improvement associated with the different forms of redesign.

(iii) Organizational ideologies

Finally in Chapter 8 job-redesign theory was analysed at the level of ideological assumptions about organizations, using the unitarist, pluralist and radical distinctions of Fox (1966). Theories and writings were analysed according to their objectives, views of the worker, unit of analysis, views of the wider organization, preferred mode of implementation of job redesign, and preferred mode of diffusion. It became clear that four major perspectives on job redesign could be distinguished at this level, once pluralists had been subdivided into pragmatic and committed varieties. This analysis once again underlined the complexity of job redesign and the difficulty of casting it into a single mould whether 'humanistic', 'conservative', or whatever. This is not to say that different approaches have little in common, for the same chapter also showed that the *practice* of job redesign often entails significant economic costs for workers, *viz* labour elimination, labour intensification, increased managerial control over work performance and non-provision of pay increases.

These findings invalidate the claim that job redesign satisfies the mutual interests of workers and employers by revealing an asymmetrical distribution of costs between the parties. It is clear that my own findings and conclusions indicate profound weaknesses in the classical theory of job design, but it therefore becomes important to enquire into the reasons for these weaknesses in order to be able to correct them. Although all job-redesign theories offer inadequate accounts of both motivation and performance, these are only symptoms of more fundamental deficiencies. The alternative theory advanced in Chapter 3 owes its superiority to its better grasp of the employment relationship, of structural features of organizations and of the environments in which organizations operate. In short, the central weakness of job-redesign theory is that it contains no adequate theory of organization, and it is from this general deficiency that its specific shortcomings all derive, of which the most crucial is its conception of the nature and significance of motivation.

(a) Motivation

Motivation, as many writers have observed, is a difficult and ill defined concept that has nevertheless been extensively discussed and researched (see the Nebraska Annual Symposia; Deci, 1975; Peters, 1960; Scott, 1975; Warr, 1976b).

We noted in earlier chapters that all theories of job redesign employ the concept of need. They consider that the excessive fragmentation of jobs leads to inadequate fulfillment of higher-order needs—for growth, challenge or responsibility—leading in turn to 'dysfunctional' organizational behaviours: absenteeism, turnover, poor job performance. Consequently the redesign of jobs aims to provide greater opportunities for need fulfillment that are expected to lead to performance and attitudinal improvements. In other words, the key to job performance lies in changes in motivation. An examination of the assumptions underlying this approach will indicate several problems and issues whose solution requires considerably more attention be given to organizational features and processes.

This concept of need is itself open to question. Needs, on a biological analogy, are usually taken to be universal, at least within a species, yet it is readily admitted by some job-redesign theorists that individuals differ in their needs. This concession in turn raises the question: why one should talk of needs rather than, say, preferences or wants. Measures of 'higher-order need' strength invariably contain no justification for the designation of need, and their designers and users have hitherto failed to indicate the grounds for believing that their instruments measure needs rather than preferences. Secondly, there is a tendency to assume that if job redesign results in improved performance this must be because of higher levels of need fulfillment, evidenced in changes in job satisfaction and motivation. This assumption might be correct if other things were equal: invariably they are not. Job performance has been improved because of changes in payment systems, work methods and other variables associated with job redesign, and the significance of motivation cannot be assumed retrospectively. Nor can it be supported by reference to evidence on improvements in job attitudes or job satisfaction, since as I showed earlier (chapter 7) the concepts of motivation and satisfaction are fundamentally distinct, and there are only very weak empirical and theoretical grounds for linking them.

The failure to distinguish needs from preferences or wants reflects the absence of an adequate theory of needs that would specify their origins, character and *modus operandi*. This same weakness is also responsible for an underestimation of material or economic preferences at work. Maslow, Herzberg and other job-redesign writers suggested that these more basic needs were rapidly approaching fulfillment for many workers because of the unprecedented growth in living standards during the post-war economic boom. Again, this assumption might be correct if other things were equal, and there are good grounds for thinking that in this context they were not. It is reasonable to suggest that material needs were stimulated by a massive increase in advertising, which was rendered more 'immediate' by the spread of television ownership in the 1950s throughout the advanced capitalist countries (Packard, 1960). Again, credit facilities were also enormously expanded in this period, especially for consumer durable goods. Inflation was relatively low in the early 1950s but began climbing in the late 1950s, reaching double figures in many countries by the early 1970s, but providing nevertheless a continual source of pressure for compensatory wage increases. And the range of consumer goods also increased rapidly in the post-war period, both objectively, and in terms of their availability to larger sections of society. Pressure for wage increases does not necessarily reflect a concern with basic material needs as such, since almost all cultural activities, which presumably reflect 'higher-order needs', require money for their pursuit. People may therefore adopt an instrumental attitude to employment in order to furnish the means for 'higher-order need' satisfaction outside work (*cf.* Dubin, 1956).

Fourthly, the emphasis on motivation arising from job content actually misrepresents the processes by which job redesign is often implemented. Where the redesign of jobs has been introduced following negotiations between management and union (or worker) representatives, it will often be agreed and understood that wage increases (and other benefits) are to be given in exchange for improvements in work pace, work volume or other performance criteria. It does, of course, not necessarily follow that this obligation is understood or accepted by the workers involved, but it is a reasonable presumption. In other words it is not primarily the performance of a redesigned and more motivating job that stimulates higher levels of employee performance but a prior contractual obligation. This is not to deny that job content may not play some role in motivation (although the evidence, except for some white-collar workers is unconvincing) or in improving job satisfaction.

One of the key conclusions from the preceding chapters is that work performance can only be fully understood once motivation has been displaced from its position of pre-eminence. Why should motivation *not* be considered a central determinant of work performance? The reasons are as follows: first, empirical studies of output regulation under incentive pay systems by Brown (1973), Klein (1964), Lupton (1963), Roy

(1952, 1954) and others provide little justification for low motivation as the cause of output restriction. There is a consensus that output restriction is practised because of the fear that any substantial rise in earnings will result in a revision by management, of job times or rates, thereby cutting the 'wage – effort ratio' (Baldamus, 1961). In short, the process reflects a lack of trust that management will not exploit a situation to their advantage when the opportunity arises.

Second, work performance is also determined by the design of work and the technology that is operated. The principal sources of inefficiency, in flowlines for instance, have less to do with worker motivation, than with materials supply and the difficulties of precisely coordinating the activity of up to 100 workers on the same production line (see Chapters 4 and 5). Indeed, assembly lines were originally designed by Henry Ford in order to eliminate the effects of human variability and error, and to substitute technical managerial control for the motivation that workers were thought to lack. In continuous process industries the output of plants or production systems often has only the most remote connection to worker motivation, and as we saw in Chapter 6, inefficiency and high costs were the result of inefficient, rigid and inappropriate systems of work allocation (or sociotechnical mismatches).

Third, environmental changes influence work performance in various ways (Perrow, 1978). Product-market competition was responsible for the reduced output of flowlines assembling electrical appliances in many of the case studies in Chapters 4 and 5. Many payment-by-result incentive systems have been eroded by pressure from local labour markets (Lerner *et al.*, 1969).

In order to understand these social, technical and economic influences on work performance we require a *theory of organization*.

(b) Organizations

Such a theory is also required in order to explain and predict the impact of job redesign on the various component groups of an organization. The 'problem' of supervision illustrates this logic very clearly, and reflects the realization that devolution of decision-making to shop-floor or office workers has implications for the role of supervisor, and has, in some cases indeed, been perceived by supervisors as a threat to their interests (Fitter, 1981; Wall, 1980). There is no reason to believe that work redesign affects only the bottom rungs of line management, since industrial engineers and work-study managers may also be affected—

beneficially or adversely. A reduction in turnover and absenteeism is likely to reduce labour recruitment, and thereby affect personnel managers. Changes in product quality will have implications for firms' customers, who may be pleased with improvements, but apprehensive about a price increase.

Finally trade unionists have expressed fears about the effects of work redesign on member commitment to unionism, and it has been suggested, for example, that the fragmentation of a production process may reduce the cohesion and unity of the work force and jeopardize union solidarity in the event of disputes with management as work groups respond to union calls in terms of their own sectional interests (see Chapters 6 and 8). Vertical role integration amongst blue-collar workers often involves the transfer of maintenance duties to production workers, and in one case the autonomy of a maintenance department was eroded because they were linked more closely to production departments and production supervision (Fitter, 1981).

In order to understand why job redesign is used in these various contexts, it is also necessary to develop a theory of managerial decision-making (see Appendix). Firms with similar sets of problems have shown various responses, of which the redesign of jobs is but one. It may be that the distribution of power among different management interests, such as finance, marketing or personnel, is crucial in understanding the process and outcomes of the decision whether or not to redesign jobs (Pettigrew, 1973). Legge (1977) has shown for instance that the personnel function often lacks influence because of its subordinate position in the hierarchy of management specialisms. Friedman (1977a,b) has shown that management in the British car industry has been more willing to make concessions to groups of workers strategically placed to disrupt production than to 'peripheral' workers lacking power.

In short we require a theory of organization that will allow us to derive and test answers to questions about the internal repercussions of job redesign; and about the ways in which external pressures are translated by managerial action into job redesign.

9.2 The future of job redesign

For some writers such questions, however interesting, are quickly becoming irrelevant. As the recession in the capitalist world continues, leaving in its wake mass unemployment, a shift in power from trade unions to employers and large-scale de-manning in industry, it is tempting to think that job redesign is a luxury that firms can no longer afford and which, indeed, they no longer find necessary because of the discipline imposed on the workforce by the pressure of the reserve army of unemployed.

Several writers have argued that job redesign is a transient phenomenon, now entering a period of decline (Blackler and Brown, 1975; Hackman and Oldham, 1980; Sirota, 1973b; Wade, 1973); others are more optimistic (e.g., Davis, 1980; Davis and Taylor, 1972). But the relevance of some of the evidence cited in such discussions is questionable. Several failed cases of redesign were reported in the 1970s (Frank and Hackman, 1975; Locke et al., 1976); several writers suggested that workers were uninterested in job redesign (e.g., Imberman, 1973); others said that the effects were short-lived (Penzer, 1973) and others questioned the validity of the theory (Parke and Tausky, 1975). More relevant therefore are the reports on managerial attitudes, and Thackray (1976) has suggested the recession is leading managers to reconsider some of the motivational assumptions that were accepted in the 1960s. To the extent that it is occurring, this rethinking is likely to be aided by articles such as Leonard and Rathmill (1977) in which two prominent exponents of 'group technology' wrote what amounts to a retraction in which they criticized many of its 'myths'.

The relevance of such evidence is questionable, because even if the points made were correct, they need not imply a decline in the use made of job redesign by managers. Much of this discussion of the future is also vitiated by serious theoretical misunderstandings, which are best illustated in Hackman (1978a); see also Hackman and Oldham, (1980). These authors distinguish two routes along which organizations may proceed. Route one is based on job redesign to increase intrinsic motivation, satisfaction and organizational effectiveness. Route two is the traditional, bureaucratic, Taylorist path, based on controls and managerial authority. Sadly, thinks Hackman, because of caution, lack of knowledge, and the ease of conventional routines, route two is likely to predominate in the 1980s. The chief problem with this 'choice' is that it offers paths which are not in fact incompatible. In practice, organizations have redesigned jobs and maintained bureaucratic controls; or redesigned jobs in some sectors, but not others (see Appendix).

The most coherent theoretical dismissal of job redesign has been produced by Braverman (1974), who argued that within capitalist economies it was possible to locate forces which dictated an inexorable process of deskilling of jobs and workers (see Wood, 1982, for discussions of 'skill' and 'deskilling'). According to Braverman there are two principal causes of deskilling. First, because managements in capitalist enterprises must respond to competition by rationalization of the labour process to yield increased labour productivity and higher rates of exploitation, they must take control of this process. Historically, control over the labour process rested with skilled workers through their monopoly of knowledge and control of labour supply (Montgomery, 1979). By acquiring this knowledge for itself, management could break the skilled workers' monopoly and reorganize work in the interests of capital, at the same time dividing up the skilled work to reduce worker oppositon and resistance. The second imperative is more purely economic, and can be expressed as the Babbage principle. Babbage (1835) assumes an employer who has hired a certain number of skilled workers each receiving the same rate of pay, but performing jobs requiring different levels of skill. His principle states that total labour costs and average labour price will be minimized by employing skilled workers only for skilled work, and by employing lesser-skilled and cheaper labour for work requiring less skill. In other words, a labour process employing, say, 10 skilled workers is converted to a process with, say, 3 skilled, 5 semi-skilled and 2 unskilled workers. The application of the Babbage principle therefore dictates that work should be broken up into small units for which cheap labour is suitable.

If we accept that less-skilled labour is cheaper than skilled, it still does not automatically follow that reduction of the *average price* of labour in an enterprise will minimize total or unit labour costs. This is because the *volume* of labour required will depend on the allocation of work and its intensity: the greater the inefficiency in allocation, the more labour will need to be hired, thus raising labour costs. In the case of job redesign reported by Walker (1950) continued fragmentation of jobs was holding up labour costs at a relatively high level because large numbers of workers were engaged on a range of jobs at low levels of labour intensity. By combining these different jobs, the intensity of labour was raised, some labour was eliminated, and labour costs reduced.

We can conclude therefore that the Babbage principle of dividing work to realize the lowest cost is in fact a special case of a general principle. The minimum labour cost is given by a division of labour that combines a low price for labour with a high intensity of working. Division of labour can be taken too far and cease to be 'economic', not just for 'personnel reasons'—absenteeism, turnover—but because, for instance, mechanization may severely reduce the work to be done in particular jobs (see Chapters 4–7 and Scoville, 1969). Where this happens, job redesign to reverse the division of labour can yield economic benefits for employers.

Clearly there are difficulties in predicting the future of job redesign. Published literature provides an unreliable guide to events because of the fads to which journal editorial policies are prone. Insofar as job redesign requires managerial decisions and therefore choice, this constitutes an added difficulty, especially at a time of international recession when many organizations are literally faced with extinction. But if theory is to be of any use at all, it must surely lead to some predictions. These may be set out in terms of the three categories of job redesign. The incidence of *vertical role integration* may well decline among white-collar workers because the labour market pressures on employers are reduced by higher levels of unemployment. This is also likely to affect worker behaviour by curbing expectations and employees may feel increasingly they are lucky simply to have a job. As and when unemployment falls, we would expect this form of job redesign to pick up again. For blue-collar workers, the future of vertical role integration is unclear. Increased mechanization in batch-production systems will stimulate recombination of work roles, and employer drives to reduce labour costs may lead in the same direction.

Flowline reorganization was analysed as very often a response to product-market competition, especially in the field of consumer durables. Insofar as a recession cuts consumer spending, and forces down prices, and probably profits, then product-market competition will be intensified unless production capacity is drastically reduced by plant closures. There have been many closures in Europe and the USA, especially in car manufacture, but there is also considerable concern about imports of consumer goods from places such as Japan and the Third World, particularly on the part of domestic-appliance manufacturers. The pressures that generated many cases of job redesign are therefore still present, and I would predict the continuation of job redesign in this sector.

Flexible work groups emerged in continuous-process industries, partly because of world overcapacity that put pressure on costs. Again the overcapacity has been increased during the recession, and chemicals and textiles plants have been closed in the UK, and elsewhere, and profits have slumped.

Certainly there is no reason to assume that mass unemployment will render job redesign superfluous because of the accompanying shift in power towards managements. Indeed it is precisely because of this power shift that managements may be better placed to push ahead with schemes of job redesign that might previously have been obstructed by unions; and may have more incentive to do so because of the seriousness of the problems faced by many firms in the midst of a severe recession (Roberts and Wood, 1981). Indeed there is already evidence that firms *are* taking advantage of the recession to introduce vertical role integration and flexible work groups in order to raise productivity and profitability (Incomes Data Services, 1981).

More generally, the relatively low standards of growth and productivity increase in the sluggish capitalist economies of the UK and USA are likely to generate pressure for greater utilization, intensification and exploitation of labour (Bingham, 1977; Jones, 1976; Wragg and Robertson, 1978). Intensification of labour is a well established practice in many branches of industry. Marx (1867) documented the growth in the number of looms 'tented' by each weaver in the nineteenth century. Mechanization in British Industry at the turn of the century was often accompanied by attempts to 'speed up' the machines (Lazonick, 1979; Phelps-Brown, 1959), and in America the moving assembly line was pioneered by Henry Ford for the same purpose. During the Depression of the 1930s, employers took advantage of their strong position to speed up machinery and conveyors (Branson and Heinemann, 1971). More recently, several reports on the British economy have sought to identify causes of, and barriers to, productivity growth. 'Restrictive labour practices', i.e., union-maintained manning levels were identified by the Donovan Commission (Royal Commission on Trade Unions and Employers Associations, 1968) as one factor, and the wave of productivity bargaining in Britain throughout the 1960s was directed towards their elimination.

Pratten (1976a,b, 1977) found that productivity differences between British and European subsidiaries of the same companies, which favoured the latter by between 15–30%, could be partly accounted for by differences in work allocation and division of labour. Higher levels of maintenance and craft manning have been found in UK chemicals and steel plants compared with foreign firms (Chemicals EDC, 1973a; Upham, 1980). Clearly then there is scope for a managerial drive on labour utilization in the UK, and job redesign as one form of intensification of labour will certainly feature as part of it. A similar tendency is discernible in the USA, and joint productivity committees and councils have issued numerous reports on ways of raising the slow rates of growth (National Commission, 1975a,b; National Centre, 1976). However, there are several countervailing forces that need to be considered. First, unions will rightly try to resist schemes of job redesign that are likely to eliminate jobs, though how successful they can be under conditions of high unemployment remains to be seen. Second, increases in labour productivity and in output may be constrained by lack of demand for the products in question, and this may hold back some managements. And third, some managements may be so preoccupied with survival that problems of work organization are either overlooked or resolved by coercion.

These developments will certainly present a challenge to unions, who are likely to be faced with pressure to sell some members' jobs in return for higher wages, security and job satisfaction for those who remain. Although some unions are likely to take a defensive posture and stall on any kind of organizational change, others may break out of this position, either towards a closer 'partnership' with management or towards a radical reappraisal of work and employment. The labour – management committees in the USA seem to represent the former trend (see Chapter 8); the 'workers' alternative plans' movement in Britain represents the second (Beynon and Wainwright, 1979; Cooley, 1980). Social scientists, too, will be faced with a challenge. If job redesign results in loss of jobs, how will scientists respond to this under conditions of mass and rising unemployment? Neutral positions will be harder to adopt, but the evidence on the strength of unitarist and pluralist ideological positions within the job redesign movement provides little encouragement for those who want to see social scientists play a more progressive role in organizations.

Appendix: management and job redesign

The relatively few writers who have discussed job redesign in its organizational context tend to adopt the view of management as a more or less homogeneous group with a set of views and interests, confronted by 'resistance' from subordinates to plans for organizational change (see Kelly and Clegg, 1981). Donaldson (1975), however, has made the valuable point that the unity of management is an empirical question, and cannot therefore be assumed *a priori*. A case will be described below that illustrates this point, as well as underlining a further important characteristic of management. Writers such as Davis (1966) and Hackman (1978a) have suggested that managements either possess or ought to possess a coherent approach to job design, perhaps even a philosophy. In the present case (as well as in many others) management attitudes to job redesign were almost wholly pragmatic: if the technique could facilitate the achievement of their objectives without incurring unacceptable costs, then it would be considered.

The material in this case was obtained from interviews, company documents and from participant observation at company meetings.

A.1 The company and its organization

The company produces glass containers, as well as moulds, plastics and ornamental glass, but all of the changes to be described here took place in the glass container division of the main manufacturing section. The company is jointly owned by Company A of America, manufacturers of glass packaging, and by Company B of the United Kingdom, although it appears to enjoy almost as much autonomy as before its takeover. The administrative centre is located in the south of England, and major plants are to be found in England and Scotland. Each plant has its own factory manager, to whom all specialist management functions are accountable, e.g., industrial engineering, production, personnel. Each specialist function in a plant is also accountable to its own superiors in Head Office and the factory manager is accountable to the Manufacturing Director, also at Head Office. In practice, the factory managers were allowed to exercise considerable discretion over various less important issues, although whether central control might have been reasserted in the event of a major disagreement is a possibility about which we can only speculate. Certainly, when one of the plants was encountering industrial-relations problems in the late 1960s, directives were issued from Head Office on ways of dealing with the problems.

The production of bottles, or other glass containers, is conventionally divided into two phases, the hot end and the cold end. The hot end consists firstly of the production of glass by mixing and heating silica, sand, limestone and cullet. The molten glass is then poured into moulds, a process supervised by the moulding-machine operator, and from there proceeds through the phase of annealing. This is a process of controlled cooling, in an oven, known as a lehr. At the end of this process the containers emerge on a conveyor belt (a lehr mat) and proceed through the 'cold end', where they are inspected, both automatically and manually, and packed. Hot-end work is paid at a higher rate than that in the cold end, and is regarded as skilled. Cold-end work requires several weeks or sometimes months of training before the operators are able to detect all of the 100 or more possible faults in a container. Nevertheless, the work at the cold end is considered to be only semi-skilled.

In 1975 the company was discussing a series of changes in jobs at a new plant that was to open in 1976, and which represented a high degree of investment and was itself highly capital intensive. The changes in work organization revolved around a new role provisionally known as the 'New Look Operative' (hereafter, NLO) which combined certain quality-control duties with responsibility for machine running and a measure of former, supervisory control over labour allocation. At the same time, adjacent work roles, such as that of the packaging-machine minder embodied a degree of specialization as compared to the older technology and organization.

Discussion within the company on this programme reached its peak at a meeting on 5 November 1975, attended by Factory Managers Divisional Personnel and Industrial Engineering and plant representatives of these specialist functions.

The discussion was centred around a specially prepared document built on two underlying principles:

New look type systems have developed by extending the principle that all mould cavities should be inspected at regular intervals at the cold end, together with the principle that, wherever possible, sorting should be divorced from packing operations.

The advantages of the system were said to be improved quality, optimal manning levels, stock reduction, and 'job enrichment of the personnel employed'. The 'New Look Operative' was also said to be 'the key man in the new system'. There can be no doubt that this role was 'enriched' as compared with the older organization of work. Under the old system, bottles emerging from the lehr passed along a motorized conveyor, through a small quantity of inspection machinery, finally to be inspected visually, and packed in cartons, by the sorters at the end of the line. During their process along the line, an operative called a Cavity Sampler, or Quality Checker, would take regular samples of bottles and check them for certain standard faults. Any relevant information was then fed back to the hot end. In addition, this operative was responsible for ensuring the continued functioning of the automatic inspection machinery, and for notifying faults to the foreman. These duties were now subsumed under the role of NLO, who was responsible in fact, for far more machinery than the Cavity Sampler, and was also assigned authority to requisition labour as required. The former sorter had most of his inspection duties removed, and was assigned to machine minding on the automatic packager.

The discussion document then gave summary descriptions of the main work roles required in the plant, and the Appendices provided comparative data on manning levels and line speeds from several plants, as well as from a parent company plant in the USA. Also in the Appendices was a sheet headed 'Flexibility and Job Enrichment', which discussed the possibilities for labour flexibility, and indicated, as its chief advantage, the reduction of line manning levels.

The Personnel function reactivated a discussion on behavioural science within the company. At the 5 November meeting, the contributions of the Personnel Officer and myself focused on the element of 'job enrichment' in the NLO document and tried to argue for its extension to other operatives. In particular the question of the specialization, or impoverishment, of the packaging machine minder was said by us to be incompatible with a stress on 'job enrichment'.

The argument for job 'enrichment' offered by Personnel was the standard argument used in the literature: improved job content will result in more satisfaction and motivation, and thus lead to higher productivity and quality of work. It also presupposed a certain theory of motivation, in which workers were seen as willing to increase effort, given the chance, and which, to some extent, downgraded the role of pay and external controls. The strongest attack on these views came from the Industrial Engineering Department, who supported the granting of more job complexity and authority to the NLO, but who wished, nevertheless to divorce sorting and packing operations. They said that workers could not reliably inspect their own work, and that the compulsory union of sorting and packing on the single-line conveyors in the cold end had led to a deterioration in quality. Figures were produced to demonstrate the deterioration, and it was said customer complaints had increased and sorter effectiveness had decreased. This result was attributed by Industrial Engineering to the process of despecialization, enforced by the inline system, although the workers themselves universally indicated in interviews that it was due to insufficient manning and increased pace of work, which made proper working difficult. Whatever the truth, Industrial Engineering in any case assumed that workers were motivated by a desire to maximize the wage – effort bargain in their own favour. This assumption was held by both Divisional and by factory industrial engineers, and clearly set them apart from the assumptions underlying job 'enrichment'.

At a more general level, it emerged that Personnel was opposed in principle to specialization of labour, and was arguing for an extension of despecialization. Industrial Engineering (IE), on the other hand, held no principled view on specialization, but argued pragmatically for specialization, or not, as particular cases warranted. The over-riding concern of Industrial Engineering was to maintain quality standards (production volume being chiefly a function of activity at the hot end), and the argument against the combination of sorting and packaging reflected both their experience and their assumptions about the workforce.

Finally, there was disagreement amongst management over the nature of job 'enrichment' in the NLO document—was it an end in its own right, or only a means to an end? The arguments of Personnel *implied* that it was an end in itself, although the alleged benefits of 'job enrichment' were stressed in terms of productivity and product quality.

No answer was made however to the claim by Industrial Engineering regarding the deleterious effects of the combination of sorting and packaging. For them, the element of 'enrichment' was seen as a means to an end, although the posited ends differed between different members of this function. Why then did they support the concept of the NLO at all? The answer, in part, is that they saw the enhanced authority of the NLO as necessary for the effective performance of his job. In the new plant, there would, at any one time be relatively few workers in the region of the cold end, and the foremen would often be occupied with other duties, possibly elsewhere in the plant. The crucial importance of product quality in the glass-container market made it imperative that decisions affecting quality be taken as quickly as possible before too much 'damage' had occurred. In addition, any delay in fetching extra labour, or mechanics, could result in the stopping of the line, and in view of the large amount of capital invested in the new plant, this was seen to be a wholly undesirable eventuality.

Apart from considerations of capital investment and product quality, there was also an argument, shared by Personnel and Industrial Engineering on the importance of eliminating labour from the production process. Under the section headed 'Flexibility and Job Enrichment' appeared the view of Personnel. The cold-end production line ought to be staffed permanently only by the NLO. Additional duties, such as visual inspection or machine-minding, would be performed by members of a labour pool, who, when not working on the conveyor line, would be engaged in resorting returned containers or covering for workers absent from other ancillary functions. They would, in short, be flexible, perform various jobs, and thus experience 'job enrichment'. The objective of this proposal was identical to that of Industrial Engineering, namely to reduce labour on the production line and avoid rigid manning levels. In a document written after the 5 November discussion, a Divisional Industrial Engineer proposed a modified NLO scheme, the precise details of which need not concern us. The object of this proposal was to ensure control over labour costs and product quality, and it finished on the following note:

> An effective monitoring control will be necessary to prevent full manning of the lines becoming the norm.

Meanwhile, the behavioural-science 'lobby' continued to organize its activity. The Group Personnel Officer organized a day school at the company HQ addressed by staff from the Department of Employment's Work Research Unit, to which senior divisional managers were invited. Although many were impressed by the speakers and their contributions, there remained a feeling that the company was not yet ready for a major project of the sort vaguely hinted at in the school. In late November, after a visit by the Group Personnel Officer and myself, the management at the new plant received a proposal from us outlining a social psychological study of the opening and early functioning of the new plant. The concern expressed during the visit at the amount of time such a project might consume crystallized into severe doubt on their receipt of the detailed proposal, and the project was subsequently cancelled.

When the rejection of the proposed project by management reached the Manufacturing Director, he acceded to their wishes, and perhaps also to the feelings of some of his senior managers, despite his guarded support for the use of behavioural science, expressed at the 5 November meeting.

Clearly, there may well have been more to management's decision than was expressed in letters and memos and at meetings, and this account must therefore be seen as tentative. It does nevertheless illustrate concretely some of the notions that Donaldson (1975) discussed in his own paper on the subject. In that paper he described job enlargement as a 'vehicle' through which different management specialists sought to achieve their particular aims. In the light of the present case we could perhaps modify this instrumental idea of 'the vehicle'. For in this case the consequence of the Industrial Engineers' instrumental attitude to job 'enrichment' was that in an adjacent situation—that of sorting/packaging—they were prepared to abandon 'enrichment' when another 'vehicle' proved more suitable for their ends. In the case of Personnel on the other hand, there was an altogether more intimate link between means and ends, a link that compelled a commitment to job enrichment in and of itself. This link was much more tenuous in the case of Industrial Engineering and hence more vulnerable to modification, or even abandonment.

References

Ackroyd, S. (1974). Economic rationality and the relevance of Weberian sociology. *British Journal of Industrial Relations* **12** (2), 236–248.

Agersnap, F., Junge, F, Westenholz, A., Moldrup, P. and Brinch, L. (1974). Danish experiments with new forms of co-operation on the shop floor. *Personnel Review* **3** (3), 34–50.

Aglietta, M. (1979). *A Theory of Capitalist Regulation.* New Left Books, London.

Aguren, S. and Edgren, J. (1980). *New Factories: Job design through factory planning in Sweden.* SAF, Stockholm.

Aguren, S., Hansson, R., and Karlsson, K. G. (1976). *The Volvo Kalmar Plant.* The Rationalisation Council, Stockholm.

Aitken, H. J. (1960). *Taylorism at Watertown Arsenal.* Harvard University Press, Cambridge, USA.

Alber, A. (1979a). The real costs of job enrichment. *Business Horizons* Feb., 60–72.

Alber, A. (1979b). Job enrichment for profit. *Human Resources Management* **18** (Spring), 15–25.

Aldag, R. J. and Brief, A. P. (1979). *Task Design and Employee Motivation.* Scott Foresman, Glenview, Illinois.

Alderfer, C. P. (1976). Job enlargement and the organisational context. In Gruneberg, M. (ed), *Job Satisfaction.*, Macmillan, London.

Anderson, J. W. (1970). The impact of technology on job enrichment. *Personnel Review* **47** (5), 29–37.

Andreatta, A. J. (1974). Job enrichment through autonomous groups. *Personnel Practice Bulletin* **30** (1), 9–13.

Andreatta, H. (1974). *Organisation Development in Action.* Productivity Promotion Council of Australia, Melbourne.

Anon. (n.d.). *Welvic II Report.* Internal unpublished company report.

Anon. (1972). Work teams at Pye beat production line problems. *Manufacturing Management* Dec.

Anon. (1974a). 50% reduction in labour turnover for Courtenay Wines. *Work Study* **23** (10), 32–33.

Anon. (1974b). Job enrichment at United Biscuits. *European Industrial Relations Review* **11,** 2–5.

Anon. (1975a). Experiments to improve the quality of working life in the

Netherlands. *European Industrial Relations Review* **17**, 8–9.

Anon. (1975b). Job enrichment at Hoogovens. *European Industrial Relations Review* **19**, 20–22.

Anon. (1975c). Job enrichment at Bamshoeve. *European Industrial Relations Review* **23**, 14–17.

Anon. (1975d). Can group assembly boost output at Lotus? *Business Administration* Dec, p. 51.

Anon. (1975e). Transition to more meaningful work—a job design case. *In* Davis, L. E. and Cherns, A. B. (Eds), *The Quality of Working Life*, Vol. 2. Free Press, New York.

Anon. (1979). Lincoln National Life stresses work restructure, employee improvement. *World of Work Report* **4** (6), 41–44.

Aquilano, N. (1977). Multiskilled work teams: productivity benefits. *California Management Review* **19** (4), 17–22.

Archer, J. T. (1975). Achieving joint organisational, technical and personal needs: the case of the sheltered experiment of aluminium casting team. *In* Davis, L. E. and Cherns, A. B. (Eds), *The Quality of Working Life*, Vol. 2. Free Press, New York.

Argyle, M. (1972). *The Social Psychology of Work*. Penguin, Harmondsworth.

Argyris, C. (1957). *Personality and Organisation*. Harper, New York.

Armenakis, A., Marbert, L. D. and Bedeian, A. (1982) An evaluation of the response format and scale structure of the job diagnostic survey. *Human Relations* (in press).

Armstrong, J. (1977). How to motivate. *Management Today* Feb, 60–63.

Arnold, H. J. and House, R. J. (1980). Methodological and substantive extensions to the job characteristics model of motivation. *Organisational Behaviour and Human Performance* **25**, 161–183.

Aronowitz, S. (1978). Marx, Braverman and the logic of capital. *Insurgent Sociologist* **8**, 126–146.

BBC (1977). *Democracy at Work*. BBC, London.

Babbage, C. (1835). *On the Economy of Machinery and Manufactures*. Republished in 1971 by Kelley, New York.

Baldamus, W. (1961). *Efficiency and Effort*. Tavistock, London.

Banks, T. (1974). Autonomous work groups. *Industrial Society* **56**, 10–12.

Barbash, J. (1977). Humanising work—a new ideology. *American Federationist* **84**, 8–15.

Baritz, L. (1960). *The Servants of Power*. Wesleyan University Press, Connecticut.

Barkin, S. (Ed) (1975). *Worker Militancy and its Consequences*. Praeger, New York.

Baumgartner, T., Burns, T. and de Ville, P. (1979). Work, politics and social structuring under capitalism: impact and limitations of industrial democracy reforms under capitalist relations of production and reproduction. *In* Burns, T. (Ed), *Work and Power*. Sage, California.

Behrend, H. (1957). The effort bargain. *Industrial & Labour Relations Review* **10**, 503–515.

Bell, D. (1960). *The End of Ideology*. Free Press, Glencoe.
Bell, D. (1972). Three technologies: size, measurement, hierarchy. *In* Davis, L. E. and Taylor, J. C. (Eds), *Design of Jobs*. Penguin, Harmondsworth.
Bendix, R. (1956). *Work and Authority in Industry*. University of California Press, Berkeley, USA.
Berg, I. (1970). *The Great Training Robbery*. Penguin, Harmondsworth.
Berg. I., Freedman, M. and Freeman, M. (1978). *Managers and Work Reform: a Limited Engagement*. Free Press, New York.
Berg, M. (1979). *Technology and Toil in Nineteenth Century Britain*. CSE Books, London.
Bernoux, P. and Duffier, J. (1974). Les groups semi-autonomes de production. *Sociologie du Travail* **16** (4), 383–401.
Beynon, H. (1973). *Working for Ford*. Penguin, Harmondsworth.
Beynon, H. and Wainwright, H. (1979). *The Workers' Report on Vickers*. Pluto, London.
Biggane, J. F. and Stewart, P. A. (1963). *Job Enlargement: a case study*. Research Series No. 25. University of Iowa, Bureau of Labour and Management, Iowa.
Bingham, J. (1977). Sour edge to job enrichment. *Industrial Management* June, pp. 7, 35.
Birchall, D. (1975). *Job Design*. Gower Press, London.
Birchall, D. and Hammond, V. (1978). Can clerical work be made more interesting? *Management Services* **22** (2), 4–7.
Birchall, D. and Wild, R. (1973). Job restructuring amongst blue collar workers. *Personnel Review* **2** (2), 40–56.
Birchall, D. and Wild, R. (1974). Autonomous work groups. *Journal of General Management* **2** (1), 36–43.
Birchall, D., Elliott, R. A. and Wild, R. (1973). *Organisational, cultural and societal differences, and their effect on the application and effectiveness of job and work, and organisational changes*. Henley, Unpublished MS.
Birchall, D., Carnall, C. and Wild, R. (1978). The development of group working in biscuit manufacture—a case. *Personnel Review* **7**, 40–49.
Bjork, L. E. (1978). An experiment in work satisfaction. *In* Davis L. E. and Taylor J. C. (Eds), *Design of Jobs, 2nd edn*. Goodyear, Santa Monica.
Blackler, F. H. M. (1981). Job redesign and social policies. *In* Kelly, J. E. and Clegg, C. W. (Eds), *Autonomy and Control at the Workplace*. Croom Helm, London.
Blackler, F. H. M. and Brown, C. A. (1975). The impending crisis in job design. *Journal of Occupational Psychology* **48**, 185–193.
Blackler, F. H. M. and Brown, C. A. (1978). *Job Redesign and Management Control*. Saxon House, Farnborough.
Blackler, F. H. M. and Brown, C. A. (1980). *Whatever Happened to Shell's Philosophy of Management?* Saxon House, Farnborough.
Blair, J. (1974). Three studies in improving clerical work. *Personnel Management* Feb.

Blake, J. and Ross, S. (1976). Some experiences with autonomous work groups. *In* Weir, M. (Ed), *Job Satisfaction*. Fontana, London.

Blau, P. (1963). *The Dynamics of Bureaucracy*. University of Chicago Press, Chicago.

Blauner, R. (1964). *Alienation and Freedom*. University of Chicago Press, Chicago.

Blood, M. and Hulin, C. (1967). Alienation, environmental characteristics and worker responses. *Journal of Applied Psychology* **51** (3), 284–290.

Bluestone, I. (1974). Comments on job enrichment. *Organisational Dynamics* **3**, 46–47.

Boff, R. D. (1977). Unemployment in the United States: an historical summary. *Monthly Review* **29** (6), 10–24.

Bolweg, J. (1976). *Job Design and Industrial Democracy*. Martinus Nijhoff, Leiden.

Bosquet, M. (1972). The 'prison factory'. *New Left Review* **73**, 23–34.

Bowers, D. G. (1977). Work humanisation in practice: what is business doing? *In* Heisler, W. J. and Houck, J. W. (Eds), *A Matter of Dignity: Inquiries into the Humanisation of Work*. University Notre Dame Press, Notre Dame.

Branson, N., and Heinemann, M. (1971). *Britain in the 1930s*. Panther, London.

Braverman, H. (1974). *Labour and Monopoly Capital*. Monthly Review Press, New York.

Brearley, A. (1976). *The Control of Staff-Related Overhead*. Macmillan, London.

Brekelmans, W. and Jonsson, B. (1976). The diffusion of work design changes in Volvo. *Columbia Journal of World Business* **11** (2), 96–99.

Brighton Labour Process Group (1977). The capitalist labour process. *Capital & Class* **1**, 3–26.

British Steel Corporation (1975). *Work Restructuring Exercise: Bilston Finishing and Dispatch Department*. BSC, London.

Bronda, A. (1980). FIAT. *Marxism Today* **24** (5), 4.

Brooks, T. (1972). Job satisfaction: an elusive goal. *American Federationist* **79** (10), 1–7.

Brown, G. (1977). *Sabotage: a study in industrial conflict*. Spokesman, Nottingham.

Brown, W. (1973). *Piecework Bargaining*. Heinemann, London.

Bryan, E. J. (1975). Work improvement and job enrichment: the case of Cummins Engine Company. *In* Davis, L. E. and Cherns, A. B. (Eds), *The Quality of Working Life*, Vol. 2. Free Press, New York.

Buchanan, D. (1979). *The Development of Job Design Theories and Techniques*. Saxon House, Farnborough.

Buckingham, G. L., Jeffrey, R. G. and Thorne, B. A. (1975). *Job Enrichment and Organisational Change*. Gower Press, London.

Burawoy, M. (1978). Towards a Marxist theory of the labour process: Braverman and beyond *Politics & Society* **8**, 247–312.

Burbidge, J. L. (1976). *Group Production Methods and Humanisation of Work: the*

Evidence in Industrialised Countries. Research Series 10, International Institute of Labour Studies, Geneva.

Burns, T. and Stalker, G. M. (1961). *The Management of Innovation.* Tavistock, London.

Butera, F. (1975). Environmental factors in job and organisation design: the case of Olivetti. *In* Davis, L. E., and Cherns, A. B. (Eds), *The Quality of Working Life,* Vol. 2. Free Press, New York.

Butteriss, M. (1971). *Job Enrichment and Employee Participation.* Institute of Personnel Management, London.

Butteriss, M. (1975). *The Quality of Working Life: the Expanding International Scene,* Paper 5. Work Research Unit, London.

Butteriss, M. and Murdoch, R. D. (1975). *Work Restructuring Projects and Experiments in the United Kingdom,* Report 2. Work Research Unit, London.

Carby, K. (1976). *Job Redesign in Practice.* Institute of Personnel Management, London.

Carpentier, J. (1974). Organisational techniques and the humanisation of work. *International Labor Review* **110**, 93–116.

Castles, S., and Kosack, G. (1980). The function of labour immigration in Western European capitalism. *In* Nichols, T. (Ed), *Capital and Labour.* Fontana, London.

Centers R., and Bugenthal, D. E. (1966). Intrinsic and extrinsic job motivations among different segments of the working population. *Journal of Applied Psychology* **50**, 193–197.

Champagne, P. J. and Tausky, C. (1978). When job enrichment doesn't pay. *Personnel* **55** (1), 30–40.

Channon, D. (1973). *The Strategy and Structure of British Enterprise.* Macmillan, London.

Chave, D. (1976). Neo-Taylorisme ou autonomie ouvrière: reflexion sur trois experiences de reorganisation du travail. *Sociologie du Travail* **18** (1), 3–14.

Chemicals Economic Development Council (1970). *Economic Assessment to 1972.* NEDO, London.

Chemicals Economic Development Council (1972). *Investment in the Chemicals Industry.* NEDO, London.

Chemicals Economic Development Council (1973a). *Chemicals Manpower in Europe.* HMSO, London.

Chemicals Economic Development Council (1973b). *Industrial Review to 1977.* NEDO, London.

Chemicals Economic Development Council (1976). *UK Chemicals 1975–85.* NEDO, London.

Chinoy, E. (1955). *Automobile Workers and the American Dream.* Doubleday, New York.

Clarke, R.O., Fatchett, D. and Roberts, B. C. (1972). *Workers' Participation in Management in Britain.* Heinemann, London.

Clegg, C. (1981). Modelling the practice of job design. *In* Kelly, J. E. and Clegg, C. W. (Eds). *Autonomy and Control at the Workplace.* Croom Helm, London.

Clegg, H. A. (1969). The substance of productivity agreements. *In* Flanders, A. (Ed), *Collective Bargaining*. Penguin, Harmondsworth.

Clegg, S. and Dunkerley, D. (1980). *Organization, Class and Control*. Routledge & Kegan Paul, London.

Clerc, J. (1973). Experiments in humanising the organisation of industrial work. *International Institute for Labour Studies Bulletin* **11**, 15–20.

Coch, L. and French, J. R. (1948). Overcoming resistance to change. *Human Relations* **1**, 512–532.

Conant, E. H. and Kilbridge, M. D. (1965). An interdisciplinary analysis of job enlargement: technology, costs and behavioural implications. *Industrial and Labour Relations Review* **18**, 377–395.

Cooley, M. (1977). Taylor in the office. *In* Ottaway, R. N. (Ed), *Humanising the Workplace*. Croom Helm, London.

Cooley, M. (1980). *Architect or Bee: the Human Technology Relationship*. Langley Technical Services, Slough.

Copley, F. B. (1923). *Frederick W. Taylor: Father of Scientific Management*, 2 Vols. Taylor Society, New York.

Coriat, B. (1980). The restructuring of the assembly line: a new economy of time and control. *Capital & Class* **11**, 34–43.

Corley, T. (1966). *Domestic Electrical Appliances*. Cape, London.

Cotgrove, S., Dunham, J. and Vamplew, C. (1971). *The Nylon Spinners*. Allen & Unwin, London.

Cox, D. and Sharp, K. (1951). Research on the unit of work. *Occupational Psychology* **25**, 90–108.

Crozier, M. (1964). *The Bureaucratic Phenomenon*. Tavistock, London.

Cummings, T. G. and Molloy, E. S. (1976). *Improving Productivity and the Quality of Work Life*. Praeger, New York.

Cummings, T. G. and Srivastva, S. (1977). *Management of Work: a sociotechnical systems approach*. Kent State University Press, Kent.

Cummings, T. G., Molloy, E. S. and Glen, R. (1977). A methodological critique of 58 selected work experiments. *Human Relations* **30** (8), 675–708.

Cunnison, S. (1966). *Wages and Work Allocation*. Tavistock, London.

Currie, R. M. (1972). *Work Study*, 3rd Edn. Pitman, London.

Dalton, M. (1948). The industrial rate-buster a characterisation. *Applied Anthropology* **7**, 5–18.

Daniel, W. W. (1970). *Beyond the Wagework Bargain*. PEP, London.

Daniel, W. W. and McIntosh, N. (1972). *The Right to Manage?* Macdonald, London.

Davies, D. R. and Shackleton, V. J. (1975). *Psychology and Work*. Methuen, London.

Davis, L. E. (1957). Toward a theory of job design. *Journal of Industrial Engineering* **8**, 305–309.

Davis, L. E. (1966). The design of jobs. *Industrial Relations* **6**, 21–45.

Davis, L. E. (1971a). Job satisfaction research: the post-industrial view. *Industrial Relations* **10**, 176–193.

Davis, L. E. (1971b). Readying the unready: post-industrial jobs. *California Management Review* **14**, 27–36.

Davis, L. E. (1971c). The coming crisis for production management. *International Journal of Production Research* **9**, 65–82.

Davis, L. E. (1980). Changes in work environments: the next twenty years. *In* Duncan, K. D., Gruneberg, M. M. and Wallis, D. (Eds), *Changes in Working Life*. Wiley, London.

Davis, L. E. and Cherns, A. B. (Eds) (1975). *The Quality of Working Life*, 2 Vols. Free Press, New York.

Davis, L. E. and Sullivan, C. S. (1980). A labour-management contract and quality of working life. *Journal of Occupational Behaviour* **1**, 29–41.

Davis, L. E. and Taylor, J. C. (Eds) (1972). *Design of Jobs*. Penguin, Harmondsworth.

Davis, L. E. and Taylor, J. C. (1976). Technology, organisation and job structure *In* Dubin, R. (Ed), *Handbook of Work, Organisation and Society*. Rand McNally, Chicago.

Davis, L. E. and Valfer, E. S. (1965). Intervening responses to changes in supervisory job designs. *Occupational Psychology* **39**, 171–189.

Davis, L. E. and Werling, R. (1960). Job design factors. *Occupational Psychology* **34**, 109–132.

Davis, L. E., Canter, R. R. and Hoffman, J. (1955). Current job design criteria. *Journal of Industrial Engineering* **6** (2), 5–11.

De, N. (1980). India. *In* International Labour Organisation. *New Forms of Work Organisation*, Vol. 2. ILO, Geneva.

Deci, E. L. (1975). *Intrinsic Motivation*. Plenum Press, New York.

Delamotte, Y. (1975). Union attitudes toward quality of working life. *In* Davis, L. E. and Cherns, A. B. (Eds), *The Quality of Working Life*, Vol. 1. Free Press, New York.

Delamotte, Y. (1976). *The Attitudes of French and Italian Trades Unions to the Humanisation of Work*. International Institute for Labour Studies, Research Series No. 14, Geneva.

Delamotte, Y. (1979). France. *In* International Labour Organisation, *New Forms of Work Organisation*, Vol. 1. ILO, Geneva.

Delamotte, Y. and Walker, K. (1973). Humanisation of work and the quality of working life—trends and issues. *International Institute Labour Studies Bulletin* **11**, 3–14.

den Hertog, F. (1974). *Work Structuring*. Paper read to Nato Symposium on Personal Goals & Work Design, York, England.

di Ruzza, F. (1980). The underlying principles of the economic policy of the French Communist Party. *CPGB Economic Bulletin* **7**, 13–19.

Dickson, D. (1974). *Alternative Technology and the Politics of Technical Change*. Fontana, London.

Dickson, P. (1977). *Work Revolution*. Allen & Unwin, London.

Donaldson, L. (1975). Job enlargement: a multidimensional process. *Human Relations* **28** (7), 593–610.

Drexler Jr., J. A. and Lawler III, E. E. (1977). A union-management cooperative project to improve the quality of work life. *Journal of Applied Behavioural Science* **13** (3), 373–387.

Drucker, P. (1968). *The Practice of Management*. Pan, London.

Drucker, P. (1976). The coming rediscovery of scientific management. *Conference Board Record* **13** (6), 23–27.

Dubin, R. (1956). Industrial workers' worlds: a study of the central life interests of industrial workers. *Social Problems* **3**, 131–141.

Dubin, R. (Ed) (1976). *Handbook of Work, Organisation and Society*. Rand McNally, Chicago.

Dundelach, P. and Mortensen, N. (1979). Denmark, Norway and Sweden. *In* International Labour Organization, *New Forms of Work Organisation*, Vol. 1. ILO, Geneva.

Dunham, R. (1976). The measurement and dimensionality of job characteristics. *Journal of Applied Psychology* **61**, 404–409.

Dunham, J., Aldag, R. J. and Brief, A. P. (1977). Dimensionality of task design as measured by the Job Diagnostic Survey. *Academy of Management Journal* **20** (2), 209–223.

Dunlop, J. T. and Diatchenko, V. P. (Eds) (1964). *Labour Productivity*. McGraw Hill, New York.

Dunn, J. (1974). How Dick Wood fought the freeze. *Manufacturing Management*, March.

Durand, C. (1975). Employer politics in job enrichment. *International Studies in Management and Organisation* **5**, 66–86.

Dyson, B. (1973). Hoover's group therapy. *Management Today*, May.

Edwards, R. C. (1978). The social relations of production at the point of production. *Insurgent Sociologist* **8**, 109–125.

Edwards, R. C. (1979). *Contested Terrain*. Basic Books, New York.

Elden, M. (1979). Three generations of work-democracy experiments in Norway: beyond classical socio-technical analysis. *In* Cooper C. L. and Mumford, E. (Eds), *The Quality of Working Life in Western and Eastern Europe*. Associated Business Press, London.

Eldridge, J. T. (1971). *Sociology and Industrial Life*. Nelson, London.

Eldridge, J. T. (1975). Industrial relations and industrial capitalism. *In* Esland, G., Salaman, G. and Speakman, M. (Eds), *People and Work*. Holmes McDougall, Edinburgh.

Elliott, D. (1976). Conference review: issues of value. *In* Warr, P. B. (Ed), *Personal Goals and Work Design*. Wiley, London.

Elliott, D. (1977). Can't get no job satisfaction. *Undercurrents* **20** (Feb–Mar), 31–34.

Emery, F. E. (1959). *Characteristics of Socio-Technical Systems*. Doc. 527, Tavistock, London.

Emery, F. E. (1966). *The Democratisation of the Workplace*, Doc. T813, Tavistock, London.

Emery, F. E. (1974). Bureaucracy and beyond. *Organisational Dynamics* **2**, 3–13.

Emery, F. E. (1975). *The Assembly Line: its Logic and our Future*. Australian

National University, Canberra.

Emery, F. E. (Ed) (1978a). *The Emergence of a New Paradigm of Work*. Australian National University, Canberra.

Emery, F. E. (1978b). The historical significance of the democratisation of work. *In* Emery, F. E. (Ed), *The Emergence of a New Paradigm of Work*. Australian National University, Canberra.

Emery, F. E. (1980). Designing socio-technical systems for 'greenfield' sites. *Journal of Occupational Behaviour* **1**, 19–27.

Emery, F. E. and Thorsrud, E. (1964). *Form and Content in Industrial Democracy*. Tavistock, London.

Emery, F. E. and Thorsrud, E. (1975). *Democracy at Work*. Australian National University, Centre for Continuing Education, Canberra.

Emery, F. E. and Trist, E. L. (1965). The causal texture of organisational environments. *Human Relations* **18**, 21–32.

Engelstad, P. (1972). Sociotechnical approach to problems of process control. *In* Davis, L. E. and Taylor, J. C. (Eds), *Design of Jobs*. Penguin, Harmondsworth.

Fantoli, A. (1979). Italy. *In* International Labour Organisation, *New Forms of Work Organisation*, Vol. 2. ILO, Geneva.

Faraday, J. E. (1971). *The Management of Productivity*. British Institute of Management, London.

Farquahar, H. H. (1924). A critical analysis of scientific management. *Bulletin of the Taylor Society* **9** (1), 16–30.

Fein, M. (1974). Job enrichment: a re-evaluation. *Sloan Management Review* **15** (2), 69–88.

Fein, M. (1976). Motivation for work. *In* Dubin, R. (Ed), *Handbook of Work, Organisation and Society*. Rand McNally, Chicago.

Fitter, M. (1981). Information systems and the organisational implications of job redesign. *In* Kelly, J. E. and Clegg, C. W. (Eds), *Autonomy and Control at the Workplace*. Croom Helm, London.

Fleet, K. (1974). Job enrichment, but not by bosses' head-shrinkers. *Workers Control Bulletin* 23 March.

Ford, R. N. (1969). *Motivation Through the Work Itself*. American Management Association, New York.

Ford, R. N. (1973). Job enrichment lessons from AT&T. *Harvard Business Review* **51** (1), 96–106.

Foulkes, F. K. (1969). *Creating More Meaningful Work*. American Management Association, New York.

Fox, A. (1966). *Industrial Sociology and Industrial Relations*. Donovan Commission Research Paper 3, HMSO, London.

Fox, A. (1973). A social critique of pluralist ideology. *In* Child, J. (Ed), *Man and Organisation*. Allen & Unwin, London.

Frank, L. and Hackman, J. R. (1975). A failure of job enrichment: the case of the change that wasn't. *Journal of Applied Behavioural Science* **11** (4), 413–436.

Fridenson, P. (1978). The coming of the assembly line to Europe. *In* Krohn, W. Layton, E. T. and Weingart P. (Eds), *The Dynamics of Science and*

Technology. Dordrecht, Reidel.

Friedman, A. (1977a). Responsible autonomy versus direct control over the labour process. *Capital & Class* **1**, 43–57.

Friedman, A. (1977b). *Industry and Labour: Class Struggle at Work and Monopoly Capitalism.* Macmillan, London.

Friedman, H. and Meredeen, S. (1980). *Lessons from Ford.* Croom Helm, London.

Friedmann, G. (1955). *Industrial Society.* Free Press, Glencoe.

Gainor, R. (1975). Do blue collar workers really have the blues? *Detroit News,* 5 January.

Gallegos, R. C. and Phelan, J. G. (1977). Effects on productivity and morale of a systems-designed job enrichment program in Pacific Telephone. *Psychological Reports* **40**, 283–290.

Gallie, D. (1978). *In Search of the New Working Class.* Cambridge University Press, Cambridge.

Gartman, D. (1979). Origins of the assembly line and capitalist control of work at Ford. *In* Zimbalist, A. (Ed), *Case Studies on the Labour Process.* Monthly Review Press, New York.

George, M. (1980). Why workers' plans make sense: the economics of alternative production proposals. *Economic and Industrial Democracy* **1** (1), 129–134.

Gilbreth, F. and Gilbreth, L. (1953). *The Writings of the Gilbreths.* Irwin, Homewood, Illinois.

Glaser, E. M. (1976). *Productivity Gains Through Worklife Improvement.* Harcourt Brace Jovanovich, New York.

Goldman, J. and Van Houten, D. R. (1980). Uncertainty, conflict and labour relations in the modern firm I: Productivity and capitalism's 'human face'. *Economic and Industrial Democracy* **1**, 63–98.

Goldthorpe, J. (1974). Industrial relations in Great Britain: a critique of reformism. *Politics and Society* **4** 419-442.

Goldthorpe, J., Lockwood, D., Bechofer, F. and Platt, J. (1968). *The Affluent Worker: Industrial Attitudes and Behaviour.* Cambridge University Press, Cambridge.

Gomberg, W. (1973). Job satisfaction: sorting out the nonsense. *American Federationist* June.

Gonas, L. and Levinson, K. (1980). Union strategies and structural change. *Economic and Industrial Democracy* **1**, 249–262.

Gooding, J. (1970a). Blue collar blues on the assembly line. *Fortune* **82**, July, 68–71.

Gooding, J. (1970b). It pays to wake up the blue collar worker. *Fortune* **82**, Sept, 133–135.

Gorman, L. and Molloy, E. (1972). *People, Jobs and Organisations.* Irish Productivity Centre, Dublin.

Gorz, A. (1976a). Technology, technicians and class struggle. *In* Gorz, A. (Ed), *The Division of Labour.* Harvester Press, Sussex.

Gorz, A. (1976b). The tyranny of the factory: today and tomorrow. *In* Gorz,

A. (Ed), *The Division of Labour*. Harvester Press, Sussex.

Gorz, A. (Ed) (1976c). *The Division of Labour*. Harvester Press, Sussex.

Gowler, D. (1970). Sociocultural influences on the operation of a wage payment system. *In* Robinson, D. (Ed), *Local Labour Markets and Wage Structures*. Gower Press, London.

Greenberg, P. D. and Glaser, E. M. (1980). *Some Issues in Joint Union-Management Quality of Worklife Improvement Efforts*. WE Upjohn Institute, Michigan.

Greenblatt, A. D. (1973). Maximising productivity through job enrichment. *Personnel* **50** (2), 31–39.

Gregory, D. (1978). *Work Organisation: Swedish Experience and British Context*. Social Science Research Council, London.

Gregory, D. (1981). Job redesign and trade union responses: past problems and future prospects. *In* Kelly, J. E. and Clegg, C. W. (Eds), *Autonomy and Control at the Workplace*. Croom Helm, London.

Guest, D. and Fatchett, D. (1974). *Worker Participation: Individual Control and Performance*. Institute of Personnel Management, London.

Guest, R. H. (1957). Job enlargement — revolution in job design. *Personnel Administration*, **20** (2), 9–16.

Gulowsen, J. (1972). A measure of work-group autonomy. *In* Davis, L. E. and Taylor, J. C. (Eds), *Design of Jobs*. Penguin, Harmondsworth.

Gustavsen, B. (1980). From satisfaction to collective action: trends in the development of research and reform in working life. *Economic and Industrial Democracy* **1** (2), 147–170.

Gyllenhammar, P. (1977). *People at Work*. Addison-Wesley, Reading, Mass.

Haber, S. (1964). *Efficiency and Uplift: scientific management in the progressive era 1890–1920*. University of Chicago Press, Chicago.

Hackman, J. R. (1975a). Is job enrichment just a fad? *Harvard Business Review* **53** (5), 129–138.

Hackman, J. R. (1975b). On the coming demise of job enrichment. *In* Cass, E. L. and Zimmer, F. G. (Eds), *Man and Work in Society*. Van Nostrand, New York.

Hackman, J. R. (1977). Work design. *In* Hackman, J. R. and Suttle, J. L. (Eds), *Improving Life at Work: Behavioural Science Approaches to Organisational Change*. Goodyear, Santa Monica.

Hackman, J. R. (1978a). The design of work in the 1980s. *Organisational Dynamics* **7** (1), 2–17.

Hackman J. R. (1978b). The design of self-managing work groups. *In* King, B. T., Streufert, S. S. and Fiedler, F. (Eds), *Managerial Control and Organisational Democracy*. Winston, Washington.

Hackman, J. R. and Lawler, E. E. (1972). Employee reactions to job characteristics. *In* Davis, L. E. and Taylor, J. C. (Eds), *Design of Jobs*. Penguin, Harmondsworth.

Hackman, J. R. and Oldham, G. R. (1974). *The Job Diagnostic Survey*. Department of Administrative Sciences, Technical Report No. 4, Yale University, New Haven.

Hackman, J. R. and Oldham, G. R. (1975). Development of the Job Diagnostic Survey. *Journal of Applied Psychology* **60** (2), 159–170.

Hackman, J. R. and Oldham, G. R. (1976). Motivation through the design of work. *Organisational Behaviour and Human Performance* **15**, 250–279.

Hackman, J. R. and Oldham, G. (1980). *Work Redesign*. Addison-Wesley, Reading, Mass.

Hackman, J. R., Oldham, G., Janson, R. and Purdy, K. (1976). A new strategy for job enrichment. *California Management Review* **17** (4), 57–71.

Hackman, J. R., Pearce, J. L. and Chaminis, J. (1978). Effects of changes in job characteristics on work attitudes and behaviours: a naturally-occurring quasi-experiment. *Organisational Behaviour and Human Performance* **21**, 289–304.

Hales, M. (1974a). Management science and the Second Industrial Revolution. *Radical Science Journal* **1**, 5–28.

Hales, M. (1974b). Job satisfaction and participation—is it just a con? *Workers' Control Bulletin*, 9 March.

Hallam, P. A. (1976). An experiment in group working. *In* Weir, M. (Ed), *Job Satisfaction*. Fontana, London.

Halsey, A. (1972). *Trends in British Society since 1900*. Macmillan, London.

Harding, D. W. (1931). A note on the subdivision of assembly work. *Journal of the National Institute for Industrial Psychology* **5**, 261–264.

Hartell, B. (1977). *Personal communication* 28 March.

Harvey, D. (1973). Better ways to put the pieces together. *Business Administration* April, 82–83.

Hay, S. (1973). *The Chemicals and Allied Industries*. Heinemann, London.

Heckscher, C. (1980). Worker participation and management control. *Journal of Social Reconstruction* **1**, 77–102.

Heisler, W. J. (1977). Worker alienation: 1900–1975. *In* Heisler W. J. and Houck, J. W. (Eds), *A Matter of Dignity*. University of Notre Dame Press, Notre Dame.

Hepworth, A. and Osbaldeston, M. (1979). *The Way We Work*. Saxon House, Farnborough.

Herbst, P. G. (1962). *Autonomous Group Functioning*. Tavistock, London.

Herrick, N. and Maccoby, M. (1975). Humanising work: a priority goal of the '70s. *In* Davis, L. E. and Cherns, A. B. (Eds), *The Quality of Working Life*, Vol. 1. Free Press, New York.

Herzberg, F. (1966). *Work and the Nature of Man*. Staples Press, London.

Herzberg, F. (1968). One more time: how do you motivate employees? *Harvard Business Review* **46**, 53–62.

Herzberg, F. (1974). The wise old Turk. *Harvard Business Review* **52** (5), 70–80.

Herzberg, F. (1976a). An American approach to job enrichment. *In* Herzberg, F. (Ed), *The Managerial Choice: to be efficient and to be human*. Dow Jones-Irwin, Homewood, Illinois.

Herzberg, F. (1976b). *The Managerial Choice*. Dow Jones-Irwin, Homewood, Illinois.

Herzberg, F. and RaFalko, E. A. (1975). Efficiency in the military: cutting costs with job enrichment. *Personnel* **52** (6), 38–48.

Herzberg, F., Mausner, B., Peterson, R. and Capwell, D. (1957). *Job Attitudes: Review of Research and Opinion*. Psychological Service, Pittsburgh.

Herzberg, F., Mausner, B. and Snyderman, B. (1959). *The Motivation to Work*. Wiley, New York.

Hill, P. (1971). *Towards a New Philosophy of Management*. Gower Press, London.

Hobsbawm, E. (1968). *Industry and Empire*. Penguin, Harmondsworth.

Hopwood, A. (1979a). Towards the economic assessment of new forms of work organisation. *In* Cooper, C. L. and Mumford, E. (Eds), *The Quality of Working Life in Western and Eastern Europe*. Associated Business Press, London.

Hopwood, A. (1979b). Economic costs and benefits of new forms of work organisation. *In* International Labour Organisation, *New Forms of Work Organisation*, Vol. 2. ILO, Geneva.

House of Commons Select Committee on Higher Education, Science and Arts. (1980). *The Funding and Organisation of Higher Education, Vol. 1. Report*. HMSO, London.

Hoxie, R. F. (1915). *Scientific Management and Labour*. Republished in 1966 by Kelley, New York.

Hughes, J. and Gregory, D. (1973). *Job Enrichment—a Critique*. Ruskin College, Trade Union Research Unit, Oxford.

Hughes, J. and Gregory, D. (1978). Work organisation: some issues of practice and concept. *In* Gregory, D. (Ed), *Work Organisation*. Social Science Research Council, London.

Hulin, C. (1971). Individual differences and job enrichment—the case against general treatments. *In* Maher, J. (Ed), *New Perspectives in Job Enrichment*. Van Nostrand, New York.

Hulin, C. and Blood, M. R. (1968). Job enlargement, individual differences, and worker response. *Psychological Bulletin* **69**, 41–55.

Hull, D. (1978). *The Shop Stewards Guide to Work Organisation*. Spokesman, Nottingham.

Hunnius, G. (1979). On the nature of capitalist-initiated innovations in the work place. *In* Burns, T. (Ed), *Work and Power*. Sage, California.

Imberman, A. A. (1973). Assembly line workers humbug job enrichment. *Personnel Administrator* **18** (2), 29–35.

Incomes Data Services (1979). *Changes in Work Organisation*. IDS Ltd, London.

Incomes Data Services (1981). *Productivity Improvements: Study 245, July*. IDS Ltd, London.

International Institute for Labour Studies (1974). *Selected Bibliography on Humanisation of Work and Alternative Work Organisation*. IILS, Geneva.

International Labour Organisation (1977). *Bibliography on Major Aspects of the Humanisation of Work and the Quality of Working Life*. ILO, Geneva.

International Labour Organisation (1979a). *New Forms of Work Organisation 1*. ILO, Geneva.

International Labour Organisation (1979b). *New Forms of Work Organisation 2*. ILO, Geneva.

Jacobs, C. D. (1975). Job enrichment of field technical representatives— Xerox Corporation. *In* Davis, L. E. and Cherns, A. B. (Eds), *The Quality of Working Life*, Vol. 2. Free Press, New York.

Janson, R. (1971). Job enrichment in the modern office. *In* Maher, J. (Ed), *New Perspectives in Job Enrichment*. Van Nostrand, New York.

Janson, R. (1974). Job design for quality. *Personnel Administrator* **19** (7), 14–18.

Janson, R. (1975). A job enrichment trial in data processing—in an insurance organisation. *In* Davis, L. E. and Cherns, A. B. (Eds), *The Quality of Working Life*, Vol. 2. Free Press, New York.

Janson, R. (1979), Job redesign—a results oriented strategy that works. *Advanced Management Journal* **44** (1), 21–27.

Jenkins, D. (1974). *Job Power*. Heinemann, London.

Jessup, G. (1974). *Job Satisfaction and Job Design: Paper 1*. Work Research Unit, London.

Jones, D. T. (1976). Output, employment and labour productivity in Europe since 1955. *National Institute Economic Review* **77**, 72–85.

Kakar, S. (1970). *Frederick Taylor: A Study in Personality and Innovation*. MIT Press, Cambridge.

Katzell, R. A., Yankelovich, D., Fein, M. and Ornati, O. A. (1975). *Work, Productivity and Job Satisfaction*. The Psychological Corporation, New York.

Katzell, R. A., Bienstock, P. and Faerstein, P. H. (1979). *A Guide to Worker Productivity Experiments in the United States, 1971–75*. New York University Press, New York.

Kelly, J. E. (1978a). A study of the work attitudes of computer programmers. *Personnel Review* **7** (4), 36–40.

Kelly, J. E. (1978b). A reappraisal of sociotechnical systems theory. *Human Relations* **31** (12), 1069–1099.

Kelly, J. E. (1981). Economic and structural analysis of job redesign. *In* Kelly, J.E. and Clegg, C. W. (Eds). *Autonomy and Control at the Workplace*. Croom Helm, London.

Kelly, J. E. and Clegg, C. W. (Eds) (1981). *Autonomy and Control at the Workplace*. Croom Helm, London.

Kelly, J. E. and Nicholson, N. (1980). The causation of strikes: a review of some approaches and the potential contribution of social psychology. *Human Relations* **33** (12), 853–883.

Kempner, T. (1970). Frederick Taylor and Scientific Management. *In* Tillett, A. *et al.* (Eds), *Management Thinkers*. Penguin, Harmondsworth.

Kennedy, J. E. and O'Neill, H. E. (1958). Job content and workers' opinions. *Journal of Applied Psychology* **42** (6), 372–375.

Kenton, L. (1973). The seven year switch. *Industrial Management* May.

Kilbridge, M. (1960a). Do workers prefer larger jobs? *Personnel* **37**, 45–48.

Kilbridge, M. (1960b). Reduced costs through job enlargement: a case. *Journal of Business* **33**, 357–362.

Kilbridge, M. (1961). Non-productive work as a factor in the economic division of labour. *Journal of Industrial Engineering* **12**, 155–159.

Kilbridge, M. and Webster, L. (1961). The assembly line problem. *In* Banbury, J. and Maitland, J. (Eds), *Proceedings of the Second International Conference on Operational Research*. EUP, London.

King, N. (1970). Clarification and evaluation of the two factor theory of job satisfaction. *Psychological Bulletin* **74** (1), 18–31.

Klein, L. (1964). *Multiproducts Ltd.* HMSO, London.

Klein, L. (1976). *New Forms of Work Organisation*. Tavistock, London.

Kornhauser, A. (1965). *The Mental Health of the Industrial Worker*. Wiley, New York.

Kraft, W. P. (1971). Job enrichment for production typists—a case study. *In* Maher, J. (Ed), *New Perspectives in Job Enrichment*. Van Nostrand, New York.

Kraft, W. P. and Williams, R. L. (1975). Job redesign improves productivity. *Personnel Journal* **54** (7), 393–397.

Kuriloff, A. H. (1963). An experiment in management: putting theory Y to the test. *Personnel* **40** (6), 8–17.

Kuriloff, A. H. (1977). *Personal communication* 25 March.

Kynaston-Reeves, T. (1967). Constrained and facilitated behaviour. *British Journal of Industrial Relations* **5**, 145–161.

LO (1972). *Industrial Democracy*. LO, Stockholm.

LO (1977). *Work Organisation*. LO, Stockholm.

Landes, D. (1969). *The Unbound Prometheus*. Cambridge University Press, Cambridge.

Larsen, H. H. (1979). Humanisation of the work environment in Denmark. *In* Cooper C. L. and Mumford, E. (Eds), *The Quality of Working Life in Western and Eastern Europe*. Associated Business Press, London.

Lawler, III, E. E. (1970). Job design and employee motivation. *In* Vroom, V. H. and Deci, E. L. (Eds), *Management and Motivation*. Penguin, Harmondsworth.

Lawler, III, E. E. (1971). *Pay and Organisational Effectiveness*. McGraw-Hill, New York.

Lawler, III, E. E. (1973). *Motivation in Work Organisations*. Brooks/Cole, California.

Lawler, III, E. E. (1978). The new plant revolution. *Organisational Dynamics* **7**, 3–12.

Lawler, III, E. E. and Hackman, J. R. (1971). Corporate profits and employee satisfaction: must they be in conflict? *California Management Review* **14**, 46–55.

Lawler, III, E. E., Hackman, J. R. and Kaufman, S. (1973). Effects of job redesign: a field experiment. *Journal of Applied Social Psychology* **3** (1), 49–62.

Lazonick, W. (1979). Industrial relations and technical change. *Cambridge Journal of Economics* **3**, 231–262.

Legge, K. (1977). *Power, Innovation and Problem Solving*. McGraw-Hill, New York.

Leigh, A. (1969). Making work fit. *Business Management* **99** (8), 46–48.

Leonard, R. and Rathmill, K. (1977). The group technology myths. *Management Today* Jan, 66–69.

Lerner, S., Cable, R. and Gupta S. (Eds) (1969). *Workshop Wage Determination*.

Pergamon, London.

Levitan, S. and Johnston, W. B. (1973). Job redesign, reform, enrichment: exploring the limitations. *Monthly Labor Review* **96** (7), 35–41.

Likert, R. (1961). *New Patterns of Management*. McGraw-Hill, London.

Lindestad, H. and Kvist, A. (1975). *The Volkswagon Report*. SAF, Stockholm.

Lindholm, R. (1972). *The Condemned Piecework*. SAF, Stockholm.

Lindholm, R. (1973). *Advances in Work Organisation*. SAF, Stockholm.

Lindholm, R. and Norstedt, J. P. (1975). *The Volvo Report*. SAF, Stockholm.

Littler, C. R. (1978). Understanding Taylorism. *British Journal of Sociology* **29** (2), 185–207.

Locke, E., Sirota, D. and Wolfson, A. (1976). An experimental case study of the successes and failures of job enrichment in a Government agency. *Journal of Applied Psychology* **61** (6), 701–711.

Locke, E., Feren, D., McCaleb, V. M., Shaw, K. N. and Denny, A. T. (1980). The relative effectiveness of four methods of motivating employee performance. *In* Duncan, K. D., Gruneberg, M. M. and Wallis, D. (Eds), *Changes in Working Life*. Wiley, London.

Lockwood, D. (1958). *The Blackcoated Worker*. Allen & Unwin, London.

Lupton, T. (1963). *On the Shopfloor*. Pergamon, London.

Lupton, T. (1975). Efficiency and the quality of work life. *Organisational Dynamics* **4** (2), 68–80.

Lupton, T. and Gowler, D. (1969). *Selecting a Wage Payment System*. Engineering Employers Federation, London.

Lupton, T., Tanner, I. and Schnelle, T. (1979). Manufacturing system design in Europe. *In* Cooper, C. L. and Mumford, E. (Eds), *The Quality of Working Life in Western and Eastern Europe*. Associated Business Press, London.

Lyons, T. (1972). Turnover and absenteeism: a review of relationships and shared correlates. *Personnel Psychology* **25**, 271–281.

McBeath, G. (1974). *Productivity Through People*. Business Books, London.

McDavid, I. (1975). *Participation and Involvement in BOC*. BOC Training Services Unit, Chartridge.

MacGregor, D. (1960). *The Human Side of Enterprise*. McGraw-Hill, New York.

MacKinney, A. C., Wernimont, P. F. and Galitz, W. O. (1962). Has specialisation reduced job satisfaction? *Personnel* **39**, 8–17.

Macy, B. A. (1979). A progress report on the Bolivar quality of work life project. *Personnel Journal* August, 527–530, 557–559.

Maher, J. (Ed). (1971a). *New Perspectives in Job Enrichment*. Van Nostrand, New York.

Maher, J. (1971b). Job enrichment, performance and morale in a simulated factory. *In* Maher, J. (Ed), *New Perspectives in Job Enrichment*. Van Nostrand, New York.

Maher, J. and Overbagh, W. B. (1971). Better inspection performance through job enrichment. *In* Maher, J. (Ed), *New Perspectives in Job Enrichment*. Van Nostrand, New York.

Malmberg, A. (1980). The impact of job redesign on accounting systems. *In*

Kanawaty, G. (Ed), *Managing and Developing New Forms of Work Organisation*. ILO, Geneva.

Marriott, R. (1968). *Incentive Payment Systems*. Staples Press, London.

Marx, K. (1844). *Economic and Philosophical Manuscripts. In* Marx, K., *Early Writings*. Penguin, Harmondsworth.

Marx, K. (1867). *Capital*, Vol. 1. Progress, Moscow. Republished 1970.

Meidner, R. (1980). Our concept of the Third Way. *Economic and Industrial Democracy* **1** (3), 343–370.

Merkle, J. A. (1968). The Taylor strategy: organisational innovation and class structure. *Berkeley Journal of Sociology* **13**, 59–81.

Maslow, A. H. (1943). A theory of human motivation. *Psychological Review* **50**, 370–396.

Miller, E. J. (1975). Sociotechnical systems in weaving, 1953–70; a follow-up study. *Human Relations* **28**, 349–386.

Miller, E. J. and Rice, A. K. (1967). *Systems of Organisation*. Tavistock, London.

Mills, T. (1976). Altering the social structure in coal mining: a case study. *Monthly Labour Review* **99**, 3–10.

Miner, J. B. and Dachler, H. P. (1973). Personnel attitudes and motivation. *Annual Review of Psychology* **24**, 379–402.

Mobley, W. (1977). Intermediate linkages in the relationship between job satisfaction and employee turnover. *Journal of Applied Psychology* **62**, 237–240.

Montgomery (1979). *Workers' Control in America*. Cambridge University Press, New York.

Montmollin, M. de (1974). Taylorisme et anti Taylorisme. *Sociologie du Travail* **16** (4), 374–382.

Moors, S. H. (1977). *New Forms of Work Organisation in Three Belgian Cases*. Belgian Productivity Centre, Brussels.

Morley, I. (1979). Job enrichment, job enlargement and participation at work. *In* Stephenson, G. and Brotherton, C. (eds), *Industrial Relations: A Social Psychological Approach*. Wiley, London.

Morrow, A. A. and Thayer, G. C. (1977). Collaborative work settings: new titles, old contradictions. *Journal of Applied Behavioural Science* **13** (3), 448–457.

Morse, J. J. (1973). A contingency look at job design. *California Management Review* **16** (1), 67–75.

Morse, N. and Reimer, E. (1970). The experimental change of a major organisational variable. *In* Vroom, V. and Deci, E. L. (Eds), *Management and Motivation*. Penguin, Harmondsworth.

Mukherjee, P. (1975). *The Effects of Group Production Methods on the Humanisation of Work*. International Centre for Advanced Technical & Vocational Training, Turin.

Mumford, E. and Banks, O. (1967). *The Computer and the Clerk*. Routledge Kegan Paul, London.

Mumford, E. and Henshall, D. (1979). *A Participative Approach to Computer Systems Design*. Associated Business Press, London.

Murray, H. (1978). *Socio-technical Systems in Mining (1951, 1955, 1969): Three Follow-up Studies.* Social Science Research Council, London.

Myers, C. S. (1929). *Industrial Psychology.* Thornton Butterworth, London.

Myers, C. S. (1932). *Business Rationalisation.* Pitman, London.

Myers, M. S. (1970). *Every Employee a Manager.* McGraw-Hill, New York.

Myers, M. S. (1971). Overcoming union opposition to job enrichment. *Harvard Business Review* **49**, 37–49.

Myers, M. S. (1975). *Managing With Unions.* Addison-Wesley, New York.

Nadler, D. A., Hanlow, M. and Lawler III, E. E. (1980). Factors influencing the success of labour-management quality of work life projects. *Journal of Occupational Behaviour* **1**, 53–67.

Nadworny, M. (1955). *Scientific Management and the Unions 1900–1932.* Harvard University Press, Cambridge.

Nash, J. (1976). Job satisfaction: a critique. *In* Widick, B. J. (Ed), *Auto Work and its Discontents.* Johns Hopkins University Press, Baltimore.

National Centre for Productivity and Quality of Worklife (1976). *Guide to Productivity Improvement Projects.* NCPQWL, Washington.

National Commission on Productivity and Work Quality (1975a). *Employee Incentive Schemes to Improve State and Local Government Productivity.* NCPWQ, Washington.

National Commission on Productivity and Work Quality. (1975b). *Fourth Annual Report.* NCPWQ, Washington.

Nelson, D. (1975). *Managers and Workers.* University of Wisconsin Press, Wisconsin.

Newton, K., Leckie, N. and Pettman, B. O. (1979). The quality of working life. *International Journal of Social Economics* **6** (4), 199–234.

Nichols, T. (1975). The 'socialism' of management: some comments on the new human relations. *Sociological Review* **23** (2), 245–265.

Nichols, T. (Ed). (1980). *Capital and Labour.* Fontana, London.

Nichols, T. and Beynon, H. (1977). *Living with Capitalism.* Routledge and Kegan Paul, London.

Nicholson, N., Brown, C. A. and Chadwick-Jones, J. K. (1976). Absence from work and job satisfaction. *Journal of Applied Psychology* **61** (6), 728–737.

Noble, D. (1979). Social choice in machine design. *In* Zimbalist A. (Ed), *Case Studies on the Labour Process.* Monthly Review Press, New York.

Nord, W. (1978). Dreams of humanisation and the realities of power. *Academy of Management Review* **3**, 674–679.

Noren, A. E. and Norstedt, J. P. (1975). *The Orrefors Report.* Swedish Employers Confederation, Stockholm.

Norstedt, J. P. and Aguren, S. (1974). *The Saab-Scania Report.* SAF, Stockholm.

Novara, F. (1973). Job enrichment in the Olivetti Company. *International Labor Review* **108** (4), 283–294.

Ohman, B. (1980). Wage-earner funds. Background, problems and possibilities. *Economic and Industrial Democracy* **1** (3), 417–432.

Oldham, G. R. and Hackman, J. R. (1980). Work design in the organisational context. *In* Staw, B. and Cummings L. L. (Eds), *Research in Organisational*

Behaviour, Vol. 2. JAI Press, Greenwich, Conn.

Oldham, G. R., Hackman, J. R. and Pearce, J. (1976). Conditions under which employees respond positively to enriched work. *Journal of Applied Psychology* **61** (4), 395–403.

Ollman, B. (1971). *Alienation*. Cambridge University Press, Cambridge.

Orpen, C. (1979). The effects of job enrichment on employee satisfaction, motivation, involvement and performance: a field experiment. *Human Relations* **32** (3), 189–217.

Ottaway, R. (Ed) (1977). *Humanising the Workplace*. Croom Helm, London.

Owen-Smith, E. (1971). *Productivity Bargaining*. Pan, London.

Packard, V. (1960). *The Wastemakers*. Penguin, Harmondsworth.

Palloix, C. (1976). The labour process: from Fordism to neo-Fordism. *In* CSE, *The Labour Process and Class Strategies*. Stage One Books, London.

Palmer, B. (1975). Class, conception and conflict: the thrust for efficiency, managerial views of labour and the working class rebellion 1903–22. *Review Radical Political Economics* **7**, 31–49.

Parke, E. L. and Tausky, C. (1975). The mythology of job enrichment: self-actualisation revisited. *Personnel* **52** (5), 12–21.

Paul, W. P. and Robertson, K. B. (1970). *Job Enrichment and Employee Motivation*. Gower Press, London.

Peacock, B. (1979). Job redesign in the bindery: a case study. *In* Sell, R. G. and Shipley, P. (Eds), *Satisfactions in Work Design*. Taylor & Francis, London.

Pelling, H. (1976). *A History of British Trade Unionism*. Penguin, Harmondsworth.

Penzer, W. (1973). After everyone's had his job enriched, then what? *Administrative Management* Oct, 20–22.

Perrow, C. (1978). *Complex Organisations: a critical essay*. Scott Foresman, Glenview, Illinois.

Persson, T. (1978). The cost of new assembly methods at the Saab-Scania petrol engine plant. *In* Gregory, D. (Ed), *Work Organisation*. Social Science Research Council, London.

Peters, R. S. (1960). *The Concept of Motivation*. Routledge & Kegan Paul, London.

Pettigrew, A. (1973). *The Politics of Organisation Decision-making*. Tavistock, London.

Phelps-Brown, E. H. (1959). *The Growth of British Industrial Relations*, Macmillan, London.

Philips, (1969). *Work Structuring*, Philips, Eindhoven.

Pierce, J. L. and Dunham, R. B. (1976). Task design: a literature review. *Academy of Management Review* **1** (6), 83–97.

Pignon, D. and Querzola, J. (1976). Dictatorship and democracy in production. *In* Gorz, A. (Ed), *The Division of Labour*. Harvester Press, Sussex.

Pocock, P. (1973). Participation in Preston. *Personnel Management* **5**, 31–33.

Powell, R. M. and Schlacter, J. L. (1971). Participative management: a panacea? *Academy of Management Journal* **6**, 165–73.

Powers, J. E. (1972). Job enrichment—how one company overcame the obstacles. *Personnel* **49** (3), 19–22.

Poza, E. J. and Markus, M. L. (1980). Success story: the team approach to work restructuring. *Organisational Dynamics*, 3–25.

Pratten, C. F. (1976a). *A Comparison of the Performance of Swedish and UK Companies*. Department of Applied Economics, Occasional Papers No. 47, Cambridge.

Pratten, C. F. (1976b). *Labour Productivity Differentials within International Companies*. Department of Applied Economics, Occasional Papers No. 50, Cambridge.

Pratten, C. F. (1977). The efficiency of British industry. *Lloyds Bank Review* **123**, 19–28.

Prestat, C. (1972). *A Case of Autonomous Groups*. Unpublished MS.

Quinn, R. P. and de Mandilovitch, M. S. (1974). A new survey—no more, no less. *American Federationist* **81** (1), 22–24.

Ramsay, H. (1976). Participation: the shopfloor view. *British Journal of Industrial Relations* **14** (2), 128–141.

Randall, R. (1973). Job enrichment ensures savings at Travellers. *Management Accounting* **21**, 68–72.

Rasmus, J. (1974). Why management is pushing 'job enrichment'. *International Socialist Review* Dec, 23–25, 43–44.

Reif, W. E. and Schoderbeck, P. D. (1966). Job enlargement: antidote to apathy. *Management of Personnel Quarterly* **5**, 16–23.

Reilly, P. J. (1923). Reduction of waste in operating departments of large retail stores. *Bulletin of the Taylor Society* **8** (1), 31–37.

Report of the Committee of Enquiry on Industrial Democracy (1977). *Cmnd 6706*. HMSO, London.

Rice, A. K. (1953). Productivity and social organisation in an Indian weaving shed. *Human Relations* **6**, 297–329.

Rice, A. K. (1958). *Productivity and Social Organisation*. Tavistock, London.

Rice, A. K. (1963). *The Enterprise and its Environment*. Tavistock, London.

Rice, M. (1977). The state of the unions. *In* Ottaway, R. N. (Ed), *Humanising the Workplace*. Croom Helm, London.

Riesman, D. (1953). *The Lonely Crowd*. Doubleday, New York.

Rinehart, J. W. (1975). *The Tyranny of Work*. Longman, Ontario.

Roberts, C. and Wood, S. (1981). Collective bargaining and job redesign. *In* Kelly, J. E. and Clegg, C. W. (Eds), *Autonomy and Control at the Workplace*. Croom Helm, London.

Robey, D. (1974). Task design, work values and worker responses: an experimental test. *Organisational Behaviour and Human Performance* **12**, 68–77.

Roeber, J. (1975). *Social Change at Work*. Duckworth, London.

Rose, M. (1975). *Industrial Behaviour: Theoretical Development Since Taylor*. Allen Lane, London.

Rosenhead, J. *et al. Job Enrichment: Its a Con*. Unpublished MS.

Ross, A. H. and Hartmann, P. (1960). *Changing Patterns of Industrial Conflict*. Wiley, New York.

Ross, K. and Screeton, J. (1979). Introducing autonomous work groups in Philips. *In* Guest, D. and Knight, K. (Eds), *Putting Participation into Practice*. Gower Press, London.

Roy, D. (1952). Quota restriction and gold bricking in a machine shop. *American Journal of Sociology* **57**, 427–442.

Roy, D. (1954). Efficiency and the 'Fix'. *American Journal of Sociology* **67**, 255–266.

Roy, S. K. (1967). A re-examination of the methodology of A. K. Rice's Indian textile mill work reorganisation. *Indian Journal of Industrial Relations* **5**, 170–191.

Royal Commission on Trade Unions and Employers' Associations (1968). *Report*. HMSO, London.

Runciman, W. (1966). *Relative Deprivation and Social Justice*. Penguin, Harmondsworth.

Rush, H. (1971). *Job Design for Motivation*. Conference Board Report 515, New York.

Ryan, T. (1947). *Work and Effort*. Ronald Press, New York.

Salancik, G. and Pfeffer, J. (1978). A social information processing approach to job attitudes and task design. *Administrative Science Quarterly* **23**, 224–253.

Salveson, M. (1955). The assembly-line balancing problem. *Journal of Industrial Engineering* **6**, 18–25.

Savall, H. (1981). *Work and People: An Economic Evaluation of Job Enrichment*. Oxford University Press, Oxford.

Schein, E. (1978). *Organisational Psychology*. Prentice Hall, Englewood Cliffs, New Jersey.

Schlesinger, L. and Walton, R. E. (1977). The process of work restructuring and its impact on collective bargaining. *Monthly Labor Review* **100** (4), 52–55.

Schrank, R. (1974). On ending worker alienation: the Gaines pet food plant. *In* Fairfield, R. P. (Ed), *Humanising the Work Place*. Prometheus Books, New York.

Scott, Jr., W. E. (1975). The effects of extrinsic rewards on intrinsic motivation: a critique. *Organisational Behavioural and Human Performance* **15**, 117–129.

Scoville, J. (1969). A theory of jobs and training. *Industrial Relations* **9**, 36–53.

Seeborg, I. S. (1978). The influence of employee participation in job redesign. *Journal of Applied Behavioural Science* **14** (1), 87–99.

Sheppard, H. L. and Herrick, N. Q. (1972). *Where Have All the Robots Gone?* Free Press, New York.

Sirota, D. (1973a). Production and service personnel and job enrichment. *Work Study* Jan, 9–15.

Sirota, D. (1973b). Job enrichment—another management fad? *Conference Board Record* **10** (4), 40–45.

Sirota, D. and Wolfson, A. D. (1972). Job enrichment—surmounting the obstacles. *Personnel* **49** (4), 8–19.

Skillen, A. (1977). *Ruling Illusions: Philosophy and the Social Order*. Harvester Press, Sussex.

Slee Smith, P. (1973). *Job Involvement and Communications*. Business Books, London.

Smith, A. (1776). *The Wealth of Nations*. Republished in 1974 by Penguin, Harmondsworth.

Smith, D. M. (1968). Job design: from research to application. *Journal of Industrial Engineering* **19** (10), 477–481.

Smith, C. T. B., Clifton, R., Makeham, P., Creigh, S. W. and Burn, R. V. (1978). *Strikes in Britain*. Department of Employment, London.

Smith, H. R. (1976). The half-loaf of job enrichment. *Personnel* **53** (2), 24–31.

Smith, P. C. (1955). The prediction of individual differences in susceptibility to industrial monotony. *Journal of Applied Psychology* **39** (5), 322–29.

Smith, P. C. and Lem, C. (1955). Positive aspects of motivation in repetitive work. *Journal of Applied Psychology* **39** (5), 330–333.

Social Trends 1973. HMSO, London.

Sohn-Rethel, A. (1976). The dual economics of transition. *In* CSE, *The Labour Process and Class Strategies*. Stage One, London.

Sohn-Rethel, A. (1978). *Intellectual and Manual Labour*. Macmillan, London.

Srivastva, S., Salipante, P., Cummings, T., Notz, W., Bigelow, J. and Waters, J. (1975). *Job Satisfaction and Productivity*. Kent State University, Kent.

Staehle, W. H. (1979). Federal Republic of Germany. *In* International Labour Organization, *New Forms of Work Organization*, Vol. 1. ILO Geneva.

Stark, D. (1980). Class struggle and the transformation of the labour process: a relational approach. *Theory and Society* **9**, 89–130.

Stone, E. (1975). Job scope, job satisfaction and the Protestant ethic: a study of enlisted men in the US navy. *Journal of Vocational Behaviour* **7**, 215–234.

Stone, E. (1976). The moderating effect of work-related values on the job scope—job satisfaction relationship. *Organisational Behaviour and Human Performance* **15**, 147–167.

Strange, S. (1979). The management of surplus capacity: or how does theory stand up to protectionism? *International Organisation* **33** (3), 303–334.

Strauss, G. (1970). Human Relations—1968 style. *Industrial Relations* **7**, 262–276.

Susman, G. (1970). The impact of automation on work group autonomy and task specialisation. *Human Relations* **23**, 567–577.

Susman, G. (1973). Job enlargement: effects of culture on worker responses. *Industrial Relations* **12**, 1–15.

Susman, G. (1976). *Autonomy at Work: a Socio-technical Analysis of Participative Management*. Praeger, New York.

Swedish Employers' Confederation (1975). *Job Reform in Sweden*. SAF, Stockholm.

Takezawa, S. (1976). *The Quality of Working Life: Trends in Japan*. International Institute of Labour Studies, Geneva.

Tausky, C. and Parke, E. L. (1976). Job enrichment, need theory and reinforcement theory. *In* Dubin, R. (Ed), *Handbook of Work, Organisation and Society*. Rand McNally, Chicago.

Taylor, F. W. (1893). Notes on belting. *In* Taylor, F. W. (Ed), *Two Papers on Scientific Management*. Routledge & Sons, London (1919 edition).

Taylor, F. W. (1895). A piece rate system. *In* Taylor, F. W. (Ed), *Two Papers on Scientific Management*. Routledge & Sons, London (1919 edition).

Taylor F. W. (1903). Shop Management. *In* Taylor, F. W. *Scientific Management*. Harper & Bros, New York (1947 edition).

Taylor, F. W. (1906). *The Art of Cutting Metals*. American Society of Mechanical Engineers, New York.

Taylor, F. W. (1911). Testimony before the Special House Committee. In Taylor, F. W. *Scientific Management*. Harper & Bros., New York (1947 edition).

Taylor, F. W. (1912). Principles of scientific management. *In* Taylor, F. W. *Scientific Management*. Harper & Bros., New York (1947 edition).

Taylor, J. C. (1971). Some effects of technology in organisational change. *Human Relations* **24**, 105–123.

Taylor, J. C. (1977a). Job design in an insurance firm. *Journal of Contemporary Business* **6** (2), 37–48.

Taylor, J. C. (1977b). Experiments in work system design: economic and human results. Part.I. *Personnel Review* **6** (3), 21–34.

Taylor, J. C. (1977c). Experiments in work system design: economic and human results. Part 2. *Personnel Review* **6** (4), 21–42.

Taylor, J. C. *et al.* (1973). *The Quality of Working Life: An Annotated Bibliography 1957–1972*. Centre for Organisation Studies, UCLA.

Taylor, L. K. (1973). *Not for Bread Alone*, 2nd Edn. Business Books, London.

Taylor, P. (1979). Labour time, work measurement and the socialisation of labour. *Capital and Class* **9**, 23–37.

Tchobanian, R. (1975). Trade unions and the humanisation of work. *International Labor Review* **111** (3), 199–217.

Terisse, H. (1975). *Two Experiments with Semi-Autonomous Groups at Telemecanique*. Union des Industries Metallurgiques et Minieres, Paris.

Thackray, J. (1976). US managers think again. *Management Today* Oct.

Thornely, D. H. and Valentine, G. (1968). Job enlargement: some implications of longer cycle jobs on fan heater production. *Philips Personnel Management Review* **23**, 12–17.

Thorsrud, E. (1967). *Sociotechnical Approach to Job Design and Organisational Development*, Doc. X394. Tavistock Institute of Human Relations, London.

Thorsrud, E. (1970). A strategy for research and social change in industry: a report on the industrial democracy project in Norway. *Social Science Information* **9** (5), 65–90.

Thorsrud, E. (1972). Job design in the wider context. *In* Davis, L. E. and Taylor, J. C. (Eds), *Design of Jobs*. Penguin, Harmondsworth.

Thorsrud, E. (1980). The changing structure of work organisation. *In* Kanawaty, G. (Ed), *Managing and Developing New Forms of Work Organisation*. ILO, Geneva.

Thorsrud, E., Sørensen, B. A. and Gustavsen, B. (1976). Sociotechnical approach to industrial democracy in Norway. *In* Dubin, R. (Ed), *Handbook of Work, Organisation and Society*. Rand McNally, Chicago.

Tillett, A., Kempner, T. and Wills, G. (Eds). (1970). *Management Thinkers*. Penguin, Harmondsworth.

Torner, P. (1976). *The Matfors Report*. SAF, Stockholm.

Trades Union Congress (1973). *Industrial Democracy*. TUC, London.

Travis, M. (1970). Psychology in industry: new techniques and approaches. *In* Tillett, A., Kempner, T. and Wills, G. (Eds), *Management Thinkers*. Penguin, Harmondsworth.

Trist, E. L. (1956). *Comparative Study of Some Aspects of Mining Systems in a Northern Coalfield*. Doc 434. Tavistock, London.

Trist, E. L. (1976). Critique of scientific management in terms of sociotechnical theory. *In* Weir, M. (Ed), *Job Satisfaction*. Fontana, London.

Trist, E. L. (1978). Composite cutting longwalls—their emergence and general characteristics. *In* Emery, F. E. (Ed), *The Emergence of a New Paradigm of Work*. Australian National University, Canberra.

Trist, E. L. and Bamforth, K. (1951). Some social and psychological consequences of the longwall method of coal getting. *Human Relations* **4**, 3–39.

Trist, E. L., Higgin, G., Murray, H. and Pollock, A. B. (1963). *Organisational Choice*. Tavistock, London.

Trist, E. L. and Murray, H. (1958). *Work Organisation at the Coal Face*. Doc. 506. Tavistock, London.

Trist, E. L., Susman, G. and Brown, G. W. (1977). An experiment in autonomous working in an American underground coal mine. *Human Relations* **30**, 201–236.

Tuggle, G. (1969). Job enlargement: an assault on assembly line inefficiencies. *Industrial Engineering* Feb, 26–31.

Tuggle, G. (1977). *Personal communication*, 17 March.

Turner, A. N. and Lawrence, P. R. (1965). *Industrial Jobs and the Worker*. Harvard University Graduate School of Business Administration, Cambridge.

Turner, A. N. and Miclette, A. L. (1962). Sources of satisfaction in repetitive work. *Occupational Psychology* **36**, 215–231.

Turner, H. A., Clack, G. and Roberts, G. (1967). *Labour Relations in the Motor Industry*. Allen & Unwin, London.

Umstot, D., Bell, Jr., C. H. and Mitchell, T. R. (1976). Effects of job enrichment and task goals on satisfaction and productivity: implications for job design. *Journal of Applied Psychology* **61** (4), 379–394.

Upham, M. (1980). British Steel: retrospect and prospect. *Industrial Relations Journal* **11** (3), 5–21.

Urwick, L. and Brech, E. F. (1945). *The Making of Scientific Management, Vol. 1*. Management Publications Trust, London.

Van Beek, H. G. (1964). The influence of assembly line organisation on output, quality and morale. *Occupational Psychology* **38**, 161–172.

Van Beinum, H. J. (1966). *The Morale of the Dublin Busmen*. Tavistock Institute of Human Relations, London.

Van Der Zwaan, A. A. (1975). The sociotechnical systems approach: a critical evaluation. *International Journal of Production Research* **13**, 149–163.

Van Gils, M. R. (1969). Job design and work organisation. *In* van Gorkum, P. H. *et al.* (Eds), *Industrial Democracy in the Netherlands*. Boom en Zoon, Meppel.

Van Vliet, A. and Vrenken, L. J. (n.d.) *Two Work Structuring Experiments*. Philips, Cahier No. 4, Eindhoven.

Verma, P. (1969). The chemical industry. *In* Lerner, S. *et al.* (Eds), *Workshop Wage Determination*. Pergamon, London.

Vroom, V. H. (1964). *Work and Motivation*. Wiley, New York.

Vroom, V. H. and Deci, E. L. (Eds) (1970). *Management and Motivation*. Penguin, Harmondsworth.

Wade, M. (1973). Job enrichment: no real future in sight. *Vision* Nov, 79–83.

Waldman, P. (1974). *Versatility at Work: a Study of Self-Training and Autonomous Group Working*, Paper TR6. Industrial Training Research Unit, Cambridge.

Waldman, P., Flegg, D. and Rees, R. (1976) *Self-organised Production Groups*. Industrial Training Research Unit, Cambridge.

Walker, C. R. (1950). The problem of the repetitive job. *Harvard Business Review* **28** (3), 54–58.

Walker, C. R. and Guest, R. H. (1952). *Man on the Assembly Line*. Harvard University Press, Cambridge.

Wall, T. D. (1978). Job redesign and employee participation. *In* Warr, P. B. (Ed), *Psychology at Work*, 2nd edn. Penguin, Harmondsworth.

Wall, T. D. (1980). Group work redesign in context: a two phase model. *In* Duncan K. D., Gruneberg, M. M. and Wallis, D. (Eds), *Changes in Working Life*. Wiley, London.

Wall, T. D. and Clegg, C. W. (1981). A longitudinal field study of group work redesign. *Journal of Occupational Behaviour* **2**, 31–49.

Wall, T. D. and Stephenson, G. (1970). Herzberg's two factor theory of job attitudes: a critical evaluation and some fresh evidence. *Industrial Relations Journal* **2**, 41–66.

Wall, T. D., Clegg, C. W. and Jackson, P. (1978). An evaluation of the job characteristics model. *Journal of Occupational Psychology* **51**, 183–196.

Walton, R. E. (1972). How to counter alienation in the plant. *Harvard Business Review* **50** (6), 70–81.

Walton, R. E. (1974). Innovative restructuring of work. *In* Rosow, J. (Ed), *The Worker and the Job: Coping with Change*. Prentice Hall, Englewood Cliffs, New Jersey.

Walton, R. E. (1975). From Hawthorne to Topeka and Kalmar. *In* Cass, E. L. and Zimmer, F. G. (Eds), *Man and Work in Society*. Van Nostrand, New York.

Walton, R. E. (1977). Work innovations at Topeka: after six years. *Journal of Applied Behavioural Science* **13** (3), 422–433.

Warmington, A., Lupton, T. and Gribbin, C. (1977). *Organisational Behaviour and Performance*. Macmillan, London.

Warr, P. B. (Ed) (1976a). *Personal Goals and Work Design*. Wiley, London.

Warr, P. B. (1976b). Theories of motivation. *In* Warr, P. B. (Ed), *Personal Goals and Work Design*. Wiley, London.

Webdill, G. (1976). *Report on Cycle Assembly*. Unpublished MS.

Weed, E. D. Jr. (1971). Job enrichment 'cleans up' at Texas Instruments. *In* Maher, J. (Ed), *New Perspectives in Job Enrichment*. Van Nostrand, New York.

Weinberg, A. (1974). Work experiments and improving the quality of work life in the United States. *European Industrial Relations Review* **10**, 2–5.

Weir, M. (1976). *Redesigning Jobs in Scotland*, Report No. 3. Work Research Unit, London.

Whitaker, R. (1979). Scientific management theory as political ideology. *Studies in Political Economy* **2**, 75–108.

Whitsett, D. (1971). Job enrichment, human resources and profitability. *In* Maher, J. (Ed), *New Perspectives in Job Enrichment*. Van Nostrand, New York.

Wild, R. (1974). Job restructuring and work organisation. *Management Decision* **12** (3), 117–126.

Wild R. (1975). *Work Organisation*. Wiley, London.

Wild, R. and Birchall, D. (1973). Means and ends in job restructuring. *Personnel Review* **2** (4), 18–24.

Wilkinson, A. (1971). *A Survey on Some Western European Experiments in Motivation*. Institute of Work Study Practitioners, London.

Wilson, N. B. (1973). *On the Quality of Working Life: Manpower Papers, No. 7*. Department of Employment, London.

Winpisinger, W. (1973). Job satisfaction: a union response. *American Federationist* **80** (2), 8–11.

Wood, S. J. (1979). A reappraisal of the contingency approach to organisation. *Journal of Management Studies* **16**, 334–354.

Wood, S. J. (Ed) (1982). *The Degradation of Work?* Hutchinson, London.

Wood, S. J. and Kelly, J. E. (1982). Taylorism, 'responsible autonomy', and management strategy. *In* Wood, S. J. (Ed), *The Degradation of Work?* Hutchinson, London.

Wood, W. R. (1976). *Personal communication*, 24 Nov.

Woodward, J. (1958). *Management and Technology*. HMSO, London.

Work in America (1972). MIT, Cambridge.

Work Research Unit (1980). *Future Programme 1980 and 1981*. Department of Employment, London.

Wragg, J. and Robertson, J. (1978). *Postwar Trends in Employment Productivity, Output, Labour Costs and Prices by Industry in the UK*, Research Paper 3. Department of Employment, London.

Wyatt, S. and Fraser, J. A. (1928). *The Comparative Effects of Variety and Uniformity in Work*. Medical Research Council, Industrial Fatigue Research Board, London.

Zimbalist, A. (1975). The limits of work humanisation. *Review of Radical Political Economics* **7** (2), 50–59.

Zimbalist, A. (Ed). (1979). *Case Studies on the Labour Process*. Monthly Review Press, New York.

Index

ORGANIZATIONAL AND OCCUPATIONAL PSYCHOLOGY

Series Editor: PETER WARR
MRC Social and Applied Psychology Unit, Department of Psychology,
The University, Sheffield, England

Theodore D. Weinshall
Managerial Communication: Concepts, Approaches and Techniques, 1979

Chris Argyris
Inner Contradictions of Rigorous Research, 1980

Charles J. de Wolff, Sylvia Shimmin, and Maurice de Montmollin
Conflicts and Contradictions: Work Psychology in Europe, 1981

Nigel Nicholson, Gill Ursell, and Paul Blyton
The Dynamics of White Collar Unionism, 1981

John D. Cook, Sue J. Hepworth, Toby D. Wall, and Peter B. Warr:
The Experience of Work: A Compendium and Review of 249
Measures and Their Use, 1981

Nigel Nicholson and Toby D. Wall (Editors)
The Theory and Practice of Organizational Psychology, 1981

Dean G. Pruitt
Negotiation Behavior, 1981

D. R. Davies and R. Parasuraman
The Psychology of Vigilance, 1982

Richard T. Mowday, Lyman W. Porter, and Richard M. Steers
Employee–Organization Linkages: The Psychology of Commitment,
Absenteeism, and Turnover, 1982

Richard A. Guzzo (Editor)
Improving Group Decision Making in Organizations: Approaches from
Theory and Research, 1982

George C. Thornton III and William C. Byham
Assessment Centers and Managerial Performance, 1982

Rudi Klauss and Bernard M. Bass
Interpersonal Communication in Organizations, 1982

John E. Kelly
Scientific Management, Job Redesign & Work Performance, 1982

ORGANIZATIONAL AND OCCUPATIONAL PSYCHOLOGY

In preparation

Kim S. Cameron and David A. Whetten (Editors)
Organizational Effectiveness: A Comparison of Multiple Models, 1982

Frank J. Landy and James L. Farr
The Measurement of Work Performance